REPORT

OF THE

Atlantic Avenue Commission

COMPRISING

An Account of the Work Accomplished, Reports of Hearings of Interested Parties, a History of Transit on Atlantic Avenue with Illustrations and Statistics.

CITY OF BROOKLYN

1897

EAGLE PRESS, BROOKLYN-NEW YORK.

ATLANTIC AVENUE COMMISSION.

EUGENE G. BLACKFORD, *President.*

EDWARD F. LINTON, *Secretary.*

EDWARD H. HOBBS.

WILLIAM E. PHILIPS.

WALTER M. MESEROLE.

TABLE OF CONTENTS.

Title.	Page
Final Report	5
Preliminary Report. Part I	12
Part II	20
Legislation—	
Act creating the Atlantic Avenue Commission	26
Act creating the Board for the Atlantic Avenue Improvement	27
Proposed Act supplemental to Chapter 499, Laws 1897	36
Proposed Act (additional) for Improvement of Atlantic Avenue	37
The Commission's Address to the Governor	39
Plans and Estimates of Cost of Atlantic Avenue Improvement	43
Sewers and Pipes on Atlantic Avenue	47
Proceedings and Hearings of the Commission	53
Documentary History of Transit on Atlantic Avenue	159
A Summary of the Same	213
Decisions of the Courts Respecting the Rights of the Railroads on the Avenue	216

ILLUSTRATIONS.

Description.	Page
Diagram of Proposed East River Tunnel and Transit Improvements on Atlantic Avenue	Frontispiece
Atlantic Avenue and Fort Greene Place	16
Cross Section, Atlantic Avenue from Flatbush Avenue to Bedford Avenue	32
"Gates Down," Atlantic and Bedford Avenues	46
Cross Section, Atlantic Avenue Between Bedford and Nostrand Avenues	60
"Gates Down," Nostrand and Atlantic Avenues	74
Cross Section, Between Bedford and Howard Avenues	90
View, Manhattan Junction, Vesta and Atlantic Avenues	104
Cross Section, Atlantic Avenue from Howard Avenue to Stone Avenue	120
View, Pennsylvania and Atlantic Avenues	136
View, Van Siclen and Atlantic Avenues	150
Cross Section, Atlantic Avenue, showing Tunnel from Flatbush Avenue to Tunnel Entrance at East River	166
Cross Section, showing Double Tunnel System under East River	180
Cross Section of Atlantic Avenue, as it would appear if Improved	194
Suggestion of Manner of Improving Atlantic Avenue	208

ATLANTIC AVENUE COMMISSION.

REPORT.

OFFICE OF THE ATLANTIC AVENUE COMMISSION,
2789 ATLANTIC AVENUE.

BROOKLYN, November 16, 1897.

To His Honor, the Mayor of the City of Brooklyn :

The Commission appointed under authority of Chapter 394, Laws of 1896, entitled " An Act to authorize the appointment of a Commission to examine into and report a plan for the relief and improvement of Atlantic Avenue in the City of Brooklyn," herewith submit their *final* report, covering the entire field of action of the Commission.

In view of the public importance of the subject submitted to our consideration, and the fact of a proposed expenditure of public money to an amount approximating one and one-quarter million dollars, we have regarded it proper to make our report exhaustive and complete. Therefore, we have embodied in it nearly all that has been said before us in the several hearings; also, written communications of importance—statistical and otherwise. We have caused illustrations to be made from photographs, showing the actual condition at several points along Atlantic avenue, believing that, after the proposed improvements shall have been completed, it will seem incredible that the people of this city should so long have suffered the inconvenience attending the occupation and use of one of its chief thoroughfares by a surface steam railroad.

The principal points in the history of Atlantic avenue and its occupation by the railroad are as follows :

Among the earliest railroad enterprises in this country was the Long Island Railroad, projected with the idea of making a quick connection between New York and Boston by means of a railroad, reaching from South Ferry, in Brooklyn, to Greenport, L. I., and thence by steamboat to Newport, R. I., where connection would be made with railroad lines throughout New England.

For the purpose of constructing the portion of the route which lay on Long Island, two companies were formed ; the Brooklyn and Jamaica Railroad Company, building from South Ferry to Jamaica, and the Long Island Railroad Company, building the remainder of the line to Greenport ; the time of construction covering the years 1834 to 1836.

During the next twenty years Brooklyn increased from a small village, clustered around the Fulton Ferry, to a city considerable in size and population. Along the line of the railroad, from South Ferry to Classon avenue, a street was laid out ; called Atlantic street, which gave promise of being a prominent thoroughfare. A continuance of this thoroughfare to East New York, of a width greater than any other existing in the city, was projected, and its opening and construction was carried out under the provisions of the laws quoted in full later in this report. A perusal of these documents will show the method by which the railroad between Classon avenue and East New York was removed from the strip of land which it owned and over which it had been operated for the preceding twenty years, to the center of the newly-opened street.

Up to this time the Long Island Railroad had not increased its system beyond the original project, which consisted only of a single track from Brooklyn to Greenport ; running for a long distance through an unproductive wilderness, and quite remote from most of the centers of population on the island. As a railroad, it was, of course, in every way an insignificant affair compared with the present Long Island Railroad system, which, by its various divisions and branches, gives railroad communication with practically every village and hamlet on the island.

The occupancy of this prominent thoroughfare by a railroad of such trifling importance was quickly found to be productive of a nuisance without compensating benefits, and in response to the demands of public opinion the railroad company was induced to abandon operation by steam power within the limits of the city, and to establish its terminus at Hunter's Point, the property immediately affected being assessed to produce the sum necessary to reimburse the railroad company for the curtailment of its franchise, and for the expense of the removal. The company retained the right to operate horse cars through the avenue, and continued to do so until the year 1876.

Prior to this time the corporate name of the proprietor company had been changed by successive reorganizations from the Brooklyn and Jamaica Railroad Company to the Brooklyn Central Railroad Company, the Brooklyn Central and Jamaica Railroad Company, the Brooklyn and Jamaica Railway Company, and lastly, to the Atlantic Avenue Railroad Company of Brooklyn.

By consolidation of the original Long Island Railroad with the South Side Railroad, the Flushing and North Shore Railroad and the Central Railroad of Long Island, and by the construction of many branches and extensions, the Long Island Railroad by this time had grown to be a railroad system of importance, operating all the steam railroads on Long Island, and the need of a terminus in the city of Brooklyn was a pressing one. The Common Council of the city, by authority of an act of the Legislature, restored to the Atlantic Avenue Railroad Company the right to operate with steam east of Flatbush avenue. The Long Island Railroad Company was thereby enabled, under a lease from the Atlantic avenue company, again to operate its trains by steam power on Atlantic avenue.

At the present time, therefore, the Long Island Railroad Company operates from Flatbush avenue, Brooklyn, to Jamaica, as lessee under a franchise which is owned by the Atlantic Avenue Railroad Company of Brooklyn, but the latter company's rights as landlord have been temporarily turned over by a general lease, made in April, 1896, of all its property and franchises, to the Nassau Electric Railroad Company.

The history and varying fortunes of Atlantic avenue would fill a large volume. It is not pertinent to the present occasion to go into the past at greater length. Suffice it to say that the evident intent in laying out the street from the water front to the city line, with its great width, was to make it a leading artery of communication from the interior of fertile Long Island to the great harbor surrounding the metropolis of America. Its use by the Long Island Railroad was natural, and for a time served purposes of commercial value and accommodation to the inhabitants of Brooklyn and the outlying territory. But the rapid and extraordinary growth of the city and suburbs for miles along the thoroughfare rendered its continued use, as a steam railroad, a menace to life, injurious to property, obstructive to development, and objectionable to an intolerable degree. These conditions created an intense feeling of resentment toward the railroad corporation, as well as indignation at the presumed indifference of the city authorities. Many and varied have been the attempts of the citizens for relief from these conditions. Legislatures have been appealed to in vain. Property owners along and adjacent to the line despaired of remedy. The locomotive still rushed along the street in the heart of the city, frequently killing and maiming human beings, always creating consternation. These things have too long been endured.

It remained for your administration, Mr. Mayor, to conceive of and prepare a bill, and to secure its passage at Albany, creating for the first time a body of men whose duty should be to examine into all the phases of the question, and by careful methods of inquiry arrive, if possible, at some definite practical conclusion, and recommend what should be done to solve the perplexing problem, the difficulties of which increased with each year. The task was arduous and vexatious. The views of citizens differed radically as to measures of relief, all of which will more fully appear in the verbatim reports of hearings printed herein as part of our report.

It may not be improper to say that your Commissioners addressed themselves to the subject with resolution and earnest endeavor, without compensation, actuated only by a desire to intelligently and practically "solve the problem." Many interests were involved ; rights, that were unassailable, yet conflicting, had to be adjusted on lines of equity and reason. Perhaps the most formidable obstacle to obtaining the desired relief arose from the great expense involved. Just who should bear it, and how to provide the funds, long embarrassed the Commission in their deliberations. Many ideas were advanced for removing the railroad, but few could point out the way to procure the money required in doing so.

Fortunately the Commission found in the person of the President of the Long Island Railroad, Mr. William H. Baldwin, Jr., a man of broad experience, liberal and comprehensive views, together with a spirit of co-operation that greatly lightened their labors. It was mainly through his intelligent grasp of the general situation and needs, not only of Brooklyn as a city but of the Long Island Railroad itself,—separated as both were from proper communication with New York,—and other portions of the country,—that the project of connecting the railroad system of Long Island by a suitable tunnel under the East River, permitting the landing of passengers right in the heart of the business center of New York, was revived and presented to the Commission as a most important factor in the great problem. The practicability of uniting the two projects, namely: the relief of Atlantic avenue, and quick through transit to New York City, was demonstrated. The Commission entered heartily into co-operation on these lines, with the result that on January 8, 1897, there was submitted to your Honor a report accompanied by plans with a recommendation that they be approved and a bill prepared for introduction in the Legislature providing for carrying into effect the grand scheme outlined above (the report and drawings appear herein in their proper places). The press of the two cities were supplied with copies of the report and drawings, and generously published them in full, at the time, thus giving the public the fullest knowledge of the work and recommendations of the Commission.

The response of public sentiment was marvelous. The entire press approved of and supported the idea, editorially and otherwise. Papers in other cities commented upon the great engineering enterprise favorably, all referring to the incalculable advantages to be derived by all concerned. Few dissenting voices were heard, and these mostly from a misconception of what was intended, and were speedily silenced by a presentation of the facts.

The Commission prepared and submitted with its preliminary report to the Mayor, the draft of the bill which, as carefully revised by the Corporation Counsel, was approved by the Mayor, and which, it was believed, would amply protect both the interests of the city and of the property owners along the avenue. The full text of the bill as passed by the Legislature is printed herein.

The financial difficulties were provided for in a manner entirely practical, and without assessing abutting property that had already suffered much. The contribution by Brooklyn of a sum not to exceed one and one-quarter million dollars was regarded as a light burden on the city at large, when the enormous advantages were taken into consideration.

The Commission gave much attention to the subject of improving the avenue, in addition to the treatment of the railroad. Part two of the Commission's report, submitted on March 18th, 1897, with suggestions in the form of drawings, together with a bill prepared for carrying them into effect, appear within, and more fully explain the views of the Commission. It is proper to say here, however, that the bill treating such proposed improvements was not introduced in the Legislature, on the theory that pressure of legislation might jeopardize the original bill relating to the railroad, it being the belief of the Commission that the successful accomplishment of the removal of the tracks and operation of a surface steam railroad on Atlantic avenue would involve the necessity of improvements in other respects, and could safely be left for future treatment.

The bill providing for the removal of the tracks of the Long Island Railroad from Atlantic avenue in the City of Brooklyn was introduced in the Legislature in 1897. The Commissioners appeared at several hearings before Committees of the Assembly and Senate at Albany, with the result that the bill passed both branches of the Legislature unanimously, was approved by the Mayors of New York and Brooklyn, and signed by the Governor, becoming a law May 18th, 1897, being Chapter 499,

Laws of 1897. Under its provisions a board of seven members was to be appointed by the Mayor of Brooklyn, called "The Board of the Atlantic Avenue Improvement," whose duty it should be to carry into effect the provisions of the law. On May 26th, 1897, your Honor appointed the following named gentlemen to serve as such board:

EUGENE G. BLACKFORD,
EDWARD F. LINTON,
EDWARD H. HOBBS,
WILLIAM E. PHILIPS,
WALTER M. MESEROLE,
Representing the City of Brooklyn.

WILLIAM H. BALDWIN, JR.,
CHARLES M. PRATT,
Representing the Long Island R.R.

The several members immediately qualified by taking the prescribed oath of office, and entered upon their duties.

This, together with the subjoined detailed printed matter, constitutes the history of the work of the Atlantic Avenue Commission. In closing, the Commissioners have a sense of pride in what they fully believe to be the successful formulation of a plan which, when carried into execution, will produce lasting benefits and substantial advantages to the many interests affected.

The Commissioners feel that they ought not to close this report without expressing to the Mayor and Corporation Counsel of the City of Brooklyn their acknowledgments and just appreciation of the intelligent aid and continued support given to the labors of the Commission by these public officers.

All of which is respectfully submitted.

EUGENE G. BLACKFORD, *President;*
EDWARD F. LINTON, *Secretary;*
EDWARD H. HOBBS,
WILLIAM E. PHILIPS,
WALTER M. MESEROLE,
Commissioners.

PRELIMINARY REPORT.

PART I.

OFFICE OF THE ATLANTIC AVENUE COMMISSION.
BROOKLYN, January 8, 1897.

To His Honor, the Mayor of the City of Brooklyn:

The Commission appointed by your Honor, under authority conferred by the Legislature of the State of New York, Chapter 394, Laws of 1896, entitled "An Act to authorize the appointment of a commission to examine into, and report a plan for, the relief and improvement of Atlantic avenue in the City of Brooklyn," beg leave to submit the following *preliminary* report of their deliberations and conclusions to date.

The Commissioners were appointed by your Honor May 28, 1896. On June 3d the Commission met and organized by the election of Mr. Eugene G. Blackford, President, and Edward F. Linton, Secretary. Rooms were secured for the use of the Commission in the Real Estate Exchange, No. 189 Montague street, wherein meetings have been held from time to time. Stated public meetings have been held, they having been duly advertised in the Brooklyn papers; ten such hearings in all have been had. A large number of people, including representative citizens, property owners, public officials, and disinterested civil engineers were invited and have appeared before the Commission. The interest shown has been of an intense character.

A large majority of those who appeared before the Commission were strongly opposed to a surface railroad operated by steam upon any part of Atlantic avenue. The general condition of Atlantic avenue as a thoroughfare, aside from the operation of a steam railroad thereon, was the subject of strong condemnation by all. Arguments looking to a remedy for existing ills chiefly favored depressing the tracks from Flatbush avenue to

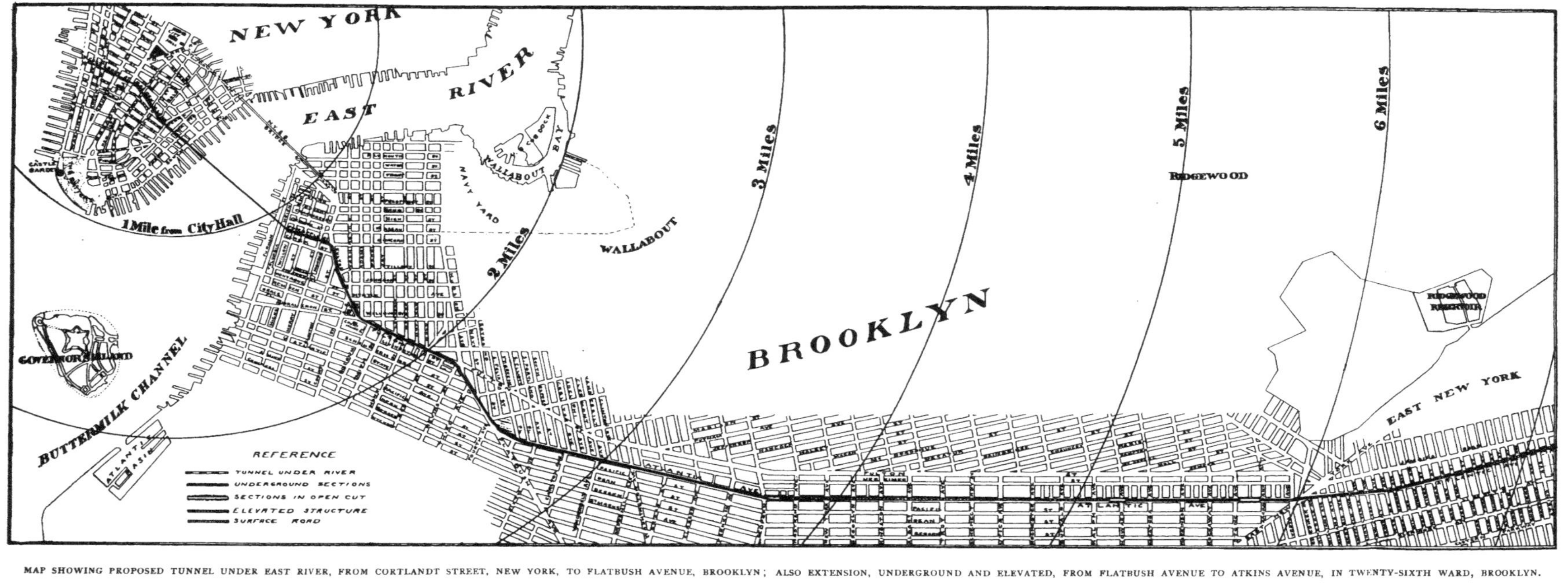

MAP SHOWING PROPOSED TUNNEL UNDER EAST RIVER, FROM CORTLANDT STREET, NEW YORK, TO FLATBUSH AVENUE, BROOKLYN; ALSO EXTENSION, UNDERGROUND AND ELEVATED, FROM FLATBUSH AVENUE TO ATKINS AVENUE, IN TWENTY-SIXTH WARD, BROOKLYN.

the City Line. In fact, this treatment of the problem seemed to be the popular wish. Very many desired to have the railroad removed entirely from the avenue. Many suggested an elevated railroad. The past history of railroad activities on Atlantic avenue was rehearsed at great length.

Estimates have been submitted by distinguished engineers and others as to the cost of depressing the tracks, as well as the cost of an elevated railroad. They have varied from $3,000,000 to $5,000,000. These estimates, however, have not included the cost of the disposition of water and sewer mains, or other substrata conditions. No practical financial plan providing for such cost has been submitted by any one.

The Commission have personally visited and carefully inspected the physical conditions of Atlantic avenue from Flatbush avenue to Woodhaven, and have found it deplorable, worse than an average country road, and unworthy of an enlightened and prosperous city of one million inhabitants. The circumstances which have contributed to this condition are too well known to require lengthy comment here.

The Commission deeming it wise to visit the City of Boston, Mass. (where the problem of congested street railroad travel was being solved, by the construction of a subway, under the direction of a Commission appointed by the authorities of that city), for the purpose of examining the method and character of the construction being carried on there, a committee of this Commission proceeded to Boston for that purpose. They were received with marked courtesy by the authorities and the Subway Commission, and were conducted by the engineer in charge through the entire work. The sum to be expended in that work will exceed $7,000,000. Much valuable knowledge was obtained, and the visit is regarded as of advantage in the work of the Atlantic Avenue Commission.

This Commission have given the matter committed to their care much thought and study. The sad and untimely death of Mr. Austin Corbin, President of the Long Island Railroad, in midsummer, embarrassed the Commission somewhat by the consequent delay in consultation with authorized representatives of that corporation. Immediately after the appointment of Mr. W. H.

Baldwin as President of the Long Island Railroad several interviews were had with him. We found him to be a broad-minded gentleman with progressive views, desirous of co-operating with the Commission in its work in every possible way. These interviews have resulted in the practical acceptance by the Long Island Railroad Company of plans formulated by the Commission, which are comprehensive in character and which treat the whole subject of transportation on Atlantic avenue, having regard for the im portance of communication throughout Long Island, as well as to the commercial interests and rights of the City of Brooklyn. The Commission have recognized certain legal rights of the rail road companies as well as the imperative need of a radical change from present conditions. The problems involved have been especially difficult of solution. Yet the Commission feel that they have found a practical plan which will meet with almost universal approval, certainly one which will meet nearly every demand along reasonable lines of financial and engineering possibilities, and which will at the same time afford permanent relief from past and present inconveniences of a most serious and annoying character, with the least disturbance of property interests and the lowest cost of construction.

The Commission submit herewith detailed plans and drawings showing the proposed disposition of the railroad tracks, reference to which will more fully illustrate the recommendations of the Commission.

We have carefully considered the various plans presented to us for the improvement of Atlantic avenue, and have also taken into consideration the grave engineering difficulties attending the abatement of the present objectionable features of the operation of a steam railroad on the surface of the avenue, and have arrived at the conclusion that the solution of the question must be attained by the employment of a composite scheme of construction, by which a large proportion of the expense and difficulty contemplated has been avoided, notably by non-interference with the existing sewers and the large 48-inch water main, which is one of the most important for supplying water to the City of Brooklyn. The plan which the Commission recommends, while it eliminates the grade crossings at the various streets, reduces to a minimum the interference with traffic of all sorts on Atlantic avenue during the carrying out of the improvements.

The project of connecting Brooklyn with New York by means of a tunnel from Flatbush Avenue Depot in Brooklyn to Cortlandt street in New York was taken into consideration in connection with the study of the Atlantic avenue problem, and the tunnel construction should be considered as an important item in the report of the Commission. The proposition is to have a low level station at Cortlandt street, New York, about seventy feet below ground, connecting with the elevated roads in that city and the streets by means of elevators; the tunnels being carried thence on that level to a station at Maiden Lane and Pearl street, connecting with the Second and Third avenue railroads; thence under the East River, under Pineapple street and Fulton street to a station near the City Hall, Brooklyn; thence under Fulton street and Flatbush avenue to Flatbush Avenue Depot, going into a depressed station at Flatbush Avenue Station about eighteen feet below grade. The tunnel will be carried under the Brooklyn streets within the curb lines to a station at the City Hall, which will be 115 feet below the street grade, and will rise by an easy grade from that point, so that the bottom of the tunnel shall come above the main relief sewer at Flatbush avenue and Hanson place, before passing into the depressed station. Continuing from Flatbush Avenue Depot, the tracks are to be depressed to Bedford avenue, a distance of 6,700 feet; the depression being covered by means of girders and masonry arching, restoring the surface of the street for public use for its full width. From the east side of Bedford avenue the railroad tracks will rise rapidly in an open cut to the grade of the street, and, continuing to rise, will pass onto an elevated railway structure, which, at Nostrand avenue, will attain such height that full head room will be provided for all street traffic without interference.

The physical characteristics of the ground between Bedford and Nostrand avenues are such that the rising grade of the railroad and the falling grade of the street combine to favor this transition from a depressed to an elevated structure, so that no obstruction is caused to any existing cross street, and full advantage is taken of the length of this block between Bedford and

ATLANTIC AVENUE AND FORT GREENE PLACE, SHOWING RAILROAD USE OF STREET.

Nostrand avenues (which is the longest on Atlantic avenue). At Nostrand avenue an elevated station is proposed, and the elevated structure continues thence a distance of 8,010 feet to Ralph avenue.

The posts of the elevated structure are to be twenty-two feet and three inches apart, and the street being 120 feet wide will allow ample space for all road traffic necessary. The extreme width of the elevated structure at the top surface is thirty-two feet, and being designed to be of medium height, will not interfere with the light and air of the adjacent owners, as is the case with existing elevated railroads, which generally cover a large proportion of the width of comparatively narrow streets. This plan saves great expense in construction, as it does not interfere with the many sewers in that section, nor with the water mains or the grade of the intersecting streets. The elevated section terminates between Ralph and Howard avenues, at which point the grade of the street rises rapidly going east; the tracks of the railroad are then to be carried through a tunnel for a distance of 2,910 feet to Stone avenue, thence the tracks rise to the present grade at Sackman street.

At Vesta avenue, in the Twenty-sixth Ward (which is better known as the Manhattan Crossing), owing to the complication of the tracks of the Manhattan Beach division, the railroad from Long Island City, the elevated road, the Canarsie Railroad and various sewers and water mains, the expense of changing the level of the railroads at this point would be of such magnitude that it has been deemed wise not to remove them from the surface.

Plans are being prepared for providing new depot accommodations at this location that shall greatly improve the present unsatisfactory conditions, as well as give better and safer facilities for the public street traffic.

At Snediker avenue, one block east of Manhattan Crossing, the railroad tracks will rise and continue as an elevated structure to Atkins avenue, where the tracks return to the surface grade, a distance of 6,070 feet. It will thus be observed on the entire route west of Atkins avenue, along Atlantic avenue, excepting at Manhattan Crossing, all grade crossings are eliminated, and the use of the surface of the street is restored to the public without obstruction. It is also proposed to operate a line of railway by the trolley system, on the surface of the streets, thus replacing the existing "rapid transit" trains by a much more convenient and efficient service for short distance riders, while at the same time it will distribute the passengers on the through trains to points intermediate between stations, and the through trains will be enabled to give true rapid transit by reason of the few stoppages.

The motive power for both systems will be electricity. The through service by short trains at frequent intervals and high speed will give accommodation never before offered. The freedom of this system from the nuisance of noise, smoke, steam and coal gas, will do away with many of the objections to former plans for the treatment of the problem.

The most important factor in this whole question will be the reduction of time in transit between New York City, Brooklyn and outlying suburbs; some idea of this great saving to passengers may be had when it is stated that the running time from the Cortlandt street terminus in New York to the City Hall station in Brooklyn will be 4 minutes; to Flatbush avenue, 6½ minutes; to Nostrand avenue, 9½ minutes; to Manhattan Crossing, in the Twenty-sixth Ward, 14 minutes, and to Jamaica, 21 minutes.

It will be seen by the foregoing that the Commission present as a result of their labors, a complete plan of real rapid transit, as well as a provision for local transit, not only as far as Atlantic avenue and the outlying portions of Long Island reached thereby are concerned, but includes the vastly more important connection with the active business part of New York City by a complete, practical system, the importance of which to Brooklyn cannot be over-estimated. The Commission believe that the solution of the problem of Atlantic avenue is second in importance only to the connecting of New York and Brooklyn by bridges spanning the East River. They feel especially happy because of the fact that they are able, in presenting their report, to include an actual connection with New York under the East River. The Commission feel warranted in saying that a corporation, now in existence, will construct the tunnel, and assume the cost thereof, provided the City of Brooklyn will participate in the expense of constructing the proposed railroad facilities from Flatbush Avenue to Atkins avenue in the Twenty-sixth Ward.

We are able to state positively that the total cost of construction of the proposed railroad from Flatbush avenue to Atkins avenue, ready for use and operation, will not exceed two and one-half million dollars. Estimates have been furnished to the Commission by competent engineers, and the figures verified by Mr. Walter M. Meserole, a member of the Commission, who is himself a civil engineer. This estimate may be reduced somewhat; at all events, it will not be increased. The City of Brooklyn's share in the expense of such construction will not exceed one-half the amount named.

The Commission are not at this date prepared to suggest a method by which such moneys shall be provided by the City of Brooklyn. We are fully aware that it will require grave and thoughtful consideration in view of the constitutional limitation of the debts of cities. At the same time, when the vast public and commercial interests are so admirably to be provided for, we believe that the financial problem will really be found less difficult of solution than the engineering problems have been, and that the public will respond to the needs of the occasion.

The Commission expects to further report its recommendations of possible needed legislation. We feel sanguine of the acceptance by all parties in interest of the result of our labors so far, in solving the problem submitted to us, which will also accomplish real rapid transit, not only from Brooklyn to all parts of Long Island, but will reach the central business portions of New York City, and this, too, at a cost very much less than any sum heretofore mentioned in connection with the subject. The question of the treatment of the avenue—outside of the railroad tracks—in the line of street improvements, will receive the earnest consideration of the Commission in due time.

In closing this report, the Commission desire to express their high appreciation of the aid and encouragement afforded by your

Honor, as well as by many citizens and the various City Departments, during our work.

Respectfully submitted,

EUGENE G. BLACKFORD, *President;*
EDWARD F. LINTON, *Secretary;*
EDWARD H. HOBBS,
WILLIAM E. PHILIPS,
WALTER M. MESEROLE.

PART II.

OFFICE OF THE ATLANTIC AVENUE COMMISSION,

BROOKLYN, March 18, 1897.

To His Honor, the Mayor of the City of Brooklyn:

The Commission appointed "to examine into and report a plan for the relief and improvement of Atlantic avenue, in the city of Brooklyn," herewith make *further* report of their conclusions and recommendations in reference to the improvement of said avenue.

The report submitted to your Honor January 8, 1897, covered the detail of organization, public hearings and the general condition of Atlantic avenue as a thoroughfare, but was devoted principally to what the Commission regarded as the chief factor in the problem, namely: The presence and operation of the Long Island Railroad by steam on the surface of the avenue. Reference to our preliminary report will more fully convey information on that part of the subject.

The Commission are gratified to know that their report so favorably impressed your Honor, that by your direction a bill has been prepared by the Law Department of the city and is now pending in the Legislature at Albany. The purpose of the bill being to relieve the avenue of the objectionable features attending the operation of a surface steam railroad thereon, it is to be hoped the bill will become a law. The Commission are still firmly of the belief that the carrying out of its provisions will be of incalculable advantage to the city of Brooklyn at large, and especially to the very large district immediately affected, as well as to the entire territory of Long Island, whose future growth and development are a matter of large concern to the commercial interests of the city of Brooklyn.

Having thus treated the question of the steam railroad, the Commission have since actively addressed themselves to the remaining features of the problem submitted to them.

It was undoubtedly originally intended that Atlantic avenue should be a great artery of communication from the water front through the city of Brooklyn to the district comprising Long Island to the eastward. This great purpose, however, has been defeated; the usefulness and material interests of the avenue have been dwarfed by the presence of the surface steam railroad, and its improvement as a thoroughfare has been sadly neglected. The property owners along the line have suffered, values have depreciated, and its condition has been, and is now, most deplorable. Therefore, the Commission believe the time has come when these disadvantages that afflict the city in many ways, as well as property fronting upon and adjacent to the avenue, should be remedied; that their work would be incomplete unless provision were made looking to the improvement of the avenue in all respects, so that it shall be, in fact, a fine thoroughfare of large contributive advantage to all interests, and that the work of improvement should immediately follow the proposed change in the character of the railroad operation.

The Commission find upon examination of the avenue between Flatbush avenue and the City Line, a varied condition of improvement, or lack of improvement, as the case may be. That portion between Flatbush avenue and Bedford avenue is paved with granite block pavement. That portion between Bedford avenue and Vesta avenue, a distance of over two miles and a half, is in a miserable condition. It appears that in former years the avenue was graded, curbed and partially improved by thin macadamizing, and the property subjected to assessments therefor, but said improvement has long since disappeared by reason of neglect and accumulations of deposits upon the surface. The roadway between Vesta avenue and Berriman street in the Twenty-sixth Ward, a distance of a mile and a quarter, is paved fifteen feet in width from each curb, with granite blocks, but by reason of the introduction of sewer, water and gas mains, has been so frequently torn up and disarranged as to practically ruin the pavement, requiring new treatment to restore it to even a favorable condition. The portion of the avenue between Berriman street and the City Line, a distance of one mile, is graded and curbed, but otherwise is in a condition of such deterioration as to be useless for vehicle traffic.

The Commission believe that a comprehensive plan of improvement should be adopted, treating the entire avenue from Flatbush avenue to the City Line, so that its condition shall be practically alike in all parts. The cost of such improvement may properly be divided into equitable parts and assessed upon the three interests served, namely: the city at large, the abutting property owners, and the Long Island Railroad Company.

The justification of such proper division of contributing to the cost of such improvement may be found in the fact that the city government is somewhat responsible for the ills that have existed on the avenue for many years.

The abutting property owners have from time to time paid assessments for the varied kind of improvements that have been made. The Long Island Railroad Company and the property owners will be large beneficiaries because of such improvement; therefore, we think that all three should contribute a fair share toward defraying the cost thereof.

The Commission are not prepared at this time to suggest a definite apportionment of the cost among the three interests named, but are confident that further consideration will result in intelligent and satisfactory treatment of the subject. The Commission are not inclined to even specify what the character of the improvement shall be, other than in general terms. They are of the opinion that the broad purpose and intention of those who laid out the avenue originally should be established.

Upon further study of the subject, if it shall be determined to have a pavement smooth in character, that would attract the many thousands of our citizens who are using the bicycle for recreation and business purposes, the avenue would be of great further advantage and use to large and growing numbers of people to whom heretofore Atlantic avenue has been an impassable and unknown thoroughfare.

In connection with this subject, it is pertinent and timely to call attention to the activity of our neighbors in Queens County (within the lines of the proposed Greater New York), in the matter of "good roads." Within the next two years there will be expended over a million dollars for macadamizing the country roads through Queens County.

The improvement of Atlantic avenue will connect directly with this comprehensive system. The present means of reaching these fine roads is by way of Glenmore avenue, opened and improved in 1896, but by reason of this avenue being the only connection, it has already become overcrowded by wagon traffic, and the roadbed so cut up as to be almost useless to bicyclists.

A feature that has impressed the Commission as an important and strong reason why the avenue should be improved, as outlined above, is the fact that the Twenty-sixth Ward, now containing a population of over 50,000 inhabitants, and rapidly growing in importance, is practically without proper lines of communication with the central business portions of the City of Brooklyn, by reason of the fact that, at the entrance to the ward, the principal thoroughfares leading to the water front (and thence to New York City) concentrate at this point and involve such a network of railroads and other features of congestion as to imperatively demand an adequate outlet and means of intercommunication, such as the improvement of Atlantic avenue will afford. There is no practical solution of the question, other than that Atlantic avenue shall be such chief thoroughfare to and from this important section of Brooklyn.

The Commission have considered it proper, for the information of your Honor, to submit an approximate estimate of the cost of improving the avenue, and for that purpose referred the matter to the member of the Commission who is a civil engineer. We embody his communication herein :

OFFICES OF WALTER M. MESEROLE,
CIVIL ENGINEER AND CITY SURVEYOR,
2789 ATLANTIC AV. AND 189 MONTAGUE ST.,

BROOKLYN, N. Y., March 12, 1897.

To the Atlantic Avenue Commission:

GENTLEMEN.— In compliance with your resolution passed March 6th, I have to make the following report relative to the expense of paving and otherwise improving the surface of Atlantic avenue between Fort Greene place and the City Line, at Enfield street.

My estimate will provide for a pavement of vitrified brick, or asphalt, on concrete foundation, or granite blocks on sand foundation.

The total length of the proposed improvement is 30,525 feet, which, being doubled, gives 61,050 front feet. Deducting the intersections aggregating 10,000 feet for the two sides of the street, leaves 51,050 front feet of property to be assessed.

While I have estimated the various items of cost carefully, I do not deem it necessary to more than give the approximate total cost of said improvements in round figures, which is $612,000.00.

Respectfully submitted,

WALTER M. MESEROLE.

The Bill now pending before the Legislature relating to the treatment of the railroad provides for the appointment of a Commission under whose direction the work shall be carried out.

We are of the opinion that the proposed further improvement of the avenue should be under the direction and charge of the same Commission, for the following reasons:

The work can be done most economically in connection with the work of changing the grade of the railway tracks, and under the same authorities, because there will be no duplication of work; the backfilling of excavations will be done by the same parties who are to be responsible for the integrity of the pavement; the organization of temporary railroad tracks and construction trains will be useful for removing surplus earth and bringing in the materials for paving, very materially saving in the item of freight, and the advantages of a single authority in dealing with pipe corporations, grades, rights of adjacent owners, etc., will be secured.

If this work were done under any City Department, the cost of supervision would be large and much additional labor would be entailed on the officials of that Department, while this Commission, being organized for the work, can handle it with very little added expense.

The Commission being of the opinion that legislation will be required to authorize the improvement of the avenue, as herein suggested, we therefore respectfully recommend that a bill be prepared by the Law Department of the City of Brooklyn, and introduced in the Legislature at Albany for the purpose of providing for the entire co-operative plan of improving the avenue.

Respectfully submitted,

E. G. BLACKFORD, *President;*
E. F. LINTON, *Secretary;*
E. H. HOBBS,
W. E. PHILIPS,
W. M. MESEROLE.

LEGISLATION.

ACT CREATING THE ATLANTIC AVENUE COMMISSION.

LOCAL—KINGS COUNTY.

[Five folios.]

LAWS OF NEW YORK—BY AUTHORITY.

[Every law, unless a different time shall be prescribed therein, shall not take effect until the twentieth day after it shall have become a law. Section 43, article II, chapter 8, General Laws.]

CHAPTER 394.

AN ACT to authorize the appointment of a commission to examine into and report a plan for the relief and improvement of Atlantic avenue in the city of Brooklyn.

Accepted by the city.

BECAME a law April 27, 1896, with the approval of the Governor. Passed, three-fifths being present.

The People of the State of New York, represented in Senate and Assembly, do enact as follows:

Section 1 The mayor of the city of Brooklyn is hereby authorized, immediately after the passage of this act, to appoint five persons, residents of the city of Brooklyn, who shall constitute a commission for the purposes hereinafter mentioned, and who shall serve without compensation. One of said persons shall be a civil engineer and one shall be a lawyer. Said commissioners shall organize by the election of a president and a secretary and shall have power to summon witnesses, administer oaths and send for persons and papers, and any person swearing falsely before them shall be deemed guilty of perjury, and upon conviction be fined as for that crime. Said commission may employ such engineers and other assistants and incur such incidental expenses as may be necessary and proper, not to exceed, however, in the aggregate the sum of five thousand dollars, which shall be taken out of the revenue fund of said city.

§ 2. Said commission shall inquire into the condition of Atlantic avenue in said city with reference to the railroads operated thereon, and in other respects shall give public hearings and invite suggestions from parties interested therein as to the best methods for the relief and improvement of the same. It shall formulate a plan for the relief of said avenue and the improvement of the same, and shall report such plan, together with such recommendations as to it may seem proper, to the mayor of said city on or before the first day of December in the year eighteen hundred and ninety-six, and thereupon the said mayor shall cause a bill to be prepared to carry out said plans and recommendations and shall present the same to the legislature at its meeting in the year eighteen hundred and ninety-seven.

§ 3. This act shall take effect immediately.

STATE OF NEW YORK, } ss.:
Office of the Secretary of State.

I have compared the preceding with the original law on file in this office, and do hereby certify that the same is a correct transcript therefrom and of the whole of said original law.

JOHN PALMER,
Secretary of State.

ACT CREATING THE BOARD FOR THE ATLANTIC AVENUE IMPROVEMENT.

LOCAL—KINGS COUNTY.

[Forty-five folios.]

LAWS OF NEW YORK—BY AUTHORITY.

[Every law, unless a different time shall be prescribed therein, shall not take effect until the twentieth day after it shall have become a law. Section 43, article II, chapter 8, General Laws.]

CHAPTER 499.

AN ACT to regulate and improve Atlantic avenue between Flatbush avenue and Atkins avenue in the city of Brooklyn, and providing for the removal of the steam railroad of the Long Island Railroad company from the surface, and for changing the grade of said railroad and providing for all changes in avenues, streets and railroads that may be rendered necessary by reason of such changes, and providing means for the payment thereof.

Accepted by the city.

BECAME a law May 18, 1897, with the approval of the Governor. Passed, three-fifths being present.

The People of the State of New York, represented in Senate and Assembly, do enact as follows:

SECTION 1. The grade of the railroad of the Atlantic Avenue Railroad company of Brooklyn, now leased to and operated by the Long Island Railroad company, as at present established between Flatbush avenue and Atkins avenue, in the city of Brooklyn, shall be changed and altered by said railroad companies as follows: Commencing at Fort Greene place, the grade of said railroad shall be depressed so as to connect with the tracks in the railroad yard of the Long Island Railroad company at Flatbush and Atlantic avenues, which said yard tracks are to be depressed to a depth of not less than sixteen feet below the surface of Flatbush and Atlantic avenues, adjoining said yard. And the connection between the tracks of said Atlantic Avenue Railroad company, or of its lessee, the Long Island Railroad company, and the right of way of said companies, now in the center of Atlantic avenue, and said railroad yard, shall be depressed and altered so that it shall be by tracks running under Fort Greene place and Atlantic avenue, until they intersect the center line of the depressed right of way and tracks on said Atlantic avenue at or near South Elliott place. From South Elliott place running eastward, the grade of the right of way of said railroad companies shall be depressed so that the existing surface railroad tracks shall be below the surface of Atlantic avenue at such depth as to allow the complete restoration of the surface of said Atlantic avenue free from steam railroad tracks, fences, gates, signal posts or other appurtenances of such steam railroad now existing thereon; and the said railroad of the Atlantic Avenue Railroad company of Brooklyn, now operated by its lessee, the Long Island Railroad company, shall run under the surface of Atlantic avenue to a point at or near the easterly side of Bedford avenue in said city of Brooklyn. At or near the said easterly side of Bedford avenue the said right of way and railroad tracks shall be used and operated in an open cut, with proper retaining walls and of width not greater than the present right of way in possession of said railroad companies, the grade of said tracks and right of way rising gradually until they reach a point about midway between Bedford and Nostrand avenues in said city, where the grade of said railroad tracks and right of way and the grade of Atlantic avenue shall coincide. From said point about midway between Bedford and Nostrand avenues, running easterly, the said railroad tracks shall be removed from the surface as now operated, and raised by convenient grades on suitable and sufficient structures until they reach the west side of Nostrand avenue in said city at a point not less than fourteen feet above the street surface. From said westerly side of Nostrand avenue and until they reach the easterly side of Ralph avenue, the said railroad tracks shall run on an elevated steel structure over the right of way of said railroad companies as now in possession at such grade elevation that they shall cross over all intervening streets and avenues at such grade as to leave the same unobstructed on the surface, and open to the free passage of pedestrians and vehicles with a clear height at each crossing of not less than fourteen feet. From the easterly side of Ralph avenue in said city the said tracks shall descend by convenient grade on suitable and sufficient structures, until they reach a point about midway between Ralph and Howard avenues in said city of Brooklyn, where the grade of said right of way and tracks shall coincide with the grade of Atlantic avenue adjoining the same. From said point about midway between Ralph and Howard avenues said right of way and tracks shall be used and operated in an open cut with proper retaining walls and of width not greater than the existing right of way in possession of said railroad companies on a convenient descending grade to the west side of Cooper place in said city. From said west side of Cooper place the right of way of said railroad shall be depressed so that said right of way and tracks shall be used and operated below the grade of the surface of Atlantic avenue as now existing and in such manner as to leave the surface of Atlantic avenue free from the present steam railroad tracks, fences, gates, posts and other appurtenances of said steam railroad, until said railroad, right of way and tracks reach a point at or near the easterly side of Stone avenue in said city of Brooklyn. From said point at or near the easterly side of Stone avenue said right of way and tracks shall be used and operated in an open cut with proper retaining walls and of width not greater than the present right of way now in the possession of said railroad companies, easterly to a point at or near the westerly side of Jardine place in said city of Brooklyn, where the grade of said right of way and tracks shall again coincide with the grade of Atlantic avenue adjoining. From said westerly side of Jardine place the said right of way and railroad tracks shall be used and operated by said Atlantic Avenue Railroad company of Brooklyn, or its lessee, the Long Island Railroad company, as at present on a surface grade to a point at or near the easterly side of Snediker avenue in said city of Brooklyn. From said point at or near the easterly side of Snediker avenue in said city said tracks shall be elevated to convenient grades on a suitable and sufficient structure so as to pass over Williams avenue at a clear height of eight feet, and Alabama avenue at a clear height of twelve feet, over the right of way of said railroad companies as now in possession. From the easterly side of Alabama avenue, running easterly to a point at or near Linwood street, said railroad tracks shall be operated upon an elevated steel structure running over the present right of way of said railroad companies and crossing over all intervening streets and avenues at such grades as to leave the same unobstructed on the surface and open to the free passage of pedestrians and vehicles, with a clear height at each crossing of not less than fourteen feet. From said point at or near Linwood street said tracks shall descend by convenient grades on suitable and sufficient structures to the present railroad grade at or near Atkins and Atlantic avenues in said city of Brooklyn, and from said point at or near Atkins avenue the said right of way and tracks shall be used and operated as at present located. At the various points hereinabove set forth at which said railroads are directed to be operated in an open cut while passing from the depressed grade to the overhead grade, said open cut shall be of width not greater than the existing right of way in possession of said railroad companies, and said open cut shall be constructed with masonry walls and surmounted by suitable railings. The elevated structure herein provided for shall be of steel, supported by posts, so that the tracks and posts shall not encroach beyond the existing right of way of such railroad companies; provided, however, that the coping on said retaining walls at said open cuts may extend not more than eighteen inches over the land of the right of way in possession of said railroad companies, and the foundation piers and supports for the pillars holding said elevated structure, as well as the foundation walls of depressed and covered portions, may be constructed under the surface of Atlantic avenue outside the line of said railroad right of way as now in possession. Between the westerly side of Carlton avenue and Adelphi street the present tracks connecting the said railroads with the freight yard and station at Carlton and Atlantic avenues shall be depressed below the surface of Carlton and Atlantic avenues aforesaid so as to afford an entrance for two tracks from said right of way and tracks to said freight yard by convenient grades, in such manner as to leave the surface of Atlantic and Carlton avenues intact.

§ 2. The Atlantic Avenue Railroad company of Brooklyn, or its lessee, the Long Island Railroad company, is hereby authorized and permitted, at its election, to erect stations and platforms on either side of the railroad at any points along said depressed tracks to take the place of those existing on its through line of railroad between Brooklyn and points on Long Island, and sidings for the passage of trains, provided such stations and sidings shall be below the surface of Atlantic avenue, and for the support of the girders to sustain the said avenue over said depressed tracks and over said stations and sidings, proper structures may be extended over said right of way for such distance as shall be necessary for affording necessary support to the surface of the street. Stations and platforms along the depressed line shall be reached by stairs not less than five feet in width which shall terminate on the sidewalk on either side of Atlantic avenue. Said railroad companies are also authorized to erect and maintain a station or stations to take the place of such existing stations on either side of the elevated structure hereinabove provided for. The use of stations, platforms and sidings, when constructed, shall in no way interfere with the grade of Atlantic avenue, or the free use of said avenue by the public save so far as the same may be affected by the supports for stations along the elevated structures hereinabove provided for. All of which, however, shall be done under the approval, direction and sanction of the board hereinafter provided for.

§ 3. The Atlantic Avenue Railroad company of Brooklyn, or its lessee, the Long Island Railroad company, during the change of the grade of said railroad, as herein provided, is authorized to maintain such temporary structures, and to occupy any part or parts of Atlantic avenue, of intersecting public streets or avenues in the city of Brooklyn necessary in the premises, or for the continued operation of said railroad, all of which, however, shall be done under the approval, direction and sanction of the board hereinafter provided for.

§ 4. There shall be a board whose duty it shall be to direct and superintend the construction of the said improvement by said railroad companies, which board shall be called "The Board for the Atlantic Avenue Improvement." It shall be the duty of the said board to file a monthly statement, under oath, of the items of its expenditures, with the comptroller of the city of Brooklyn. Regular accounts of all its transactions shall be kept by the board, which shall be open to the inspection of the officers of the said railroad companies and to the comptroller and the commissioners of city works of the city of Brooklyn. The said board is authorized to pass suitable by-laws for its own regulation and government, and to select a presiding officer and secretary from its number, and to employ clerical and other necessary assistants in the performance of their duties, and to fix the compensation of such assistants. It shall keep a record of all its proceedings. The said board shall consist of seven members (one of whom shall be a practical civil engineer) all of whom shall be appointed by the mayor of the city of Brooklyn, but two of said members shall be appointed on the written nomination of the president of the Long Island Railroad company. In case of the death, removal or resignation of either of the members of the board, the vacancy shall be filled by appointment by said mayor, provided that if either of the members of said board appointed by the said mayor on the written nomination of the president of the Long Island Railroad company shall die, resign or be removed, the vacancy shall be filled by the said mayor on the like nomination of the president of said company. All appointments of commissioners made in pursuance of this act shall be filed in the office of the city clerk of the city of Brooklyn. The said board are hereby authorized and directed to take the entire charge and control of the said improvement, and to direct and superintend the construction of the same, in conformity with the provisions of this act, in a substantial and workmanlike manner. Each member of the board shall receive ten dollars for every day that he shall be employed in the performance of his duties under this act, and the compensation of said commissioners and of any clerical or other assistants employed by them shall be paid from the funds provided for the expenses of said improvement. They may appoint a general superintendent of the works, who may be one of their number. The said board shall prepare plans and specifications, and an estimate of the cost of the work of said improvement, in conformity with this act, which, when approved by the commissioner of city works, shall be filed in the office of the comptroller of the city of Brooklyn, and a duplicate thereof in the office of the said commissioner of city works of said city. The members of said board before entering upon the performance of their duties, shall severally take and subscribe an oath of affirmation before a judge of a court of record in the city of Brooklyn faithfully to perform the trusts and duties required of them by this act, and as a member of the said board, which oath shall be filed in the office of the city clerk of the city of Brooklyn. No work shall be done upon any street, nor shall any street be opened without the consent of the commissioner of city works of the city of Brooklyn.

§ 5. When the said plan, specification and estimate shall be made and filed as aforesaid, the said board shall prepare a statement showing the items of the expense and cost of the said improvement, and what is to be deemed properly included therein, and said expense and cost of such items shall be borne and paid by the Atlantic Avenue Railroad company of Brooklyn or its lessee, the Long Island Railroad company, and the city in which said road is located, in equal proportions, one-half each by said city and by said railroad corporations, as the construction of said improvement progresses. The said board, before the work of said improvement is commenced, shall file a statement showing the division of the cost made as aforesaid between the railroad corporations above named and the said city, but in no event shall the proportion of said cost to be borne by said city exceed the sum of one million two hundred and fifty thousand dollars, and any amount in excess thereof shall be borne and paid by the said railroad companies. When and as often as it shall appear by the certificate of the superintending engineer of the work of the said improvement, duly certified by the aforesaid board, that the sum of twenty-five thousand dollars has been expended thereon by either of said railroad companies, specifying the por-

CROSS SECTION, ATLANTIC AVENUE, SHOWING CUT AND COVERED WAY, WITH RESTORED STREET SURFACE FROM FLATBUSH AVENUE TO BEDFORD AVENUE.

tions and division of the said improvement where said expenditure has been made, the comptroller of the said city shall draw his warrant upon the treasury of the said city, in favor of the treasurer of the railroad company, bearing and paying said expense, for one-half the said sum, which shall be duly signed and countersigned by the proper officers of said city, upon whom there is devolved the duty of signing and countersigning warrants, and deliver it to the said railroad company for and on account of the one-half of the expense and cost of the said improvement to be borne and paid by the city as aforesaid.

§ 6. For the purpose of raising the sum or amount of the cost of said improvement to be borne and paid by the said city, it shall be the duty of the mayor and comptroller, or other proper officers thereof, from time to time, upon the requisition of said board of improvement, to issue bonds of said city not exceeding the amount above specified, bearing such rates of interest as they may deem proper, which interest shall be payable semi-annually, which bonds shall be issued as are other city bonds, and the proceeds of which shall be used for the purpose of paying the one-half part of all amounts called for by the certificate of the superintending engineer, approved by said board and provided for in the preceding section of this act. Such bonds shall be known as the "Atlantic avenue improvement bonds," and shall be issued at not less than par, for such period as said mayor and comptroller may determine, not exceeding twenty years.

§ 7. The proceeds of the sale of said Atlantic avenue improvement bonds so sold, as provided in the preceding section, shall be set apart, when collected, as a trust fund, for the purposes of said improvement, and for paying the portion of the cost thereof hereinabove imposed upon said city. To provide for the payment of the interest upon said bonds there shall be included in the tax budget and raised by tax upon the real and personal property in said city which, during each year until said bonds are paid, is subject to taxation, a sum sufficient to pay such interest after deducting therefrom any interest that may have been earned and received during the said year from said trust fund or the sinking fund hereinafter provided for. To provide for the payment of the principal of said bonds, there shall be included in the tax budget and raised by tax upon the real and personal property in said city which, during each year until said bonds are paid, is subject to taxation, a sum equal to one-twentieth part of the entire principal of said bonds, which amount shall be set apart as a special sinking fund to be denominated the "Atlantic avenue improvement sinking fund," and shall be appropriated and applied for and towards the payment of the principal of said bonds, and shall be under the management and control of the mayor, comptroller and treasurer of said city, or a majority of them, who shall be commissioners of said fund, and shall apply the same solely to the use and purpose aforesaid until the principal of said bonds shall be fully paid and discharged. The moneys directed to be paid unto the said sinking fund shall be invested by the commissioners of said fund in the several respective public stocks or bonds of said city or of the State of New York.

§ 8. The cost of construction of all stations and sidings upon said railroad and other betterments to the railroad hereafter made, whether provided for in this act, or not, shall be borne by the said railroad corporations, or one of them, and shall not be included in the estimate to be made by said board of the cost of the proposed improvement herein authorized.

§ 9. Said depressed right of way and tracks and the elevated portions of said railroad hereinabove provided for, shall be employed for the uses and purposes of the said the Long Island Railroad company to the same extent and as fully and completely as the railroad at present constructed which is operated by the said company, provided that the operation of passenger trains on said railroad on said improvement shall be by some power other than steam locomotives, but steam locomotives may be used to move freight trains and, in cases of emergency, preventing the use of other power, to move the passenger trains over said improvement. It shall not be lawful for any person or persons other than a public officer in the execution of his duty as such, with his agents or assistants, to enter or pass upon or through the said depressed right of way or the elevated structure or any portion thereof, in any other way than in the proper cars of such corporation provided for that purpose, without the consent of said corporation, under a penalty of fifty dollars for each offense, to be recovered by said railroad corporation.

§ 10. If in the preparation of the plans for said improvement, it shall be found that the alteration in the grade of the right of way and railroad tracks hereinabove referred to shall interfere with any water main or pipe running longitudinally along said avenue, the said board for the Atlantic avenue improvement may locate said underground and depressed right of way and tracks at such point or points along said avenue as shall avoid said water mains or pipe, but the entire width of the depressed right of way and tracks shall not exceed the width of the present right of way occupied by the tracks and fences upon the surface of Atlantic avenue. Said board of improvement shall prepare a map and plan showing the location of the right of way and tracks of the railroad company as now in possession, together with the location of any water main running longitudinally along said avenue and which might be affected or interfered with by the construction of the depressed track herein provided for, and shall also indicate on said plan the underground and depressed right of way as located by them, and in consideration of a license from the said the Long Island Railroad company to the city of Brooklyn or its successor to keep and maintain the said longitudinal water mains or pipes as at present constructed, the said city is hereby authorized and directed to execute all necessary instruments for vesting in said Atlantic Avenue Railroad company of Brooklyn, or its lessee, the Long Island Railroad company, their successors and assigns, the full and complete right and privilege, during the continuance of said license, of using and occupying, for railroad purposes, such portions of the depressed right of way under the surface of Atlantic avenue as may be necessary by reason of such change in location, in so far as the said city shall have any right, title or interest therein. Whenever, in the prosecution of the said improvement, it shall become necessary to remove or change the position of the water or sewer pipes upon the said avenue, the same shall be done by the department of city works of the said city, and so as not to interfere with the prosecution of the work of the said improvement, and the cost thereof may be included in the estimate to be made by the said board, of the amount to be paid jointly by the said railroad companies and the city in which said road is located, or the same shall be paid wholly by the said city according as the said board may determine; and whenever, in the prosecution of the said improvement, it shall become necessary to change the location of the gas pipes upon or under the said avenue, the same shall be done by and at the expense of the corporation or corporations owning or operating the same.

§ 11. During the progress of said work, the Atlantic Avenue Railroad company of Brooklyn and its lessee, the Long Island Railroad company, are hereby authorized to lay down such temporary tracks on Atlantic avenue as may be necessary for carrying on the railroad business during the progress of the work, and such tracks shall be removed when the work shall have been completed.

§ 12. Whenever it shall be found advisable or necessary to alter the grade of the streets crossing the said Atlantic avenue under or over said railroad, the same may be done by said companies, but so as not to interfere with the free use of said streets by the public, and under the supervision of and with the sanction of said board for the improvement of Atlantic avenue and not otherwise.

§ 13. The said board shall determine when the work of said improvement shall commence, but they shall not so determine until they are satisfied that an underground double track railroad will be built from the westerly terminus of the said railroads to some convenient point at or near Maiden Lane in the city of New York as now constituted and that a company competent and able to build such an underground railroad has secured all the necessary consents and franchises therefor, has entered upon the performance of said work and has obligated itself to unite with the Long Island Railroad company in operating trains to and over the railroads aforesaid, and until the said the Long Island Railroad company has secured all the necessary rights, consents and franchises to construct the improvement herein provided for and has agreed to pay the proportionate cost thereof as hereinabove provided. After such determination is made the work shall be prosecuted to completion with reasonable expedition. When completed, the Long Island Railroad company as the lessee of the said Atlantic Avenue Railroad company of Brooklyn, its successors, or assigns, are authorized and directed to run their trains over the said improvement, and the route of said railroad as constructed and authorized by law, and no trains or cars of other companies without permission of the said Long Island Railroad company shall be run therein or thereon.

§ 14. The board appointed pursuant to the provisions of this act shall act upon any and all questions by a majority vote of its members.

§ 15. This act shall take effect immediately.

STATE OF NEW YORK, } ss.:
Office of the Secretary of State. }

I have compared the preceding with the original copy on file in this office, and do hereby certify that the same is a correct transcript therefrom and of the whole of said original law.

JOHN PALMER,
Secretary of State.

Bill introduced in the Legislature April 2, 1897; passed both branches. Was approved by Mayor of Brooklyn. Did not become a law by reason of failure of the Governor to attach his signature.

The intent of the bill being supplementary to Chapter 499, Laws of 1897:

STATE OF NEW YORK.

No. 1400. Int. 1075.

IN SENATE,

April 2, 1897.

Introduced by Mr. Wieman—read twice and ordered printed, and when printed to be committed to the committee on affairs of cities.

AN ACT to regulate the use of lands, forming part of the right of way of any railroad company, the road of which has been removed from the surface in, or adjacent to, streets and highways in all cities of the first class in this state.

The People of the State of New York, represented in Senate and Assembly, do enact as follows:

SECTION 1. Whenever the right of way, grade or tracks of any steam railroad company in or adjacent to any street or highway in any city of the first class are required by law to be changed or altered by elevating or depressing the same for the purpose of discontinuing the use of steam power upon the surface of such highway or street, such alteration or change of grade shall not be deemed to curtail or affect any right which such railroad company or its lessees or assigns may have to maintain and operate a surface passenger railway within the limits of the right of way so depressed or elevated, and over or under the railroad tracks so depressed or elevated, with all turnouts, sidings and tracks necessary to secure the continuous connection and operation of such surface railroad.

§ 2. In the event that any such turnouts, sidings or tracks shall extend beyond the lines of the right of way of such railroad corporations so depressed or elevated in or upon any of the streets or highways aforesaid, such turnouts, sidings or tracks so extending beyond the lines of such right of way shall only be constructed upon condition that the consent of the owners of one-half in value of the property bounded on, and the consent also of the local authorities having the control of that portion of such street or highway upon which it is proposed to construct such turnouts, sidings or tracks, shall be first obtained; or, in case the consent of such property owners can not be obtained, the appellate division of the supreme court in the department where such construction is proposed, may, upon application, appoint three commissioners who shall determine, after a hearing of all the parties interested, whether such turnouts, sidings and tracks so extending beyond the limits of such right of way and on said highway ought to be constructed or operated: and their determination, confirmed by the court, may be taken in lieu of the consent of the property owners.

§ 3. Any such surface railroad shall be operated by some power other than steam locomotives, and shall not be used except for passenger traffic.

§ 4. This act shall take effect immediately.

Bill prepared by Counsel for the Commission, to be introduced in Legislature, providing for grading and paving Atlantic avenue from Flatbush avenue to City Line, was not introduced for reasons stated in final report of the Commission.

AN ACT to regulate and to improve Atlantic avenue in the city of Brooklyn and to provide the means of payment therefor.

The People of the State of New York, represented in Senate and Assembly, do enact as follows:

SECTION 1. The Board for the Atlantic Avenue Improvement appointed pursuant to the provisions of the act of the legislature of the State of New York, passed at the session of the year eighteen hundred and ninety-seven, entitled " An Act to regulate and improve Atlantic avenue between Flatbush avenue and Atkins avenue in the city of Brooklyn, and providing for the removal of the steam railroad of the Long Island Railroad Company from the surface, and for changing the grade of said railroad, and providing for all changes in avenues, streets and railroads that may be rendered necessary by reason of such changes, and providing means for the payment thereof," are hereby charged with the execution of the duties and vested with the powers conferred upon it by the provisions of this act.

§ 2. The said Board shall prepare a plan for the improvement of Atlantic avenue from Flatbush avenue to the City Line of the city of Brooklyn, by paving and repaving said avenue uniformly throughout with an improved pavement, which plan shall fix the widths of the roadway and such permanent improvements throughout said avenue from Flatbush avenue to said City Line, as in its judgment shall be for the benefit, beauty and utility of said avenue, and shall show the treatment for the various portions thereof as shall, in its opinion, best serve said purposes. When said plan shall have received the approval of the mayor to be endorsed in writing thereon, the said Board shall have power to cause said avenue to be improved in accordance therewith. All such work shall be done by contract or contracts, let to the lowest responsible bidder in accord with the provisions regulating other work now done by contract in said city, save and except the making, execution and superintendence of such contract or contracts, shall be in all respects within the exclusive cognizance and control of the said Board. And said Board shall have power to employ such engineers, surveyors, clerical and other assistants as may be necessary in the premises, and to fix and to regulate their respective compensations.

§ 3. During the work and improvement hereby committed to said Board, it shall have the exclusive government, management and control of said Atlantic avenue from Flatbush avenue to the said City Line, subject, however, to the laws of the state and to the powers of the common council in relation thereto, not inconsistent with this act, and no person or corporation shall have power to open the street for any temporary purposes, except with the consent and under the supervision of said Board.

§ 4. To meet the cost in the first instance, of the work and improvement authorized by this act, the Mayor and the Comptroller of the city of Brooklyn shall from time to time, as may be required, issue bonds of said city, to an amount not exceeding $700,000, as other city bonds are issued, and the proceeds thereof shall be paid into the city treasury, to be used as required for the payment of such work, improvement and the expenses thereof, and for no other purpose. Such bonds shall be known as the Atlantic Avenue Improvement Bonds, Series Number Two, and shall be issued in such amounts, at such rates of interest and in such series and be made payable at such times as the Mayor and Comptroller may determine. None of said bonds shall be sold at less than par. The proceeds of said bonds shall be paid out of the city treasury from time to time as may be required, upon vouchers duly approved by the said Board or a majority thereof.

§ 5. When said work and improvements shall have been fully completed and paid for as above provided, the said Board shall thereupon so certify in writing to the Mayor and the Comptroller of said city, and thereupon the said Comptroller shall certify to the Board of Assessors of the city of Brooklyn one-half of the total cost of said work and improvement, and thereupon one-quarter of the said total cost of said work and improvement as so certified, shall be borne and paid by the Atlantic Avenue Railroad Company of Brooklyn, or its lessee, the Long Island Railroad Company, or its successors or assigns, and shall be duly assessed by said Board upon the property of said company in, on or along the line of such improvement upon said avenue and one-quarter of the said total cost of said improvement shall be borne and paid by the property lying within one-half block from each side of said avenue and shall be assessed thereon by said Board of Assessors according to benefit, in accord with the provisions and procedure of law now regulating the levying of assessments in said city, and in levying such assessments the said Board shall take into consideration, in each and every instance, whether the parcel, lot or piece of land to be assessed shall have at any time theretofore been assessed for any previous paving of said Atlantic avenue and shall have power to make such allowance therefor as it may deem proper in determining the amount of such assessment to be imposed thereon. Said assessments when duly confirmed shall be a lien upon the property assessed and shall be collected as are assessments for local improvements in said city. If at any time the functions and powers of any of the officers named in this act, other than the said Board, shall cease and determine by act of law previous to the fulfillment of the powers and duties cast upon the said Board by the provisions of this act, then the duties herein conferred upon the said Mayor shall devolve upon the Mayor within whose jurisdiction the territory within which such avenue exists shall be placed, and the other duties cast upon such other officers shall devolve upon such officer or officers as shall by act of law have succeeded to the duties of such officer or officers respectively.

§ 6. The said Board shall act upon all questions by a majority vote of its members, and shall not be entitled to any further or additional compensation for the performance of the duties imposed upon it by the provisions of his act, save and except if the performance of such duties shall require its attention subsequent to the full and final performance of any duties required of said Board under the provisions of the act named in the first section of this act; then and then only each member of said Board shall receive $10 a day for every day that he shall be so employed, and the compensation of said commissioners and of such engineer, surveyors, clerical and other assistants, shall be charged upon the fund provided for the payment of such work and improvement by the fourth section of this act.

§ 7. All acts and parts of acts inconsistent with this act are hereby repealed.

§ 8. This act shall take effect immediately.

THE COMMISSION'S ADDRESS TO THE GOVERNOR.

BROOKLYN, May 10, 1897.

To the Governor:

The undersigned respectfully ask your excellency to officially approve the bill, which, near the close of the last session of the Legislature, passed both houses, entitled:

"An Act to improve Atlantic avenue, between Flatbush ave-
"nue and Atkins avenue, in the City of Brooklyn, and providing
"for the removal of the steam railroad of the Long Island Rail-
"road Company from the surface of the said avenue."

In this connection we beg to state that we were the Commissioners appointed by the Mayor of the City of Brooklyn, under authority of Chapter 394 of the Laws of 1896, entitled:

"An Act to authorize the appointment of a Commission to "examine into and report a plan for the relief and improvement "of Atlantic avenue in the City of Brooklyn," which act contained directory provisions that the said Commission should inquire into the condition of Atlantic avenue with reference to the railroad operated thereon; and that it should give public hearings and invite suggestions from parties interested therein as to the best methods for the relief and improvement of the same; and that the Commission should formulate a plan for the relief of the said avenue and the improvement of the same, and should report to the Mayor such plan, together with such recommendation as to it might seem proper, and that thereupon the Mayor should cause a bill to be prepared to carry out the plans and recommendations of the Commission, and submit the same to the Legislature at the session of 1897.

The Commission was appointed early after the adjournment of the Legislature, and at once entered upon the contemplated inquiry. Public hearings were advertised in the Brooklyn daily papers, and were held at frequent intervals during a period of several months. Notices were sent out to the people along the avenue, and every facility was given by the Commission to the inhabitants of the city to be affected by any improvement of the avenue, to come before the Commission and freely to express their views.

The hearings before the Commission were largely attended, and the sentiment was well nigh universal that the avenue ought to be improved, and that the operation of a railroad on the surface thereof by steam power should be discontinued.

Some favored the removal of the railroad from the surface altogether; some favored a depressed cut, some an underground road, while others favored an elevated road in preference to the condition of things now existing.

The Commission likewise had many conferences with the officials of the railroad company having certain vested rights in the avenue, and invited and received suggestions and advice from engineers and others whose judgment in such matters would be of much value. After many months of patient labor, and after fully considering the engineering problems involved in the various schemes of improvement presented, and the financial questions which must be met, especially in so far as the city of Brooklyn was concerned, and having, as we thought, an unselfish regard for the best interests of all those who were to be most directly affected by any improvement, we recommended the scheme which is embodied in the bill now before the Governor for his official action.

As will be seen, the general plan proposed by the bill contemplates an underground road for a part of the distance, and an elevated road for another portion, the restoration of the surface of the avenue to the public use, and the removal of steam as a motive power, both as relates to the surface of the avenue and the operation of the railroad to be constructed under the provisions of the bill. We have never for a moment doubted that the carrying out of the improvement contemplated by the bill would be of incalculable benefit to the city of Brooklyn, and especially so to all that class of citizens living along the line of the projected improvement.

This will be the more apparent when it is observed that it was made evident to the Commission that in connection with the improvement of Atlantic avenue, though not a part of it, nor within our jurisdiction to consider, a tunnel will be constructed under the East River, extending from Flatbush and Atlantic avenues, the westerly terminus of the improvement contemplated by the bill, to the lower portion of New York City, thus giving a continuous and uninterrupted route from lower New York City over the whole length of Long Island.

Such opposition as has been developed to the scheme contemplated by the bill comes from a few property holders abutting on the avenue between Bedford and Howard avenues, a distance of about eight city blocks, where the railroad is to run upon an elevated structure of sufficient height as to allow the free use of the cross streets, and this opposition is not to the improvement of the avenue by the removal of steam from the surface, but rather to the placing thereon of an elevated structure, a preference being expressed for a structure all underground.

This opposition, however, is not formidable, either in numbers or the amount of property held by them along the avenue. We have carefully analyzed the personnel of this opposition and of the holders of all the property abutting on the line of the improvement, and we have ascertained that only about fifteen out of one thousand holdings along the avenue, viz.: One and one-half per cent. of the whole, oppose the plan proposed by the Commission and embodied by the bill, while the vast majority of the property holders directly to be affected, both in numbers and value of property, are enthusiastic in their approval of the proposed scheme.

It will not be deemed out of place to state in this connection that the newspaper press of the two great cities, the reflectors of public opinion, with unanimity, characterize the undertaking proposed by the bill, in connection with the tunnel under the East River, as a scheme of the greatest public benefit, and pregnant with advantage to all this portion of the State. No public measure in years has been supported and approved so generally, by all classes of our citizens, as that proposed by this bill.

It will be remembered that notwithstanding the Legislative committees heard all the opponents of the bill, nevertheless, it passed in the Senate unanimously, and in the Assembly with a single negative vote.

We, therefore, earnestly request the Governor to permit this bill to become a law by giving to it the sanction of his name.

Very sincerely yours,

EUGENE G. BLACKFORD, *President;*
EDWARD F. LINTON, *Secretary;*
EDWARD H. HOBBS,
WILLIAM E. PHILIPS,
WALTER M. MESEROLE,

Commissioners.

PROPOSED ATLANTIC AVENUE IMPROVEMENT.

THEIR CHARACTER AND ESTIMATED COST.

DECEMBER 11, 1896.

MR. MESEROLE,
189 Montague Street, Brooklyn, N. Y.

DEAR SIR.—In accordance with instructions of Mr. W. H. Baldwin, President of the Long Island Railroad, I take pleasure in handing you herewith a set of drawings for your use and information, being copies of those presented by Mr. Baldwin before your Commission.

The drawings are as follows:

(1) Tunnel Brooklyn, New York and Jersey City Terminal Railway Company; map of location.
(2) Tunnel Brooklyn, New York and Jersey City Terminal Railway Company; profile.

ATLANTIC AVENUE IMPROVEMENTS.

(3) Map of location and profile of suggested scheme of improvements. Exhibit No. 1.
(4) Exhibit No. 2. Plan and profile showing departure from depressed portion of elevated structure.
(5) Exhibit No. 3. Cross section of depressed railroad covered.
(6) Exhibit No. 4. Cross section of open cut gauntlet.
(7) Exhibit No. 5. Cross section of elevated railroad.
(8) Exhibit No. 6. Cross section of tunnel section.

Yours truly,

CHARLES M. JACOBS.

SUMMARY OF ESTIMATES.

Flatbush avenue depressed station (including excavation, retaining walls, portals, underpinning surface stations, new flooring, grading, platforms, tracks, shade roofs, new entrance stairs, and baggage elevators, etc	$144,261 31
6,700 feet depressed track from Fort Greene place portal and 105 feet west of Bedford avenue portal	724,544 70
Portal and approach of grade changing sheet grade, etc., and approach to elevated R. R. abutment	81,634 85
Spur connections to Carlton avenue freight yard depressing and altering Carlton avenue freight yard	50,660 50
Elevated R. R. stations at Nostrand avenue (extra)	11,000 00
8,010 feet elevated R. R. complete, from Nostrand avenue to Ralph avenue abutment	482,402 25
Excavation and change of grade of street at Albany avenue	1,100 00
Portal, abutment and approach connection from elevated R. R. to tunnel near Howard avenue	60,500 00
2,910 feet tunnel executed in open cut from portal near Howard avenue to portal near Stone avenue	275,926 20
Approach to grade, open cut fenced in, including portal	34,060 40
Changing position of fence on street and safety gates	22,000 00
	$1,888,090 21

SCHEDULE OF PRICES, ON WHICH ESTIMATES ARE BASED.

Excavation, including digging, timbering, trenches to support road, hoisting and conveying débris, loading into cars, railroad haul, and discharging cars........................	75c. cu. yd.

Concrete, in place in walls, including boarding of wall spaces, facing cement, finish, etc	$6.00 cu. yd.
Dressed stone, in copings, caps and pedestals	75c. sq. ft.
Steel I beams, and brick and concrete arching for street floor over depressed tracks	90c. sq. ft.
Railroad track	$1.50 lin. ft.
Main track, drain	$2.00 lin. ft.
Brick work, lining for arched top, tunnel section, including Portland cement, mortar, timber, centering, etc., in place	$9.00 cu. yd.
Pointing brick work (extra)	20c. super yd.
Cast-iron, where required, including patterns	3c. per lb.
W. I. bolts	3½c. lb.
Steel superstructure, in elevated R. R. section, including falsework and erection complete	2½c. lb.
Timber oak, in guard rails, ties, etc	$30.00 M. ft.
Hand railing, W. I. gas pipe rails and stanchions	75c. lin. ft.

CHARLES M. JACOBS.

MR. MESEROLE'S REPORT.

BROOKLYN, March 12, 1897.

To the Atlantic Avenue Commission:

GENTLEMEN.—In compliance with your resolution passed March 5th, I wish to make the following report relative to the expense of paving and otherwise improving the surface of Atlantic avenue, between Fort Greene place and the City Line at Enfield street.

The scheme of improvement contemplated includes the pavement of two roadways, each 30 feet wide, with an unpaved strip between, through which the trolley road will be operated. At all intersecting streets, whether they cross or end at Atlantic avenue, the intersections will be paved out to the Court Yard lines across this strip and up the intersecting streets to the Court Yard lines of Atlantic avenue.

"GATES DOWN," ATLANTIC AND BEDFORD AVENUES, SHOWING BLOCKADE OF BICYCLISTS, CARRIAGES, ETC.

The estimate covers four lines of new curb, two being, as usual, along the sidewalks, and two surrounding the unpaved strips. It covers all necessary excavations to cut down the sidewalks to the uniform width of 18 feet, to bring the roadway to the proper grade and to excavate to the bottom of the proposed pavement. An item is also included to cover the transplanting of trees and the removal of other obstructions.

The price allowed for pavement will cover Vitrified Brick or Asphalt on Concrete foundation, or Granite Blocks on sand foundation.

Excavation, 160,000 cubic yards, at 30c.	$48,000 00
Curb, 115,000 lineal feet, at 75c.	82,250 00
Pavement, 230,000 square yards, at $2.00.	460,000 00
Transplanting trees and incidentals.	10,000 00
Executive and engineering expenses.	12,000 00
Total	$612,250 00

The total length of the improvement is 30,525 feet, which being doubled gives 61,050 front feet; deducting the intersections, aggregating 10,000 feet for the two sides of the street, leaves 51,050 front feet of property to be assessed.

Respectfully submitted,

WALTER M. MESEROLE.

SEWERS AND PIPES ON ATLANTIC AVENUE.

BROOKLYN, N. Y., October 26, 1896.

PETER MILNE, Esq.,
Chief Engineer.

DEAR SIR.—In response to your directions of October 23d, I transmit herewith lists giving sizes, kinds and approximate depths of sewers crossing Atlantic avenue from South Ferry to City Line. Also sizes, kinds and approximate depths and location of sewers on each side of Atlantic avenue, between the same limits. These lists answer your questions Nos. 1 to 4, inclusive, as far as possible with present information.

In answer to question No. 5, would say that the building of the Greene avenue sewer was accomplished with satisfaction generally, and price for the tunnel sewer where it crosses Atlantic avenue was $69 per foot. Man-holes are extra.

Respectfully,

C. H. MYERS, *E. S.*

BROOKLYN, N. Y., Oct. 23, 1896.

MR. PETER MILNE,
Chief Engineer.

DEAR SIR.—Replying to yours of even date, will say

1st.—There are two force mains crossing Atlantic avenue, one of which is 42 inches and the other 48 inches in diameter.

2d.—The depth of the excavation under the surface of the street varies from 8 feet to 12 feet.

3d.—The brick conduit on the inside is 10 feet wide by 8 feet 8 inches high and on the outside 15 feet wide by 10 feet 8 inches high.

4th.—The depth of the excavation to the bottom of the conduit planking is about 31 feet.

Respectfully,

I. M. DE VARONA,

Engineer of Water Supply.

SEWERS IN ATLANTIC AVENUE, SOUTH SIDE, BETWEEN SOUTH FERRY AND THE CITY LINE.

Distance from Curb.	Between	Size. Inches.	Approx. Depth. Feet.
	River—Ferry	36	8
About 11 feet.	Ferry—Columbia	12	9.5
"	Columbia—Hicks	12	11
"	Hicks—Boerum	12	12
"	Boerum—Smith	12	10
"	Smith—Hoyt	12	9
"	Hoyt—Flatbush	12	12
About 16 feet.	Flatbush—Fifth av	18	13
"	Fifth av.—Sixth av	18	12
"	Sixth av.—Carlton	15	12
"	Carlton—Vanderbilt	15	12

Distance from Curb.	Between	Size Inches.	Approx. Depth. Feet.
About 16 feet.	Vanderbilt—Underhill	12	12
"	Underhill—Grand	12	12
"	Grand—Classon	36	13
"	Classon—Franklin	..	..
"	Franklin—Bedford pl.	12	12
"	Bedford pl.—Bedford av.	..	..
"	Bedford av.—New York	12	12
"	New York—Brooklyn	12	11.5
"	Brooklyn—Kingston	15	12
"	Kingston—Albany	12	12
"	Albany—Troy	12	12
"	Troy—Schenectady	12	12
About 12 feet.	Schenectady—Saratoga	12	11
"	Saratoga—Hopkinson	12	12
"	Hopkinson—Rockaway	12	11.5
"	Rockaway—Stone	12	12
"	Stone—Sackman	12	11.5
"	Sackman—Vesta	12	12
"	Vesta—Snediker	12	12
"	Snediker—Hinsdale	12	12
"	Hinsdale—Williams	12	12
"	Williams—Alabama	12	12
"	Alabama—Georgia	12	12
"	Georgia—Sheffield	12	12
"	Sheffield—Pennsylvania	12	12
"	Pennsylvania—New Jersey	12	12
"	New Jersey—Wyona	12	11
"	Wyona—Bradford	12	12
"	Bradford—Miller	12	11
"	Miller—Van Siclen	12	12
"	Van Siclen—Hendrix	12	12
"	Hendrix—Jerome	12	12
"	Jerome—Elton	15	12
"	Elton—Linwood	12	12
"	Linwood—Essex	12	12
"	Essex—Shepherd	18	12
"	Shepherd—Berriman	18	12
"	Berriman—Atkins	15	12
"	Atkins—Montauk	12	12
"	Montauk—Milford	12	12
"	Milford—Logan	30	12
"	Logan—Fountain	12	12
"	Fountain—Conduit	..	..
"	Conduit—Market	12	12
"	Market—Crescent	12	12

Distance from Curb.	Between	Size. Inches.	Approx. Depth. Feet.
About 12 feet.	Crescent—Railroad	12	12
"	Railroad—Lincoln	12	12
"	Lincoln—Sheridan	15	12
"	Sheridan—Grant	18	12
"	Grant—Enfield	18	12

SEWERS IN ATLANTIC AVENUE, NORTH SIDE, BETWEEN SOUTH FERRY AND THE CITY LINE.

Distance from Curb.	Between	Size. Inches.	Approx. Depth. Feet.
About 11 feet.	Furman—Columbia	36	11
"	Columbia—Hicks	18	13
"	Hicks—Henry	18	14
"	Henry—Clinton	18	18
"	Clinton—Court	18	15
"	Court—Boerum	12	12
"	Boerum—Smith	24	11
"	Smith—Hoyt	12	9
"	Hoyt—Bond	12	12
"	Bond—Flatbush	12	12
16 to 31 feet.	Flatbush—Ft. Greene	36	15
About 16 feet.	Ft. Greene—S. Portland	36	13
"	S. Portland—Clermont	24	13
"	Clermont—Vanderbilt	12	13
"	Vanderbilt—Clinton	15	13
"	Clinton—Grand	12	12
"	Grand—Franklin	12	12
"	Franklin—Bedford	..	..
"	Bedford—New York	12	12
"	New York—Brooklyn	12	11
"	Brooklyn—Kingston	15	12
"	Kingston—Schenectady	12	12
About 12 feet.	Schenectady—Buffalo	12	11
"	Buffalo—Havens pl.	12	12
"	Havens pl.—Vesta	15	12
"	Vesta—Alabama	12	12
"	Alabama—Sheffield	30	13
"	Sheffield—Pennsylvania	12	12
"	Pennsylvania—New Jersey	24	11
"	New Jersey—Miller	30	14
"	Miller—Van Siclen	12	11
"	Van Siclen—Jerome	15	12
"	Jerome—Ashford	18	12
"	Ashford—Elton	54	12
"	Elton—Shepherd	24	13
"	Shepherd—Dresden	18	12

Distance from Curb.	Between	Size. Inches.	Approx. Depth. Feet.
About 12 feet.	Dresden—Hale	15	12
"	Hale—Fountain	12	12
"	Fountain—Chestnut	36	12
"	Chestnut—Market	12	12
"	Market—Pine	18	12
"	Pine—Crescent	15	12
"	Crescent—Lincoln	12	12
"	Lincoln—Nichols	15	12
"	Nichols—Grant	18	12
"	Grant—Enfield	12	12

Sewers Crossing Atlantic Avenue.

	Size. Inches.	Approx. Depth. Feet.
Brick sewer crosses Atlantic av. diagonally from point on south side near Ferry to Furman st	36, brick	8–10.2
Smith st	Old brick sewer, size unknown	8.5
Hoyt st	15, pipe	12
Bond st	12 into 15, pipe	12
Nevins st	15 pipe	11.6
Third av	24, pipe	12.9
Fourth av	180, brick	about 40
Flatbush av	60, brick	17.2
Grand av	36, brick pipe, and 24 and 15, connections	13.1
Franklin av	36, brick	12
Nostrand av	36, brick	14.1
New York av	30, brick	12.9
Brooklyn av	42, brick, and 15, pipe connections	14.1
Troy av	30, brick	13.5
Schenectady av	30 into 36, brick	14.3
Utica av	18, pipe	13.4
Rochester av	30, brick	13.5
Buffalo av	36, brick	13.1
Ralph av	30, brick	13.0
Howard av	18, pipe	12.0
Saratoga av	15, pipe	13.2
Hopkinson av	12, pipe	12.0
Rockaway av	15, pipe	11.7
Stone av	15 into 18, pipe	12.0
Sackman st	15, pipe	12.0
Vesta av	18, pipe	12
Snediker av. into Williams pl	18, pipe	12
Sheffield av	30, brick	13
Miller av	18, pipe, and 30, brick, into 36, brick	13

	Size. Inches.	Approx. Depth. Feet.
Elton st.	30 by 54, into 54, brick	11.3
Norwood av. into Montauk st.	30, brick	13
Logan st.	24, pipe	13.0
Fountain av.	42, brick	13.0
Market st.	30, brick	13.0
Railroad av.	12, pipe	12.0
Grant av.	60, brick	9.5

Atlantic Avenue 48-inch Main, Laid 1868—Length 25,800 Feet from Court Street to Junction of East New York Avenue and Snediker Avenue.

Court st. to Smith st.	1,050 feet,	15 feet from northeast curb.
Smith st. to Flatbush av.	3,600 "	17½ " " " "
Flatbush av. to Fifth av.	400 "	10-15 " " " "
Fifth av. to 100 feet west of Cumberland st.	1,400 "	17-22 " " " "
100 feet west of Cumberland st. to Classon av.	3,750 "	22 " " " "
Classon av. to Snediker av.	15,600 "	16 " " " "
Total	25,800 feet.	

36-inch extension, Court st. to Clinton, 450 feet long, 15 feet from curb.

6-inch pipe, Clinton st. to East River, 1,900 feet long, 6 to 7 feet from curb.

48-inch main, average depth 4½ feet, except at summits of Atlantic av.

At Classon av.	300 feet long, 6 feet deep.
Albany av.	300 " " 6 " "
Hopkinson av.	300 " " 6 " "

BUREAU OF EXTENSION AND DISTRIBUTION.

Pipes Crossing Atlantic Avenue.

6-inch Pipes.	8-inch Pipes.	12-inch Pipes.	20-inch Pipes.
Furman st.	Henry st.	Hoyt st.	Court st.
Clinton st.	Court st.	Flatbush av.	Fourth av.
Hoyt st.	Boerum pl.	Ralph av.	Nostrand av.
Hoyt st. (branch).	Smith st.	(3 12-inch Pipes.)	Saratoga av.
Sixth av.	Bond st.		Rockaway av.
Carlton av.	Nevins st.		(5 20-inch Pipes.)
Carlton av.	Third av.		
Vanderbilt av.	Fourth av.		30-inch Pipes.
Franklin av.	Washington av.		Clinton st.
Bedford av.	Grand av.		Washington av.
(10 6-inch Pipes.)	Classon av.		(2 30 inch Pipes.)
	New York av.		
	Schenectady av.		
	Utica av.		
	(14 8-inch Pipes.)		

Average depth. 4½ feet to Classon avenue,
" " 4 feet east of Classon avenue.

Totals—Ten 6-inch, fourteen 8-inch, three 12-inch, five 20-inch, and two 30-inch pipes.

PROCEEDINGS AND HEARINGS OF THE COMMISSION.

MAYOR'S OFFICE, June 3, 1896.

The Commission met pursuant to appointment, at the office of the Mayor at 11 A. M.

Present—E. G. Blackford, E. F. Linton, E. H. Hobbs, W. E. Philips, W. M. Meserole, Commissioners.

The meeting was called to order by his Honor, Mayor Wurster. Mr. Blackford was appointed temporary chairman; and Mr. Linton temporary secretary.

The Commission proceeded to effect a permanent organization by the election of Mr. Blackford as president and Mr. Linton as secretary.

Messrs. Hobbs and Meserole were appointed a committee to procure suitable office rooms for the Commission.

Messrs. Linton and Philips were appointed a committee to secure clerk and stenographer for the Commission.

A resolution was adopted that no expense shall be incurred by the Commission except such as may be paid out of the money provided for by the bill creating the Commission.

Adjourned to meet at Bedford Bank on Monday, June 8th, at 4 P. M.

BEDFORD BANK, June 8, 1896.

The Commission met pursuant to adjournment.

Present—E. G. Blackford, E. F. Linton, E. H. Hobbs, W. E. Philips, W. M. Meserole, Commissioners.

The Minutes of the last meeting were read and approved.

The Committee appointed to procure offices reported that suitable rooms could be had in the Real Estate Exchange, 189 Montague street, and they were authorized to secure them.

The Committee were continued, with authority to procure furniture.

The Committee appointed to secure a clerk reported as follows: Mr. Philips presented the name of Frank H. Cothren, 173 South Oxford street. Mr. Linton presented the name of Richard Pickering, 2787 Atlantic avenue. The report was received.

Mr. Meserole moved that the election of clerk to the Commission be deferred until the next meeting. Carried.

Moved that Mr. Meserole be authorized to procure maps. Carried.

Adjourned to meet at the office of Mr. Meserole, in the Real Estate Exchange, June 15th, at 4 P. M.

E. F. LINTON, *Secretary.*

OFFICE OF MR. MESEROLE, June 15, 1896.

The Commission met pursuant to adjournment.

Present—E. G. Blackford, E. F. Linton, W. E. Philips, W. M. Meserole, Commissioners.

The Minutes of the last meeting were read and approved.

Mr. Meserole reported that an office room in the Real Estate Exchange could be had for $250 until January 1, 1897. Mr. Philips moved that the Committee be authorized to rent the room. Carried.

Mr. Philips moved that the Committee appointed to procure furniture be empowered to procure furniture necessary to furnish the offices and to place the name of the Commission on the door. Carried.

Mr. Philips moved that F. H. Cothren be employed as clerk to the Commission at a salary of $25 per week, he to have all correspondence and minutes typewritten at his own expense. Carried.

Adjourned to meet at the office of the Commission, room 200 Real Estate Exchange, on Monday, June 22d, at 4 P. M.

E. F. LINTON, *Secretary.*

June 22, 1896.

The Commission met at their office, room 200 Real Estate Exchange, at 4 P. M.

Present—E. G. Blackford, E. F. Linton, E. H. Hobbs, W. E.

Philips, W. M. Meserole, Commissioners, and W. J. Kelley, Counsel for the Long Island Railroad Company.

The Minutes of the previous meeting, held at the office of Commissioner Meserole, in the Real Estate Exchange Building, June 15th, were read and approved.

Commissioner Meserole, as special committee on rooms and furniture, reported that he had executed a lease with the Real Estate Exchange for the rooms now occupied by the Commission, for a period of six months from July first next, at the yearly rental of $500.00, on condition that on ten days' notice being given by either party the lease may be cancelled. On motion of Commissioner Linton the action of Mr. Meserole was ratified.

It was moved, seconded and carried, that the Secretary certify bill for July rent ($20.84) and further, that the Secretary certify all bills that may be approved by the Commission.

Commissioner Meserole further reported that he had purchased furniture for the use of the Commission, of Finn Bros., No. 28 Centre street, New York, consisting of two dozen chairs, at $6.00, and three small tables and a gate, $11.00.

Upon motion duly seconded the report was received.

A letter from David Maire, Esq., was read by the President, and ordered to be filed.

It was suggested by Mr. Linton, that it would be advisable to have photographs taken of crossings of the Atlantic avenue railroads at times when they are most crowded.

Mr. Linton also suggested that, later on, a personal inspection of Atlantic avenue would be necessary.

Upon motion duly seconded and carried, it was decided that the office of the Commission be open from 9 A. M. to 3 P. M., and on Saturdays it will close at 12 M.

The meeting was then opened for a hearing of interested parties.

The Chairman—The object in notifying the Long Island Railroad Company to send a representative here to-day was for the purpose of a conference, rather than for a formal hearing. In consulting together we have felt that it was wise to have the Long Island Railroad submit to this Commission their ideas as to what they would be willing to do to assist in the improvement of Atlantic avenue. It is unnecessary to state that such improvement should be made: we do not wish to trespass upon anybody's rights; we feel there are so many interests involved in the treatment of this subject that we shall have to go very carefully. We want, if possible, to agree upon some plan which can be adopted by all parties interested.

The Commissioners will be very glad to hear from you, Mr. Kelley, if you have anything to suggest.

Mr. Kelley—Mr. President and members of the Commission: I came here at the request of Mr. Pratt, the Vice-President, who received a notice of your hearing, and desired me to say that it was his intention to have been here personally this afternoon, if he had not been prevented by a positive engagement.

So far as the position of the Long Island Railroad Company in connection with the Atlantic avenue matter is concerned, on behalf of the Corporation, I can only say that it is prepared to meet the Commission, or meet the City authorities and property owners in any practicable plan which may seem wise to the Commission and to the City authorities. What that plan should be, of course, is a matter which requires very considerable deliberation. The railroad company has thought it out and has figured on it, and it has been discussed both here and in Albany in past years, and I think we are all agreed that the railroad interest is an important one, that it serves a large proportion of the people and serves the city, and that, whatever plan is adopted by the Improvement Commission for submission to the Legislature, should be such as not to interfere with the usefulness of the only railroad connection which the city has with the outside country.

Now, as to the details of the improvement, as to what it should be, and how it should be accomplished, I am here on behalf of the railroad company to say that we have no suggestions to make as a corporation to the Commission. We are willing to meet the Commission and discuss any plan which may be suggested, and discuss it fairly with a desire to accomplish something. Suggestions, it seems to me, or the preparation of plans, might well be left to the Commission in the first instance, rather than to the railroad company, although in that, as in any other matter, we are prepared to do exactly as the Commission thinks proper under the circumstances.

The subject which appears to have been discussed most in the past has been that of a depressed track.

If the Commission thinks that is the proper way out of the difficulty, the plans and the figures and the results of the investigations made by the Corporation are at the service of the Commission at any time. If any different method is proposed,anything we can do to throw light on the subject will be at your service. I came here to-day with the idea that this was to be somewhat of an informal meeting and to simply say to the Commission on behalf of the management, that we are interested in the results of your deliberations and desirous to accomplish some good results from it. We think that the interests of the railroad and the interests of the city are identical. We think that the interests of property owners are not antagonistic to the proper operation of the road, and we think that a fair examination of all the facts that surround the operation of this road on Atlantic avenue and the rights which have attached to it for some sixty odd years, are entitled to consideration. The railroad was incorporated a month before or a month after the city of Brooklyn; they have gone together hand in hand for sixty odd years, and there should be nothing antagonistic in their operation.

I want, at the outset, to make the situation of the railroad clear in a desire to facilitate in every way we can the accomplishment of a good result.

The Chairman—Has not your corporation made plans and estimates as to the cost of a depressed road?

Mr. Kelley—Yes, sir; starting from Flatbush avenue and running to Manhattan Crossing.

The Chairman—You obtained no estimates for carrying it beyond Vesta avenue, or Manhattan Crossing?

Mr. Kelley—I don't think so. I think that, at the time the depressed track movement was agitated, the plans and specifications related only to Manhattan Crossing. I might say that they were submitted to the City Works Department, and I think the City Works Department have a duplicate set of them.

The Chairman—Also if it is possible for the Long Island

Railroad Company to lay before this Commission at a not very distant day, some scheme for the improvement of Atlantic avenue, that they would be bound by, or would support and do all they could to bring about.

Mr. Kelley—Well, yes, I would answer to that, that they are perfectly willing to submit plans. The only plans that are crystallized, so to speak, are the plans for the depressed track in recent years.

There was a plan prepared years ago for an elevated structure, and I think those plans are still in existence. The depressed track plans are the more recent.

The Chairman—Has the Long Island Railroad Company expressed any preference or is it ready to express any preference for an elevated or depressed track?

Mr. Kelley—The suggestions that have been made by the Citizen's Committee in recent years have related altogether to a depressed track. The railroad company some years ago assented to the depressed track idea as proposed by the property owners' committee. That, so far as I know, is what I might call the pending plan. The elevated structure was proposed in former years running to the ferry, and that was lost sight of after the depressed track feature was brought up, and, as I say, of late years we have heard only of the desire for a depressed system.

The Chairman—This Committee has already received communications from parties who are interested in the matter, some suggesting an elevated, and some very much opposed to an elevated, and some suggesting a depressed track, while others are opposed to that. And in order to handle this subject intelligently, and satisfy the people of Brooklyn, I suppose that we shall have to discuss all of the different plans and find out which has the most merit in it, and not only that, but which one is the most practicable, and we rather expect to have considerable help from the Long Island Railroad corporation in giving us the results of their knowledge and experience in the matter.

I know that the Long Island Railroad Company have made extensive surveys and maps for a depressed road. At one time I had the pleasure of looking at them in the engineer's office; and I know there were plans that were made for an elevated structure. But there is a new phase of a depressed road, which I suppose it is well to speak of at this time, and that is, a depressed road which should end at Vesta avenue or Manhattan Crossing would not be satisfactory to the Twenty-sixth Ward.

Mr. Linton—I think not, if they had to pay for a part of it.

Mr. Kelley—I don't know that the railroad corporation ever made any estimates of a plan to the City Line, although I would not say that they had not made estimates for the full distance. Of course at the time this subject was agitated before, the committee having it in charge stopped at Manhattan Crossing.

The Chairman—And your corporation could give us the statistics as to the amount of freight brought to the Flatbush Avenue Depot and carried out; that would be very useful to us.

Mr. Kelley—Yes, we can give you that.

Mr. Philips—And will you also give statistics as to the passenger traffic?

Mr. Kelley—Yes, passenger and freight traffic.

The Chairman—I don't know whether you can give us the statistics in regard to the present status of the elevated company; we would like to know whether they have any intention to build?

Mr. Kelley—Yes, I think I can give you that.

The Chairman—We would like to know something about the character of the structure which they have proposed to build, and also as to whether it was proposed to remove the tracks from the surface, in case of building an elevated road. I suppose the Atlantic Avenue Railroad Company is now superseded by the Nassau Company as the lessor of the track.

Mr. Kelley—We hold under the old deeds made by the Brooklyn and Jamaica Railroad Company, the property which was afterwards purchased by the Atlantic Avenue Railroad Company. What transactions have occurred between the Atlantic avenue and Nassau companies I only know from newspaper reports. I assume it is a lease, but I am not sure.

Mr. Philips—Wouldn't it be a good idea to have Mr. Ford down here when these maps are presented? He is the engineer.

Mr. Kelley—Yes, sir.

Mr. Linton—I don't want to know anything about any plans to depress the road or to elevate it. It seems to me there is

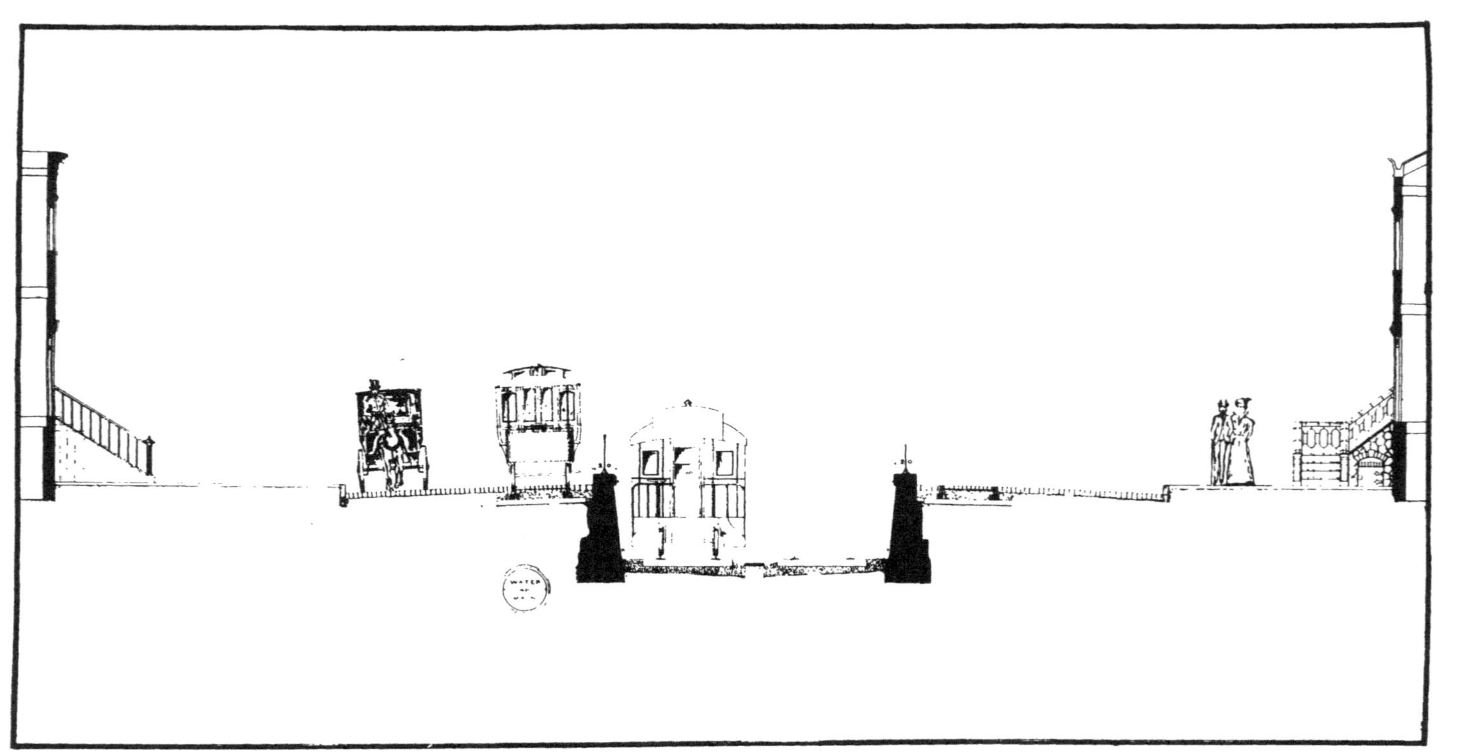

CROSS SECTION, ATLANTIC AVENUE, SHOWING OPEN CUT BETWEEN BEDFORD AND NOSTRAND AVENUES, APPROACHING ELEVATED STRUCTURE, ALSO EMERGING AT STONE AVENUE.

something that precedes that, and that is ascertaining something, if we can, that the Long Island Railroad Company itself would suggest to this Commission, and a solution of a problem which has agitated men's minds for many years. I recognize that the Long Island Railroad Company has rights; I recognize that they are a very important factor in this inquiry. I feel pretty sure that we as a Commission will accomplish nothing unless it shall be along lines of co-operation and united action with all the interests, and so it seems to me the first thing to find out is, that the Long Island Railroad might suggest themselves, with their knowledge of the track and condition, and present to the consideration of this commission, some plan that this commission might later find itself ready to recommend, and ultimately create a co-operative line of action to an end. To-day, of course, Mr. Kelley represents the Long Island Railroad here, but only in the sense of a first interview to get an idea of the situation.

Mr. Kelley—That is all. I stated before you came in that the railroad company is desirous of meeting the Commission on the lines that you suggest with a desire to accomplish something, to come to some practical solution.

Mr. Linton—I haven't personally any view as to what should be done. I have a very great desire to know what is best to be done, and that I believe is the object of this Commission, and the Long Island Company can aid us very much, particularly along the lines they themselves enter into, so it seems important to me that we should first find something that the Long Island Railroad itself could formulate.

Mr. Kelley—I have said that we would take up the depressed track plan, and try to take up the ends of the elevated plan, and see if it is practicable in either direction. The discussion of the past few years has been for a depressed road, and that the railroad took up and decided it was practicable at one time, that was some years ago when the agitation was pending at Albany.

Mr. Linton—Were you connected with the company at the time of the Rapid Transit Commission, and do you remember we gave much attention to the depression then?

Mr. Kelley—Yes, sir.

Mr. Linton—And do you remember we had a good deal of discussion with the engineer and decided that that was impracticable?

Mr. Kelley—I don't know that it was considered impracticable.

Mr. Linton—I mean from a financial standpoint.

Mr. Kelley—I think at that time the Commission reported in favor of an elevated structure, and I think the railroad company, the management at that time, acceded to that and formed a company. But there were other obstacles interposed which stopped that. In later years the depressed track was suggested; it came up through bills introduced in Albany, and the railroad company took that matter up, and thought they saw the way to carry out that proposition.

Mr. Linton—No official action was ever taken outside of the company, was there?

Mr. Kelley—No, sir, the legislation never materialized.

Mr. Linton—All those things are the basis of this Commission. I was going to ask if you recall certain figures that were named at the time, what the depressed track would cost?

Mr. Kelley—I think we have them all; I think the proceedings of your Commission at that time were printed and bound in book form.

Mr. Linton—It has been stated from time to time that it is impracticable from a financial standpoint to depress those tracks if a portion of it has to be paid by the city.

Mr. Kelley—Well, that is a matter which ought to be, and I have no doubt will be, inquired into fully by the Commission; the question of valuations and the condition of the properties now on either side of the avenue, and the effect of depression, etc, a great many matters are involved in it.

Adjourned to Monday, June 29th, at 4 P. M.

E. F. LINTON, *Secretary*.

June 29, 1896.

The Commission met at their office, room 200 Real Estate Exchange, at 4 P. M.

Present—E. G. Blackford, E. F. Linton, W. E. Philips, W. M. Meserole, Commissioners, and W. J. Kelley, Counsel for the Long Island Railroad Company.

The Minutes of the meeting of June 22d were read and approved.

A bill for $5.20 for lettering the door was presented and ordered paid. It was decided that President Blackford should interview the Comptroller, and try to arrange it so that in the future there may be a fund on hand to meet small bills, and to save the inconvenience of officially passing on each one.

Upon motion duly seconded and carried, it was decided that the Department of City Works be requested to furnish this Commission with whatever plans, maps and other material there may be in its possession pertaining to Atlantic avenue, from South Ferry to City Line, for the use and information of the Commission.

Commissioners Philips and Meserole were appointed a special committee to wait on the Commissioner of City Works to learn what they could find in his department in the way of plans, maps, etc., pertaining to Atlantic avenue.

The clerk was instructed to file with the Comptroller, the lease of the rooms now occupied by the Commission; also to ascertain the total front footage and total valuation of property on both sides of Atlantic avenue, from Flatbush avenue to Bedford avenue, and report at the next meeting.

The hearing of interested parties continued, Mr. Kelley being requested to make any statement he was prepared to make.

Mr. Kelley—I find that I undertook a little larger contract than I was able to perform when I told you I could give you all the detail that was asked for at the last meeting. We have started the work on the statistics as to travel, etc., and we have that very well worked out.

About the plans for the depressed road, I find there is but one set of those plans in our possession at this time. They were prepared by the engineer, who was out of the country until last Saturday, and I was unable to get at their whereabouts until this morning. We have only one set of these plans, but the entire duplicate set, complete, with the figures and everything else, was handed to the City, and I am told that the engineer of the City Works Department has them. We do not want to give up those plans we have, but will have an entire copy made for the Commission, if they can be obtained, of the set which is in the possession of the City. The set of plans to which I refer shows the depressed track scheme from Flatbush avenue to Manhattan Crossing, made in 1894.

Mr. Linton—What brought forth these plans?

Mr. Kelley—They were prepared at the time the original bill was introduced into the Legislature to authorize the depression of the tracks; that was in 1894, I am very sure.

Mr. Linton—And these plans were then made with a view of comporting with that bill if it was passed?

Mr. Kelley—Yes, sir. I can give you the figures which were furnished by the auditor of the railroad as to the travel and freight traffic, and these figures are subject to your examination and verification if you see fit. These figures, I will say, relate to the year ending June 30, 1895. Their year ends June 30th, and that is the time their annual report to the State Commissioner is made, and the current year not being complete, they gave me the year ending June 30, 1895. I assume that the year ending June 30, 1896, would possibly show a little increase.

The number of through passengers transported both ways between Flatbush avenue and Jamaica (this doesn't include rapid transit passengers) for that year was 4,216,806. Of that number, there were transported between Flatbush avenue and the turning off on the Coney Island division to Manhattan Beach, and turning over to Long Island City on the other side, changing at East New York, 369,710.

That is between Flatbush avenue and Manhattan Crossing, and includes the people who branch off there for Coney Island and the other direction. The 4,216,806 did not include this 369,710.

The freight tonnage moved in both directions between Flatbush avenue and East New York, that is, simply local freight between Flatbush Avenue Depot and Bedford and points west of Manhattan Crossing, was 735 tons. Between Flatbush avenue and all stations east, that is, still local freight, freight originating in Brooklyn or originating on Long Island and coming into

Brooklyn, 30,187 tons; that is in addition to the 735 tons, and that represents local freight from Brooklyn to the Island and from the Island to Brooklyn.

Foreign freight (260,000 tons), representing the cars brought in over the East New York tracks, and from Jamaica down to Flatbush avenue,—that includes all the supplies that come to Flatbush avenue station irrespective of local freight, 271,000 tons. That includes the meat and the coal and the various classes of freight that come in.

Then the suburban traffic, the rapid transit traffic, so called, in passengers is 1,610,418 in both directions on the entire division, in and out.

These figures were sent to me to-day, and there are other figures which you asked for which they were unable to give me to-day.

I would be very glad if the Commission would have the Auditor before them to explain more in detail these figures.

The Chairman—How long will it be before the Auditor will have his figures complete for this year?

Mr. Kelley—I suppose the figures will not be completed before August 1st; it generally takes them thirty days. I have asked him also to divide up the supplies and give you the tonnage on each class of freight which he has been unable to do by to-day, and also the commuters tickets and school tickets.

Mr. Linton—It would be interesting to know the number of trains moving east and west.

Mr. Kelley—That could be furnished you by the Superintendent.

Mr. Meserole—Do these figures include freight and passengers landed at East New York and points beyond New York?

Mr. Kelley—Yes, sir; but it is divided up so you can see the separation at East New York. About the train service, that you will have to get from Mr. Reynolds' office,—the General Manager, E. R. Reynolds.

Mr. Linton—Could you tell from memory whether the present service on the rapid transit part of the system was ever greater than now?

Mr. Kelley—I know it was.

Mr. Linton—What circumstances have changed that?

Mr. Kelley—Possibly the Kings County Elevated had something to do with it, but I think the main reason of curtailment of the rapid transit service is to make way for the through service. They ran rapid transit, I think, two or three each way an hour. The volume of business is the main thing, and it is curtailed by the new facilities given for that sort of traffic, so they reduced it as much as they could to accommodate the traffic and accommodate the through traffic also.

Mr. Linton—My idea was that at some time they might have carried a greater number of passengers.

Mr. Kelley—I do not know as to carrying more passengers, but more trains were run. The freight traffic has developed very largely in recent years.

The Chairman—You said a few minutes ago you thought the figures for the current year would show an increase, which was rather a surprise to me in view of the fact they claimed the trolley roads have largely affected the passenger traffic.

Mr. Kelley--They have affected it advantageously; people ride one way on the electric and they return on the steam roads.

The Chairman—One of the matters we called your attention to at the last meeting was the elevated railroad.

Mr. Kelley—About the elevated railroad plans, I have started them to look those up. I do not believe that you will find any better history of that than is furnished in the bound report of the Commission. That Commission prepared plans and specifications and everything in detail. There was a company incorporated under the auspices of the Commission, the Atlantic Avenue Elevated Railroad Company, and that company is still in existence.

The Chairman—Who is the president of that company?

Mr. Kelley—I suppose Mr. Corbin was president of it until his death.

The Chairman—I saw recently a notice in the paper which spoke of an election of directors, and from that I inferred that it was a live corporation.

Mr. Kelley—It is in existence. It has been kept up constantly organized and has paid in the required amount, etc., and has been kept up ever since as an existing corporation.

Mr. Linton—Has there been any expiration by reason of having done nothing, or that sort of limitations?

Mr. Kelley—I would not want to say; it is a living corporation.

Mr. Linton—Could it build an elevated railroad now, if it chose to?

Mr. Kelley—Yes, if it could get the permission.

Mr. Linton—Is it alive sufficiently so it is a business organization, and if they desired to build an elevated railroad, and if there were no obstructions outside of themselves, could do so?

Mr. Kelley—I presume so. Of course, the elevated plan is one with which the Commissioners are familiar. There was a good deal of opposition to it in the first place, and then the condition of things below Flatbush avenue was complicated by the action of the Atlantic Avenue Railroad Company at that time.

Mr. Linton—Who is the counsel for that company, the Atlantic Avenue Elevated Railroad Company?

Mr. Kelley—So far as it has any counsel, I suppose I represent it; it has never operated.

Mr. Linton—So far as any legal matters pertaining to it, or legal questions bearing upon that, you could answer if you knew in advance that such questions were liable to be asked.

Mr. Kelley—Oh, yes, we could find out the condition of that corporation.

The Chairman—Can you tell me who the executive officer of that elevated railroad is?

Mr. Kelley—I know Mr. Corbin was at the time of his death. There is no head appointed for it now; his vacancy has not been filled.

The Chairman—Could you give me the names of the directors elected within two or three months?

Mr. Kelley—I cannot tell you from recollection.

The Chairman—We should like to have the name of the executive of that board or the names of its directors?

Mr. Kelley—Yes, and any other detail of information that is wanted I can get, and send to the Commission by mail, and then you can determine upon whatever other additional information you want.

The Chairman—The probability is that our future meetings will be more of a formal character, in which we will summon the gentlemen by notice, and go into the matter in detail.

Mr. Kelley—The other important matter on which you asked information, was to have some suggestion from the corporation as to its views on the question. I can only say I have been unable to get those in this time, the Vice-President, Mr. Pratt, being away.

Mr. Linton—My idea of such suggestion from the railroad authorities, or the company, would be based on the fact of this particular Commission going into this question now and treating it in a full and complete manner, and that any plan they might have that they thought was good for all, would be a great aid to us, and necessarily that will take some time to be thought out.

Mr. Kelley—I will take that up with Mr. Pratt now very soon.

The Chairman asked if any of the gentlemen present in the room desired to be heard.

Mr. Linton—Perhaps it is proper to say that this Commission will probably go into the question of the ownership or title of Atlantic avenue, and I am aware, by reason of my former connection with the Rapid Transit Commission, that that question came up before that organization and is exhaustively treated in their report. But my impression is that that did not cover the question of title east practically of Manhattan Crossing. Most of the matter printed there pertained to the titles which would be west of Manhattan Crossing, and in the Twenty-sixth Ward, which is practically from Manhattan Crossing to the City Line. There are some matters there which this Commission will inquire into as to title; and also as to some agreement entered into between the Long Island Railroad and the Commissioners of Highways in New Lots.

Mr. Kelley—I do not know what agreement you refer to. So far as the right of way is concerned, you can ascertain fully how that is held. There is the deed of every square foot of it, full covenant warranty deed. We have the records, and, if necessary, it can be easily shown. There are a number of permits from Highway Commissioners, but I haven't in mind the particular permits you refer to.

Mr. Linton—I am calling your attention to the fact that we will go into that later.

The Chairman—For instance, it has been claimed that the Atlantic Avenue Railroad owned the fee of the land lying between the fences on Atlantic avenue, and we shall want to go into that later; we want to know from you what rights you claim on Atlantic avenue by virtue of any ownership of fee.

Mr. Linton—I think the proper way is that we formulate our wishes in writing.

Mr. Kelley—The reason I spoke about the Highway Commissioners, I supposed there were permits obtained at the time of the construction of the Manhattan Beach Division; I haven't in mind any agreement or permit.

Mr. Linton—That is not what I refer to. The town of New Lots is now the Twenty-sixth Ward. At that time in the town of New Lots there was a Highway Commission with which the railroad made some agreement, and it has been held in the Twenty-sixth Ward that such permission was giving up the fee by having the right of way by reason of some agreement, and the railroad was to maintain the grade.

Mr. Kelley—I know there is absolutely nothing in that. The railroad title comes under the deed which has been held since 1844 and 1846.

Mr. Linton—Some agreement was said to have existed there.

Mr. Kelley—I remember myself the time the pavement was made.

Mr. Meserole—That was before the time of pavements. It was at the time they opened the avenue 120 feet to Schenck avenue. There was no right of way except some had been thrown out in spots. There was no right of way for the avenue outside of the railroad. Then there came a time when they condemned that right of way, and it was those Commissioners that Mr. Linton referred to—special Commissioners for laying out Atlantic avenue.

Mr. Kelley—If there was such a thing with that Commission, we can find it.

Mr. Meserole—That was in 1869 and 1870.

Mr. Linton—I wish you would have this particular thing in

mind, because I shall take a great deal of interest in that as a member of the Commission.

Mr. Meserole—April 16, 1869, and May 3, 1870, were the two dates.

The meeting adjourned to meet July 13th, at 3 P. M.

E. F. LINTON, *Secretary*.

July 13, 1896.

The Commission met at their office, room 200 Real Estate Exchange, at 4 P. M.

Present—E. G. Blackford, E. F. Linton, E. H. Hobbs, W. M. Meserole, Commissioners, and W. J. Kelley, Counsel for the Long Island Railroad Company.

Commissioner Hobbs presided in the absence of President Blackford, who was called away.

The Minutes of the meeting of June 29th were read and approved.

It was moved and seconded that the Secretary be authorized to procure articles needed for the office of the Commission: carried.

In order to conform to the established rules of the office of the Comptroller and Auditor, the action of the previous meeting authorizing the Secretary to certify to all bills was reconsidered, and, on motion of Commissioner Meserole, the President was authorized to certify to all bills of the Commission.

The hearing of Mr. Kelley of the Long Island Railroad was continued.

Mr. Kelley presented the following names as being those of the Directors of the Atlantic Avenue Elevated Railroad Company:

Austin Corbin, George S. Edgell, E. R. Reynolds, A. C. Bedford, E. B. Hinsdale, F. L. Cook, Charles M. Pratt, F. L. White, W. G. Bosworth, Wm. B. Kendall, Daniel Lord, Jr., D. S. Voorhees, Frank L. Babbott.

The Chairman—We have here a set of plans of the City Works Commission, copies of those made by Mr. Jacobs.

They were made in 1893, and submitted to Mr. White in

1894. Do you know whether there is another set of plans made two or three years previous to that?

Mr. Kelley—That is the only depressed track plan that we have any knowledge of; I think it is the only one that was ever made.

The Chairman—I had an impression that I saw some plans at one of the meetings held in 1891 or 1892.

Mr. Kelley—Unless there were depressed track plans prepared at the time of the Rapid Transit Commission, there are no others. It may be proper for me to state that the engineers are now at work going over those figures again to bring them down to date, and they have also set a number at work on the extension from the Manhattan Crossing to the City Line. They have instructions from the Executive Committee of the company to hasten their work as much as possible. I spoke to Mr. Jacobs as to when they would be ready, and he said he didn't think that the plans out to the City Line could possibly be ready for submission to the Commission before two weeks from to-day.

The Chairman—Is he considering the depressing of the tracks below Flatbush avenue to the river?

Mr. Kelley—Yes, sir.

The Chairman—We have some figures here given us by the engineer's office of the City Works Department in which the estimated cost is $3,162,854 for the road from Flatbush avenue to Manhattan Crossing. Those are the figures which were prepared in 1894.

Mr. Kelley—I think they exceeded the estimate which the company's engineer placed on the work at that time.

Mr. Linton—Who would be the proper party to address on the part of this Commission to the Long Island Railroad Company to have a conference and possibly to get some views from them?

Mr. Kelley—That is the very thing we are at work on now. Of course, it is an undertaking of very great magnitude. We took up the plans that were prepared in 1894, and simply want to go over them and see that the prices are right for 1896. There had been no estimates prepared on the extension, and the Executive Committee have directed that plans should be prepared and estimates furnished. Their intention is then to take these estimates up and consider them and consider any other plans which the Commission may desire them to consider, as to the cost and feasibility, and then submit to the Commission a statement of what the Railroad Corporation is able to do. We cannot make any such statement, and a conference would be fruitless until they have this information in hand. The extension through the Twenty-sixth Ward is quite a strip of property to go over; they are working on that now, and I am told that it will be ready two weeks from to-day.

Mr. Meserole—Are there any estimates of the cost of the elevated scheme?

Mr. Kelley—I do not think there are any in addition to what were submitted to the Rapid Transit Commission. The elevated plans can only be accomplished under the conditions of the Rapid Transit Act, and that Commission at that time went all over that subject, and made estimates and plans and everything else in detail. There is a bound volume of their proceedings which contains all that matter.

Mr. Meserole—I have seen it, although I have not gone over it carefully, but as far as I have gone over it, I have not discovered any estimates.

Mr. Kelley—I suppose the proceedings are filed in the County Clerk's office.

Mr. Linton—In asking what individual would be the proper one, or if not one, then more, to represent the Long Island Railroad Company, I have in my own mind the idea that there needs to be some plan of action adopted soon; that the mere asking of desultory questions is not the manner in which the thing will ultimately be accomplished, and it may be that a depressed railroad will be the solution; it may be that an elevated railroad will be the solution; it may be that some other treatment would be a solution of this problem. The problem relates to many interests and the idea of a conference was to get this body and others interested, besides the Long Island Railroad,—to have a general conference with a view of applying brains to the solution of the problem, but more particularly along the lines that would be co-operated with by the Long Island Railroad and any other corporation that has railroad interests which are affected by this question. Nothing of that kind has occurred yet, and my own mind is that such action should take place before long.

Mr. Kelley—Mr. Pratt is the gentleman; he is the first Vice-President of the Long Island Railroad Company. But I venture to suggest that there is no use in inviting a conference at present, because we are endeavoring to get the material on hand which will enable us to do what you ask.

The Chairman—When that material is all ready we would like the Long Island Railroad Company to submit a proposition on their part for the relief of Atlantic avenue from their standpoint.

Mr. Kelley—We will do that as soon as we get that information in hand. The matter was taken up at the first meeting of the Executive Committee after this Commission was organized, and it is with that in view that they have started this investigation.

The Chairman—We have a large number of people who want to come before this Commission, and we will have a large number of plans probably. We would like to have something definite which might be practicable to agree upon, and, if possible, then to bring all interests into harmony. We might not be able to accept the first proposition of the railroad, but as a starting point, we think a proposition from them as to what they would be willing to do, as to how much of an expense they would be willing to bear, would be the opening of the question to a practical solution.

Mr. Kelley—Whatever information is desired we are willing to give, but it occurs to me if there are other plans, or if there is a discussion from the various standpoints, that it might expedite matters and might make the result of the work more profitable if we had all that. If there are any other plans or if there are any other suggestions, or if there are any views to present, they should be presented so that the railroad company could have the advantage of them, as well as the Commission. We are engaged in a work of considerable magnitude in going over this ground and preparing these plans. They represent a great deal of work. We are perfectly willing to go ahead from our own standpoint, but it occurred to me at the last meeting, and presses

"GATES DOWN," NOSTRAND AND ATLANTIC AVENUES, SHOWING BLOCKAGE OF TROLLEY CARS.

on me now, that if there are other suggestions, it would be very desirable to have them made. There are arguments for and against a depressed track, and while we are perfectly willing to go ahead and prepare plans from our point of view and submit them to you, we would be very glad to get the benefit of the suggestions. It may be that they are not practicable, or it may be that they won't do us any good, but at the same time if we had the suggestions in advance there might be something in them which would be desirable or advantageous. I make that suggestion notwithstanding we are going right ahead, as I said.

Mr. Linton—It was just such a line of thought as you have suggested that led me to ask who would represent the railroad. My own feeling is that the preparing of the plans is premature; that a number of persons in authority could come here and have a more general talk, nobody committed to anything but to gather the sentiments of the Commission, and those interests which I have indicated with a view of possibly outlining a plan.

I do not think there are any plans; I know the Commission hasn't any; I don't know that any individual member of the Commission has any plan. I have floating through my brain a dream, but I am not ready to dignify it by the name of plan. But thoughts might be expressed by individuals, and out of that expression may grow the basis of the plan, for the question is a large one. It might be that the railroad company themselves would be the very first to desire to leave Atlantic avenue with their system entirely so far as even a depressed road was concerned, provided that some other adequate means might be formulated that would be accepted by them and meet the commercial interests of the case. We are in an age of invention and it doesn't follow that we must bore in the ground or go in the air to solve this problem. There has been suggested to me by a very eminent railroad man some thoughts, which, at the proper time, I would like to express, but the idea is that by a preliminary informal conference, coming together and spending an hour, we could get some form out of which we could begin to work.

Adjourned to Monday, July 20th, at 4 P. M.

E. F. LINTON, *Secretary.*

July 20, 1896.

A regular meeting of the Commission was held in their room in the Real Estate Exchange at 3 P. M.

The meeting was called to order by President Blackford; all the Commissioners being present.

The Minutes of the meeting of July 13th were read and approved.

Upon motion duly seconded, it was decided that no public hearing should be held at this meeting; the next public hearing to be held Monday, July 27th, at 3 P. M.

Adjourned.

E. F. LINTON, *Secretary.*

July 27, 1896.

The Commission met at their office, room 200 Real Estate Exchange, at 4 P. M.

Present—E. G. Blackford, E. F. Linton, E. H. Hobbs, W. E. Philips, W. M. Meserole, Commissioners; W. J. Kelley, Counsel for the Long Island Railroad, and Charles M. Jacobs, Consulting Engineer.

President Blackford called the meeting to order, and the Minutes of the meeting of July 20th were read and approved.

A letter was received from a Mr. Hatch, which accompanied maps, plans, etc., pertaining to the Greathead system of tunneling, and was read by the Secretary. It was ordered filed, and the thanks of the Commission were extended to Mr. Hatch for his interest in the matter.

It was moved and seconded, that when the blue prints of the proposed depressed road from South Ferry to the City Line are received from the Long Island Railroad, the profiles be transmitted to the Commissioner of City Works, with the request that he inform the Commission as to the sewers and water mains that will be interfered with by the proposed construction, and the expense of their removal and reconstruction. Carried.

The representatives of the Long Island Railroad Company were then called upon for statements and plans of the company's ideas of the Atlantic avenue improvements.

Mr. Kelley—I will state, Mr. President and gentlemen of the Commission, that I have here the plans that have been referred to at the previous meetings of the Commission, plans showing a depressed track between Flatbush avenue and the City Line station, and Mr. Charles Jacobs, the Consulting Engineer of the company, is also here to answer any inquiries which the Commission may wish to make in regard to the matter.

Mr. Blackford—I suppose that Mr. Jacobs has prepared estimates as to the additional cost of carrying the depressed track from Manhattan Crossing to the City Line.

Mr. Jacobs—Yes, sir.

Mr. Blackford—Have you considered at all the depressed road from Flatbush avenue to the ferry?

Mr. Kelley—We have considered it, but we have not any plans here showing it. We have material to make the plans up with if the Commission desire it.

Mr. Blackford—Have the estimates been made out, or will they be reported?

Mr. Kelley—Whichever you wish.

Mr. Blackford—We will be glad to have Mr. Jacobs read those and file them with us, if he will.

Mr. Jacobs here reads.

Mr. Blackford—In the Manhattan Beach Crossing, does this plan propose that the Manhattan Beach trains cross at the present grade?

Mr. Jacobs—Oh, no, sir. I will show you the plan of this division (shows plan).

Mr. Linton—Does your plan provide for how many tracks?

Mr. Jacobs—Two.

Mr. Linton—Let me understand about Carlton avenue. Do I understand you that the bridge will be depressed there?

Mr. Jacobs—Oh, yes.

Mr. Meserole—A point that I am going to ask you now is, if you provide sidings in the present width of the street from curb to curb?

Mr. Jacobs—No, no, we take up fifty-six feet.

Mr. Kelley—All the passageways for vehicles will be——

Mr. Meserole—What sort of bridges have you provided for?

Mr. Jacobs—Sixty feet wide.

Mr. Meserole—Solid floor and paved?

Mr. Jacobs—Why, certainly.

Mr. Blackford—Paved with asphalt?

Mr. Jacobs—Certainly.

Mr. Blackford—In the construction of these sidings, you say they are about 600 feet long?

Mr. Jacobs—From where they turn out to where they turn in.

Mr. Blackford—You would have to excavate from curb to curb?

Mr. Jacobs—Yes, sir.

Mr. Blackford—And put arches over?

Mr. Jacobs—Yes.

Mr. Blackford—You speak of girders, roofed up girders?

Mr. Jacobs—Oh, yes.

Mr. Blackford—Not arched?

Mr. Jacobs—Oh, no, it is girder work.

Mr. Meserole—Your estimate provides for everything included in this side?

Mr. Jacobs—That estimate, yes.

Mr. Linton—You gave the number of bridges west of Manhattan and east of Manhattan; do you provide bridges for each street that makes a clear crossing in both cases east and west of Manhattan?

Mr. Jacobs—The streets are broken and there are three, the one is a sixty foot bridge.

Mr. Linton—I understand you said it was thirteen bridges and I was surprised at the limited number. Where would your first large station be?

Mr. Jacobs—We haven't located the stations.

Mr. Blackford—Mr. Jacobs, have you any information to show the character of the soil beneath the surface there?

Mr. Jacobs—We have.

Mr. Blackford—You know whether it is easily excavated or whether you are going to have boulders?

Mr. Jacobs—There is nothing extraordinary.

Mr. Linton—In designating these stations, the thirteen stations of certain kind, and four stations, those four stations are what, do you call them side stations?

Mr. Jacobs—Sidings.

Mr. Linton—Would those stations be located as any possible place for a through train to stop?

Mr. Jacobs—Oh, yes.

Mr. Linton—And, therefore, would differ from the minor stations?

Mr. Jacobs—They are simply the old rapid transit stations that exist at present and four stations.

Mr. Linton—Otherwise they would not have any character but the fact that they are stations.

Mr. Jacobs—I didn't know but whether they had some more reference.

Mr. Kelley—I think the question Mr. Linton is getting at would be, if there would be more stops for through trains? There are sidings now you understand where the rapids let the through trains pass.

Mr. Meserole—There are sidings now?

Mr. Kelley—Yes.

Mr. Meserole—Probably only at three points?

Mr. Kelley—I don't know how many.

Mr. Meserole—One, of course, at Carlton avenue at the freight yards there, and there are some sidings; I don't know whether they belong to the Brighton Beach crossing.

Mr. Kelley—And there are a couple at East New York. Those you speak of are turn-outs; they are not sidings. The sidings where they allow trains to pass are at East New York, but I don't know how many there are.

Mr. Blackford—Then there are no sidings west of East New York?

Mr. Linton—The sidings are at the Howard House and Linwood street. As such you have turn-outs and sidings in the freight yards. The sidings, you understand, that are provided between the Flatbush avenue station are only two——

Mr. Meserole—The road is hampered in its operations for want of sidings?

Mr. Jacobs—Yes, sir.

Mr. Linton—And you haven't located these sidings?

Mr. Jacobs—No, sir.

Mr. Blackford—Did you ever make any estimate for the department?

Mr. Jacobs—No, sir; we never made any estimate.

Mr. Blackford—How far would the old tunnel be available?

Mr. Jacobs—It would be available as a portion of the excavation.

Mr. Blackford—That is all?

Mr. Jacobs—That is all, I think. I believe, from the drawings we have of them, it is too narrow to pass the cars.

Mr. Blackford—Too narrow to cut two tracks using cars you use now?

Mr. Jacobs—Yes, sir.

Mr. Meserole—And you have no cross sections?

Mr. Jacobs—We have no cross sections.

Mr. Linton—Have you any means to-day of telling me the distance between Flatbush avenue and the South Ferry.

Mr. Jacobs—Yes, sir; 7,200 feet.

Mr. Linton—Won't you let one of your men give us that. Why can't it be approximated, what in actual figures it would cost, so much per mile?

Mr. Kelley—I think, Mr. Commissioner, if you want any figures on that, you had better let us figure it.

Mr. Linton—My whole theory is to have saved you the trouble of doing that—that an estimate might suffice for the whole purpose.

Mr. Blackford—State that, Mr. Jacobs. What is that problem, the station at the foot of Atlantic avenue, because we come down there to high water level and after you have a depressed station there, it would have to be perfected to exclude tide water.

Mr. Jacobs—All that would have to come to the surface to make a terminal.

Mr. Blackford—Do you recollect how far the old tunnel was from the ferry?

Mr. Jacobs—Yes; it was about 600 feet. It begins at Hicks street.

Mr. Blackford—About Hicks street?

Mr. Jacobs—Yes.

Mr. Linton--You perhaps would not be prepared to-day to answer if that tunnel, as it is constructed, would be available for the depressed road if it would be constructed to the ferry?

Mr. Blackford--He has already said so.

Mr. Jacobs--I do not believe it would be available.

Mr. Blackford--Not sufficient space for the two tracks?

Mr. Jacobs—I have not personally examined the same, but judging from the profile we have, it appears to be too small for two tracks.

Mr. Blackford--The carrying of the depressed road to the point where the old tunnel commences down to the ferry, would that involve this problem you speak of, the depressed station that would come below high water mark?

Mr. Jacobs--If you depressed a station at that point, it would get out of the high water mark.

Mr. Blackford—Or you could enter 600 feet on the surface and you would not encounter that?

Mr. Jacobs--Yes.

Mr. Kelley--Or you would encounter the problem of getting the station on the surface.

Mr. Blackford--Of course there would have to be quite a large amount of real estate bought.

Mr. Jacobs--It would require quite a cost and is one of those questions that cannot be determined.

Mr. Blackford—But as a matter of fact, is not the river the true terminal of the road?

Mr. Jacobs—Certainly; yes, sir. The Pennsylvania road, the Jersey Central come to the river, and they are desirable as far as the city is concerned.

Mr. Blackford--Never personally examined the tunnel?

Mr. Jacobs--No, sir.

Mr. Meserole—Not the ground?

Mr. Jacobs—No, not the ground.

Mr. Blackford—The mere construction of the depressed road from Flatbush avenue to the point 600 feet from the ferry house you could obtain the cost of that approximately from the proportion of the expense of the other, that is, not counting the expense of the tunnel?

Mr. Jacobs—Certainly; but I should judge you would rather have that figured out.

Mr. Kelley—We are perfectly willing to give you that information.

Mr. Blackford—Certainly, Mr. Kelley, we are willing to take it up in all its possible phases, and as Mr. Jacobs has answered that question, and if we are to consider it, we ought to have the cost. In the construction, in the estimate for the construction of the depressed road, the retaining walls should be of brick or stone.

Mr. Jacobs—Stone.

Mr. Blackford—And in that case you estimated for stone that it would all have to be purchased and brought there?

Mr. Jacobs—Certainly.

Mr. Blackford—Not counting upon any being there?

Mr. Jacobs—No, sir; except leaving any concrete I might find as material there, but in making an estimate, you cannot allow for such things, it is a question on its merits.

Mr. Blackford—In that estimate for carrying the line estimate to the river, we should take in the terminal facilities.

Mr. Kelley—Well, of course; that is a practical question with the railroad company.

Mr. Linton—In making this estimate, the excavating, in that has been given all the possible cost of the material by selling it?

Mr. Jacobs—As soon as you begin to dispose of the material, then comes the question of hauling and——

Mr. Linton—Have you given in that where this material might be disposed of?

Mr. Jacobs—No, sir; I have not considered that. I have made estimates upon the price with the thought that the contractor would take hold and deal with it.

Mr. Meserole—This estimate covers the work on the Manhattan Beach division?

Mr. Jacobs—Yes, sir.

Mr. Linton—Mr. Kelley, I want to ask you a question. In presenting these plans here, I would like to know if they are presented by the railroad company as an entire set of plans, or a treatment they favor provided other questions of a financial character are met satisfactorily to the railroad?

Mr. Kelley—The railroad doesn't initiate this matter at all. We are brought before the Commission under a notice from the Chairman to discuss this question, as it is called "Improving Atlantic Avenue." Our position is, we are there now in possession of our property and operating our railroad. If there is to be a change, then the question comes up, what change is practicable, what change is best adapted to the needs of the public, what can be done? This is the plan of what can be done in the way of a depressed track, and the railroad company presents it as a plan prepared by it of a depressed track improvement.

Mr. Linton—That doesn't come quite to the point of my question. Of course, I understand there are financial matters which cannot be determined, but with the proviso, if the financial matters can be met by the parties to-day, would the railroad company meet and co-operate?

Mr. Kelley—Yes, sir; if this matter can be accomplished through legislation, in a general way, that was presented three or four years ago, and arrangements made with the successors of the Brooklyn and Jamaica Railroad, who own the road and own the fees, then the Long Island road is willing to do its share toward accomplishing the improvement.

Mr. Blackford—That is the point I am getting at; I don't want to put the railroad to a great deal of expense and unnecessary trouble.

Mr. Kelley—We can give you a plan, a depressed plan of the railroad from Flatbush avenue to the ferry with the cost to go into it, but it would require very laborious work.

Mr. Blackford—I do not think that is necessary; the principal question we want to deal with is the additional expense. We shall expect the treatment of the depressed road from that point to the ferry to be the same as the depressed road, so what would answer the purposes of this Commission would be a rough sketch. Knowing the difference, we would come approximately to it.

Mr. Meserole—All I think we need is a profile of that section; no detail is necessary.

Mr. Kelley—Of course, I do not say that the railroad company is prepared to say they will go into that depressed road to the ferry. I am not authorized to say that to-day. It is an extension of the existing system which may be improved with its terminus at the ferry, but when it comes to running the railroad from Flatbush avenue to the ferry, it presents another proposition.

We are perfectly willing to take that up if the Commissioners think it is a phase of the subject, and will do so.

Mr. Blackford—The purpose of this Commission, as far as it has been developed, is to take up every phase that has been brought to their notice for the improvement on Atlantic avenue and that has been one of the phases that has been presented and I do not feel there is any necessity for detail plans as you state but that an estimate of the cost and that would hardly be complete without a supplemental plan with the cost of the terminal.

Mr. Kelley—We can prepare a statement to that effect and send it to you.

Mr. Blackford—How long would that take you?

Mr. Jacobs—We could have it next Monday.

Mr. Kelley—I would suggest, if it is agreeable to the Commission, I can send it to you.

Mr. Blackford—That will be satisfactory.

Adjourned.

E. F. LINTON, *Secretary.*

October 8, 1896.

A meeting of the Commission was held in their rooms in the Real Estate Exchange Building at 4 P. M.

Present—E. G. Blackford, E. H. Hobbs, W. E. Philips, W. M. Meserole, Commissioners, and W. J. Kelley, Counsel for the Long Island Railroad Company.

Commissioner Blackford called the meeting to order, and it was decided to hold the next public hearing on Monday, October 12, at 4 P. M., and that a notice of the same should be published in the following Brooklyn papers: *Eagle*, *Standard Union*, *Times*, *Citizen* and *Freie Presse*.

The Chairman announced that a number of gentlemen were present who desired to be heard in the matter of the Atlantic avenue improvement, and called upon Mr. Barnes.

Mr. Barnes—As you have called upon me first, I would say that I am not entirely familiar with the present status of the matter, as to how far the Commission has progressed, and whether or not this is toward the last of your meetings, or if you have others in view.

The Chairman—In brief, Mr. Barnes, the Commission has simply been sitting and obtaining all the information it can from the Long Island Railroad, through their counsel, Mr. Kelley, who is present this afternoon, in regard to certain matters in connection with the railroad company, and as to the proposed cost of depressing the railroad, and the public hearings from now on will be for the purpose of giving anyone who has an interest in the matter an opportunity to be heard as to any ideas they may have respecting the continuance of the present conditions upon Atlantic avenue.

Mr. Barnes—I have looked into the history of the present occupancy of Atlantic avenue by a steam railroad, and it seems to me that the Long Island Railroad Company, as at present using it, are usurping some of the rights of the people; but I believe that that view has not been sustained by the Court. I have prepared a little memorandum which I take the liberty of leaving with you, as covering about the position that the estate of A. S. Barnes, which I am representing, would be likely to take, and if you will allow me I will read it:

ATLANTIC AVENUE COMMISSION,
EUGENE G. BLACKFORD, ESQ., *President.*

DEAR SIR.—The estate of A. S. Barnes, which I represent, has real estate in the following wards of Brooklyn: Fourth, Ninth, Twentieth and Twenty-third, on which it pays taxes, and as citizens and taxpayers to a considerable amount, we desire to be heard by your Committee.

The Long Island Railroad is now operating with steam on Atlantic avenue through a lease of the Atlantic Avenue horse Railroad, which obtained the right to use steam by act of Legislature in 1876. This same Long Island Railroad Company, or its legitimate predecessors, abandoned the right to use steam in 1859, and received the sum of $125,000 in money as a consideration for an agreement with citizens and taxpayers of Brooklyn never to run surface trains by steam on Atlantic avenue in perpetuity.

As a result, and on the strength of this agreement of 1859, confirmed by Act of Legislature (Ch. 484, Laws of 1859), Atlantic avenue was widened, a public driveway and promenade were constructed, numerous improvements were made, a row of trees was planted down the center of the avenue, fine buildings were erected, Prospect Park was purchased and laid out, to which all parts of the city has free and safe access; and the value of the property steadily increased.

In 1870, the Brooklyn and Jamaica Railroad foreclosed their mortgage on the Long Island Railroad Company and bought in the road. Under this proceeding the new company attempted to re-introduce steam on Atlantic avenue. But the Courts intervened and declared that the bond-holders purchased only such right as the Long Island Railroad possessed.

In 1874-1877 the Atlantic Avenue Railroad operated as a horse railroad.

In 1876, by Act of Legislature (Ch. 187, Laws of 1876), the right to operate a steam railroad, subject to regulations of the Common Council, was conferred upon the Atlantic Avenue Railroad.

Then followed the lease of the Atlantic Avenue Railroad Company to the new Long Island Railroad Company, and under this lease, steam was restored to Atlantic avenue. What was the result? This broad avenue has been destroyed as a driveway and promenade, the beautiful row of trees and grass plots in the center have been destroyed. Heavy rails were laid in the center of the street, a wall of iron was set up on either side of the tracks. One part of the city was thus practically severed from the other. The north side, with its fine residences, ferries and business places, from the south side, with the Park and Greenwood; and vice versa.

The citizens who paid their money for the relief of the avenue from steam have never been reimbursed. Their property has been damaged in value to an extent of fully one-half.

The railroad has practically and morally broken its faith, and hundreds of lives have been sacrificed at the crossings. Now, what is it possible to do?

The railroad company states that the cost of sinking the

tracks from Flatbush avenue to Manhattan Crossing would be alone $4,000,000, and that the removal of pipes, engineers' fees, etc., would be extra. The sinking of the tracks would certainly benefit the city by an increase of taxable value of property all along and on both sides of the line.

Let the city, therefore, if necessary, loan the railroad company $4,000,000 at a nominal rate of interest, say three per cent., to carry out this improvement, and itself (the city) pay the cost of moving pipes and engineers' fees.

Very respectfully yours,

HENRY B. BARNES,

Executor.

The Chairman—I suppose the difficulty about that, Mr. Barnes, is that the city cannot legally do it, neither lend its money nor its credit to a railroad corporation. It is competent for the city to make this cut and depress the road and bear a part or the whole cost as it should see fit. One thing I would like to ask is, whether in your opinion the property holders, both on the line of Atlantic avenue and in the district that might be benefited by the sinking of the tracks, would submit to an assessment?

Mr. Barnes—If it were shared by a sufficiently large number of property holders, not immediately on the avenue. I contend that the city is interested in this matter on both sides of the avenue. Those living on the south side to the extent of their desire to get across the avenue to the ferries and those on the north side to get to the Park.

Mr. Philips—He means there is one section of the city more to be benefited than another, and they should make some arrangement to pay more than the city at large. Wouldn't it be right that they should be assessed for $2,000,000, and the balance assessed on the city at large?

Mr. Barnes—Our estate would certainly be willing to be taxed in our proportion.

The Chairman—Do you think that the present depreciation of real estate in price is attributable to the railroad?

Mr. Barnes—I think it is directly due to that.

The Chairman—The Barnes estate owns property directly on the avenue?

Mr. Barnes—Yes.

The Chairman—What would be the effect of building an elevated railroad instead of depressing the tracks?

Mr. Barnes—Either would be acceptable.

The Chairman—Have you any practical experience in the effort to sell property on Atlantic avenue?

Mr. Barnes—It is absolutely impossible to sell.

The Chairman--Even at the depressed valuation?

Mr. Barnes—It can be sold at a little less than the assessed valuation.

The Chairman—What I want to get at is, how much effect the railroad has had upon the property on Atlantic avenue?

Mr. Barnes—As soon as steam was restored to the avenue the price of property materially depreciated. The property on the corner of Clinton avenue and Atlantic, on which is a large house and stable, and I think either twenty or thirty lots, all available to the tenant, is rented and all we can get is $1,250. Our taxes are over $1,600.

The Chairman—Have you any other property in the same condition on Atlantic avenue?

Mr. Barnes—Yes, we have three stores on Vanderbilt and Atlantic avenues.

The Chairman—In your opinion, Mr. Barnes, what would be the effect on the City of Brooklyn at large, if the steam railroad was prohibited from coming through Atlantic avenue, stopping at Jamaica or East New York?

Mr. Barnes—I think there would be sufficient increase in the value of property to make it worth while.

The Chairman—What do you think would be the effect on business?

Mr. Barnes—I do not think it would affect the business interests of the city.

The Chairman—How about the personal convenience of citizens of Brooklyn getting back and forth from the Long Island resorts?

Mr. Barnes—I am not competent to judge of that. I am not living in Brooklyn.

Mr. Meserole—Can you tell how the improvements were paid for?

Mr. Barnes—The improvements on the avenue were paid for by the city. I don't know how the assessments were made, whether upon the property owners or not.

Mr. Meserole—You don't know whether the property paid for it?

Mr. Barnes—I believe in most every case the property does pay.

Mr. Meserole—There were a great many improvements that were never paid for. I was wondering if Atlantic avenue was one of them?

Mr. Barnes—I suppose that was paid for.

Mr. Kelley—I am familiar with the Barnes estate, and am interested in the statement Mr. Barnes has read. The Barnes estate raised all the points which Mr. Barnes has mentioned. Some of them are not intentionally inaccurate, but I presume there were some errors in looking up the records. For instance, in reference to the foreclosure of the Long Island Railroad Company. There never has been any foreclosure; there was a foreclosure of the Brooklyn and Jamaica Railroad, which is the predecessor or lessor of the Atlantic Avenue Railroad Company in Brooklyn, and of course the question of the disposition of the assessment which was paid at the time the tunnel was closed and steam removed from the entire length of Atlantic avenue has been discussed a great many times and the disposition of that money is shown by the city records. But to get down to the question of values, and the effect of the railroad on values. But before we come to that, the Barnes estate, before steam was adopted, began a suit to enjoin the operation of the railroad, in which the question of the railroad to operate by steam was decided, and that is one of the cases in which the Court re-affirmed the right of the railroad to operate by steam, and in the suit brought by Mr. Barnes, the Court also re-affirmed the question that the Long Island Railroad Company has never contracted not to operate by steam. That was one of the points involved in that

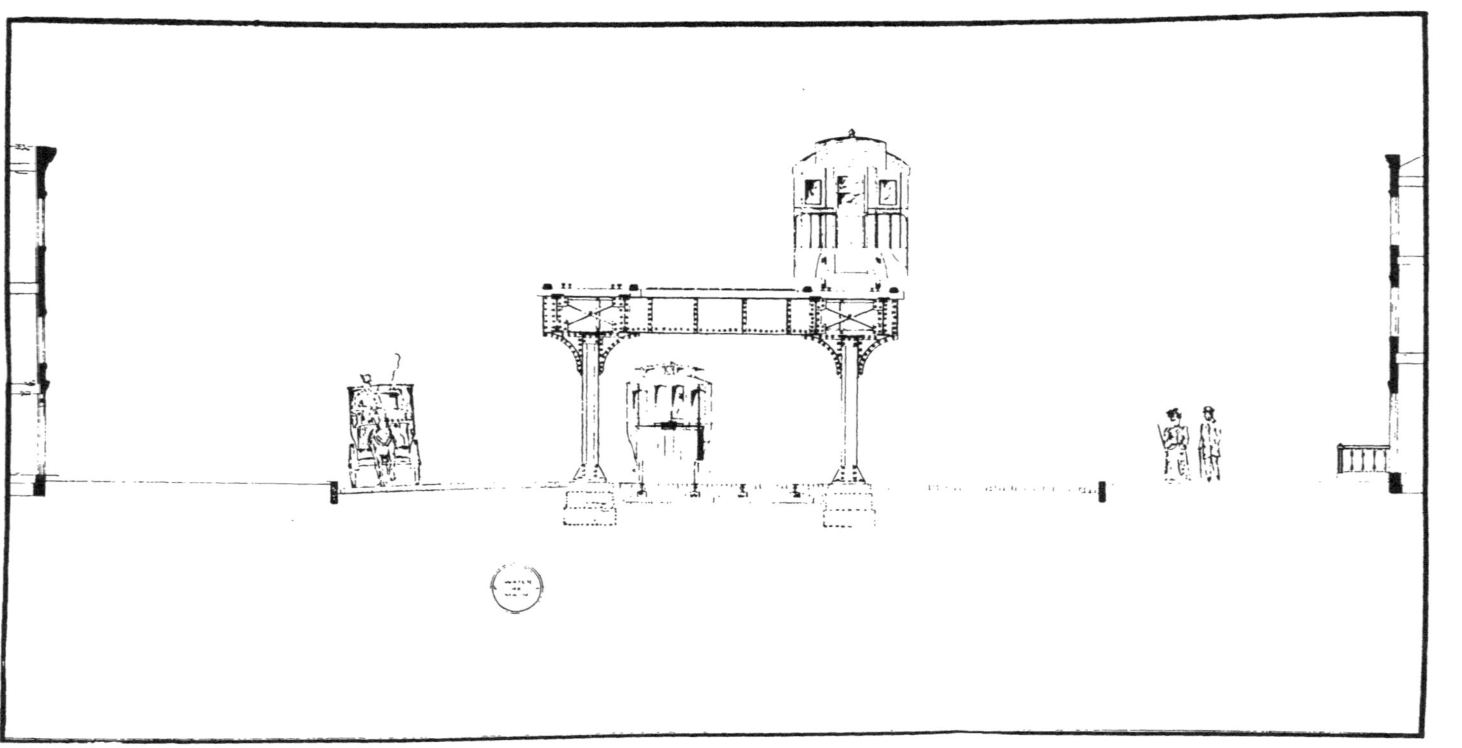

CROSS SECTION, SHOWING ELEVATED STRUCTURE, WITH TROLLEY LINE ON SURFACE, BETWEEN BEDFORD AND HOWARD AVENUES, AND, IN TWENTY-SIXTH WARD, FROM WILLIAMS AVENUE TO ATKINS AVENUE.

litigation. But, passing that, and coming to the question of value which Mr. Barnes discusses, I want to call your attention to the fact that even in the Twenty-sixth Ward, where steam has always been in use, the most valuable property in the ward is on Atlantic avenue.

In regard to the Barnes estate, the house which is said to bring in less than the taxes is peculiarly situated for a mansion. It is a very large and beautiful house, surrounded by extensive grounds, but is hardly in the place where it would bring the greatest return for the kind of house it is. In the same way, the dwelling houses which the estate has erected opposite the homestead, while they are very fine houses, they are not calculated to bring the greatest receipts for that place.

Immediately opposite the Barnes property on the south side of Atlantic avenue, there is more or less activity in real estate. There is a row of houses there and a pretty fair price was paid for them. The railroad company purchased a block of land immediately to the west of Mr. Barnes' property, between Carlton and Sixth avenues, and we found we paid pretty much up to the real value of the property, even though it was taken by condemnation proceedings. There has been depreciation in some kinds of property. You can't put a house like Mr. Barnes' down here on Court street or in the Twelfth Ward; it won't bring the revenue it would bring if located in some parts of the Twenty-fourth Ward, where they have residences of that kind, or as much as if located further down on Carlton avenue.

What I am trying to get at is, that for other classes of property there is more or less activity. Houses have gone up along Atlantic avenue; improvements have been made immediately opposite Mr. Barnes' property. For certain classes of property the trade on Atlantic avenue is active, in flats and apartment houses.

In East New York it is Atlantic avenue that furnishes the cream of values in that region. I don't make these remarks in criticism, but simply thought of them while he was reading his statement.

Mr. Barnes—We have a house on Atlantic and Marcy, and no one but colored people will live there; we have vacant lots on the corner of Atlantic avenue and those we can't dispose of.

Mr. Philips—It does appear that on Flatbush avenue property up to Nostrand avenue, all the life and business is on the south side of the Park.

Mr. Barnes—I think that is accounted for because they have access to the Park.

Mr. Beck—I think the matter has been pretty thoroughly discussed, but I differ with Mr. Kelley when he says that the Atlantic avenue tracks improve the property on the avenue. I think the condition of the avenue deplorable. I would suggest the depressing of the tracks, with a terminus at South Ferry. The Long Island Railroad would thereby obtain such advantages that they could well afford to bear the entire expense for the building of the road, with perhaps the exception of the expense of the sewer pipes and the engineers' fees. The railroad company could very easily obtain all the money they require without borrowing from the city.

The Chairman—You are the President of the W. C. Vosburgh Manufacturing Company?

Mr. Beck—I am.

The Chairman—Have they a factory on Atlantic avenue?

Mr. Beck—No; our factory is on State street.

The Chairman—Your place of residence is within a few hundred feet of Atlantic avenue?

Mr. Beck—About 170 feet.

The Chairman—Have you any knowledge as to what effect the railroad has upon the value of real estate in your immediate vicinity?

Mr. Beck—I have made no attempt to sell. The house I occupy sold fifteen years ago for $14,000; I bought it for $8,500.

Mr. Philips—Is it not a fact that property worth $5,000 sold for $20,000?

Mr. Beck—Yes, because it was wanted for business purposes.

Mr. Philips—At the time of the location of the depot, the Long Island Railroad Company bought a house which Mr. Richardson formerly lived in. They offered to sell it to me for $4,800. I presume it would bring $10,000.

Mr. Kelley—I understand you to say, Mr. Beck, your house was sold for $14,000; the railroad was running then—fifteen years ago?

Mr. Beck—There wasn't as much freightage then as now.

Mr. Kelley—I think some of the depreciation was occasioned by the meat houses back of you.

Mr. Beck—But that was caused by the railroad. All property has depreciated. There is great danger in passing there. The tracks divide the city in two parts, and should be removed. This will increase the value of property for taxation purposes, and will decrease the loss of life and health.

The Chairman—What effect do you think it would have upon the interests of the City of Brooklyn, if steam were removed?

Mr. Beck—And placed in the Twenty-sixth Ward, for instance?

The Chairman—Yes, either the Twenty-sixth Ward or Jamaica.

Mr. Beck—I believe that the business interests of the city would be just as well served, provided that Long Island City remained a terminal as well.

Mr. Philips—Would it be your idea that the freight should go there as well? Any freight that was designed to go to Brooklyn would be out of the way if it went to Long Island City.

Mr. Beck—There could be a trolley on Atlantic avenue; this could be used for freight, as well as passengers.

Mr. Philips—You think the construction and operation of an elevated railroad would improve Atlantic avenue?

Mr. Beck—Not to the extent that an underground road would.

The Chairman—Mr. Kelley, is it a possible thing for you to furnish this Commission with figures of the net earnings from the Atlantic avenue division to the Long Island Railroad?

Mr. Kelley—I suppose so.

The Chairman—The net earnings from all sources?

Mr. Kelley—Well, it is possible; I don't know whether there is any objection to doing it or not; I will submit it.

Adjourned to October 12th, at 4 P. M.

E. F. LINTON, *Secretary.*

October 12, 1896.

The Commission met in their rooms in the Real Estate Exchange, at 4 P. M.

Present—E. G. Blackford, E. F. Linton, W. M. Meserole, Commissioners.

The reading of the Minutes of October 5th and 8th was dispensed with.

Mr. A. H. Hatch, of New York, spoke at some length of the Greathead system of tunneling, such as used in various European cities, and was followed by Alderman Walkley, who addressed the Commission on the subject of removing the railroad altogether from Atlantic avenue. Mr. J. F. Anderson also spoke in the same strain.

Colonel Langdon—I am neither a property owner nor householder in this city, but I have been asked to come here from the Church Charity Foundation. Had I known the case would be so ably presented I think I would not have come here at all.

Mr. Linton—We understand the suffering on the avenue; what we want to know is a remedy for it. The suffering is the reason of the existence of this Commission.

Col. Langdon—The most noiseless way is to have the railroad underground.

Mr. Linton—You mean an underground road or a depressed road?

Col. Langdon—I mean away underground. It is no trouble at all to build it. It would be a great benefit to the city, and a great thing.

Col. Langdon then read this communication:

St. John's Hospital,
Brooklyn, N. Y., October 12, 1896.

To the Atlantic Avenue Commission, Brooklyn:

Gentlemen.—As an active member of the Board of Managers of the Church Charity Foundation, I have been appointed by that Board a committee of one to appear before your Honorable Body and most earnestly, but respectfully, to request that the tracks of the Long Island or Atlantic Avenue Railroad be so sunk as to be entirely underground, like the city railway system of London, where no cars are seen or heard by the neighbors or passers-by or people passing overhead.

First let me say: the Church Charity Foundation of Long Island is a regularly chartered charitable institution supported by the contributions of benevolent members of the Episcopal Church. It consists of the Sisters House, the Home for the Aged, the Orphanage, the Orphan's Press, the Training School for Nurses and St. John's Hospital. These establishments are quartered in a group of eight buildings and occupy nearly a whole block bounded by Herkimer street, Albany avenue and Atlantic avenue, and the property is valued at nearly half a million dollars.

Fronting on Atlantic avenue and within a few yards of the Atlantic Railway are the Orphan's Press, The Training School for Nurses, a cottage for private patients, and the large five-storied brick building known as St. John's Hospital.

The occupants of the Orphan's Press building number about twenty-five, including the Orphan printing apparatus and house-keeper and cooks. The occupants of the Training School for Nurses about twenty, and those of the Hospital, including doctors, nurses, servants and patients, number over a hundred.

All these people are constantly annoyed night and day by the running of the trains. These trains at certain seasons are run at intervals of about five minutes, and the noise and jar are intolerable, particularly in the seasons when windows have to be open for the air. While a train is passing, conversation cannot be carried on at all and sleep is almost impossible. Of course the sick people suffer the most, but the railway has become a menace to the health of the occupants of these buildings, and the Board of Managers of the Church Charity Foundation urgently request your Honorable Body to abate what the Board and those who live in those buildings consider a dangerous nuisance.

An elevated railway will be more objectionable than the present surface railway, except that the crossings will be absent and there will not be so many people annually killed as are killed by the present railway. An elevated railway is more productive of noise than a surface road, and the present surface road is simply intolerable.

If your Honorable Body will take the time to spend a Sunday afternoon at the Orphan's Press or the Printing House of the Church Charity Foundation, and sit by the windows and experience for yourselves for a few hours only, what the helpless occupants of these buildings have to endure for months, you would not fail earnestly to recommend the underground system for Atlantic avenue, similar to that used under the streets of London.

I do not consider the expense of this change should weigh in the slightest degree against the comfort of the occupants of these buildings and the patients in the hospital.

I cannot describe the workings of the underground railway in London, but I have often traveled in that railway and can vouch for the comfort it gives to the dweller in London while in no way does it annoy or injure any citizen.

LOOMIS L. LANGDON,
Colonel U. S. Army.

A communication was also read by Mr. C. Augustus Haviland, which stated that the railway on the avenue had caused a great depreciation in values.

Rev. J. E. Fray, of the Duryea Church, on Clermont avenue, near Atlantic, spoke of the annoyance caused by the exhausting of steam by the engines of the Long Island Railroad, and stated that he had complained to the management without receiving any satisfaction.

Mr. Kornder, dry goods merchant, corner Fulton and Adelphi streets, said that the presence of the railroad interfered very seriously with his business, in that it cuts him off entirely from one part of the city, his business being largely local.

It was decided to hold the next hearing at the rooms of the Commission in the Real Estate Exchange, Monday, October 19th, at 4 P. M., and that notice of the same be published in the Brooklyn *Eagle*, *Standard Union*, *Times*, *Citizen* and *Freie Presse* on the Tuesday, Thursday and Saturday previous.

Adjourned.

E. F. LINTON, *Secretary.*

October 19, 1896.

A meeting of the Commission was held in the Real Estate Exchange at 4 P. M.

Present--E. G. Blackford, E. F. Linton, E. H. Hobbs, W. E. Philips, W. M. Meserole, Commissioners.

The Chairman stated that the Commission was prepared to hear any one who had anything to say in regard to the relief of Atlantic avenue.

Mr. Wells stated that counsel whom he had hoped would be present was unable to attend to-day, but would be present at the next meeting, to make a statement before the Commission.

Mr. Henry Heins, of 1383 Atlantic avenue:

Mr. Chairman, I have had an idea that a good many would be satified if they could have Atlantic avenue paved all the way up. If your Commission could work in that way and draw up a bill to that effect I think it would be satisfactory.

The Chairman—Your suggestion is, then, that you would like to have Atlantic avenue paved?

Mr. Heins—Yes; I suppose we are not going to get the road off there; that is one thing sure, isn't it?

The Chairman—We don't know what we are going to get.

Mr. Heins—Supposing you cannot get it, what I wish to ask is, if the avenue could be paved?

The Chairman—There is no doubt that there would be a necessity of having the avenue paved eventually.

Mr. Heins--That is right, and I think we would be satisfied if it could be fixed up in good condition. I am in the grocery business at the corner of Brooklyn and Atlantic avenues. The only thing that we ever hear is, "When are we going to get Atlantic avenue paved?" Nobody asks, "When is the road going to come off?" Every single day we have to hear the same thing, because we have that terrible dust and dirt.

The Chairman—Do you think it would be any improvement to have the tracks depressed?

Mr. Heins—Yes, of course it would be a great improvement. I don't think, however, we would get depressed tracks, so I would suggest that it be paved. I think the property owners along there are entitled to a little consideration, and I don't suppose they ought to pay toward it, because they have put up with more disagreeable streets than many in the city, and other men in business on the avenue can tell you the same.

The Chairman--Where you are now is probably the worst street in the city.

Mr. Heins--That is a fact. I think if any of the officials should come there they would be surprised.

The Chairman--Has it ever been paved?

Mr. Heins—No. I asked an alderman about it, and he said if it had ever been paved, it would have to be repaved, but we can't produce any part where it has been paved.

Mr. Philips—I think it has been paved to Bedford avenue.

The Chairman—The last paving was between Franklin and Bedford avenues, by Commissioner White.

Mr. Heins—In front of the railroad offices, the company paved it, and it favored their office; the end of the street was there. Anybody can put twenty feet of paving in front of his property.

Mr. Hobbs—The Legislature can provide for its being paved at no expense to the property owners.

Mr. Meserole—On which side of the avenue is your store?

Mr. Heins—The north side.

Mr. Meserole—Where do most of your customers live?

Mr. Heins—They live on the other side; they have to cross.

Mr. Meserole—Does this drive trade away?

Mr. Heins—Yes, it does.

Mr. Meserole—Do you think they go any great distance away?

Mr. Heins—Well, people of that kind will look for clean streets.

Mr. Meserole—I mean more especially the danger of crossing the railroad. Do you think that hurts your trade at all?

Mr. Heins—Yes, it does, because they are afraid to have their little ones cross there. But as I said before, more than half I think would be satisfied if the whole thing were fixed up; if the railroad company would fence it in. It is disagreeable to pass there. Half of the fence is broken down and the crossings are not kept in repair, and wagons are liable to get broken.

The Chairman—How would you like to have an elevated road?

Mr. Heins—I wouldn't like that; I would rather have it the way it is, and improved, or a depressed road; an elevated road is not going to benefit us.

The Chairman—Of course the pavement is necessary; but we want to get views from people doing business and residing along the line of the railroad, as to what they favor; if they prefer a road depressed or elevated.

Mr. Heins—We prefer it depressed, but have no objection to the trolley cars.

Mr. Thomas H. Wray, of 1163 Dean street—I represent property in Dean street. I trust that this Commission has a good strong backbone, and I feel that it would be very foolish for us to argue either for a depressed road or an elevated road. It seems to me that the only thing that can be done that will be satisfactory to the people in the neighborhood is to get rid of the Long Island Railroad, and take the tracks off the street altogether. I do not see why the City of Brooklyn cannot perform that act.

It seems to me that the only way to do is simply this: The Long Island Railroad should either make their station at East New York or at Jamaica. We have attained a wonderful degree of efficiency in the trolley cars, and it seems to me it would be better for the Long Island Railroad and also for the passengers if the trolley cars should run from the headquarters of the Long Island Railroad at East New York rather than as they do at the present time, for this reason:

We can get off a trolley car just when we want to, and we can get on a trolley car just where we want to; it will not take very much more time to travel from East New York than it would to travel from Flatbush avenue. A large number have children, and we do not send all of our children to the public schools. Many people desire to patronize the private schools.

I have grandchildren and desire to send them down to the Adelphi Academy, or the Packer Institute, but we can't do it because we are afraid to let the children cross the tracks of the railroad.

And then there is another thing: I believe that if the Commission could accomplish it, the taking steam from Atlantic avenue would increase, enormously increase, the valuation of property. I think it would be something over twenty millions of dollars more than it is at the present time. And I say that it is a disgrace to the City of Brooklyn, and the State of New York, that a magnificent avenue like Atlantic avenue should be in the condition it is in to-day. I am glad to think that this Commission is composed of gentlemen who will not abstain from doing what they think is best in the matter.

I urge this because I feel we are entitled to some consideration, not only from the Railroad Company but from the City of Brooklyn and the Legislature of our State.

I think if the Long Island Railroad were taken off the avenue, we would have one of the finest avenues in the State.

I believe it would mean more money for the railroad company. There would be no necessity of having fifty or a hundred gatemen. There would be no necessity of their running to Flatbush avenue. They have Long Island City, where they can carry their freight; they do not need the Flatbush depot for freight work, and the passengers could be carried by trolley cars from East New York far more pleasantly than they are carried to-day, half by steam and half by trolley.

Mr. Linton—Are you acquainted with East New York?

Mr. Wray—I know East New York well.

Mr. Linton—What point in East New York would you think would be a good place for steam to end and the trolley to begin?

Mr. Wray—I think they ought to commence at the City Line in East New York. I think the City of Brooklyn ought to take hold of this matter and claim that the city belongs to them, and from the City Line let them run the trolley cars and build their railroad depot.

Mr. Linton—Isn't it a fact that a great population living on Long Island also have some rights?

Mr. Wray—Yes, most decidedly, and their rights would be attained by using the trolley cars. They have to take a trolley car when they get to the Flatbush Avenue Depot. Cars could run to South Ferry and Fulton Ferry and the Bridge.

If you take a map of this neighborhood, say both sides of Atlantic avenue, you will note that one side is built up and that the other is not. There is a large number of beautiful houses in this vicinity, but all around is any quantity of land, waiting for purposes of investment, and just as soon as you rid Atlantic avenue of the Long Island Railroad you will find that money will come in for the purpose of building up those magnificent streets, the finest section in the city to-day.

Mr. Linton—Suppose there were an elevated road there.

Mr. Wray—I don't think it would have the same effect that the removal of the road would have.

Mr. Linton—I am speaking now of the development. I am asking what would be the possible effect upon that if an elevated road were there?

Mr. Wray--I think it would be better than it is to-day, but I do think that Atlantic avenue belongs to the City of Brooklyn, and I do think that the Legislature ought to be asked to get rid of that road altogether from Atlantic avenue. We have now attained such success in the trolley business that it would not suffer. Please understand that I do not represent the trolley companies at all.

The Chairman—What is your opinion with regard to the depressing of the tracks?

Mr. Wray—That you will never get it done, that is all. It will cost too much money, and where is it to come from? You can't expect the Long Island Railroad to do it; they can't afford to. But they can afford to take the tracks from the avenue, which will cost very little, and build their depot at the City Line, and I think it will pay them better than it does to-day.

Mr. Linton—I would like very much to know what would serve the various interests to the best degree, the Long Island population, the Long Island Railroad Company, which is a great transporting corporation, and the people along the line. It is not that a man has a personal taste about a particular thing; that isn't a solution of the problem. The great problem in all its bearings is the thing about which we very much want knowledge.

Mr. Wray—So far as I can understand it, I don't think it would be detrimental to the Long Island people. It would take them, perhaps, a quarter of an hour longer to get down to the ferries, and as far as the Long Island Railroad is concerned, I think they will make money by it.

Mr. Linton—Have you ever found people who preferred to go rapidly to going slowly?

Mr. Wray—Yes, I have. I go myself sometimes faster than I ought to.

Mr. Linton—But you speak of fifteen minutes longer; do you regard that as a trifle? There are those who would regard it seriously.

Mr. Wray—I don't know that they would.

Mr. Linton—But a workingman would regard it very much to add a half an hour to his day's work.

Mr. Wray—You see they have to get off the car at Flatbush avenue if they are going to the Bridge.

Mr. Linton—Not necessarily.

Mr. Wray—I am merely arguing the advantage it would be to the City of Brooklyn to have the road stop at the City Line instead of carrying it to Flatbush avenue.

Mr. Kelley—How would you get the freight down?

Mr. Wray—Don't you carry it to Long Island City?

Mr. Kelley—A good deal of it comes down to this part of the city.

Mr. Wray—Well, those things would have to be taken into consideration.

David J. Malloy, 103 Arlington avenue:

Gentlemen of the Commission, in this matter of the Atlantic Avenue Railroad, I think you have one of the most important subjects affecting the whole City of Brooklyn.

I have known of this road and its effects on the city since the road was taken off in 1859. Up to that time Atlantic avenue from South Ferry to Court street was as important a business street as Fulton street; it had some of our leading merchants on it, both in dry goods and other businesses, and our leading wholesale merchants were at the foot of Atlantic avenue. Journeay & Burnham, at that time, were there, and, up to 1862, were the leading dry goods house in Brooklyn.

One of the reasons for this was that they had the business of Long Island. It was brought to the end of Atlantic avenue.

Some people thought it would be a grand good thing to change the terminal of the Long Island Railroad, not stopping to look at the interests of Brooklyn, but simply looking at selfish interests. The Legislature passed a bill removing steam from Atlantic avenue.

Mr. Richardson did one of the best things ever done for the City of Brooklyn when he restored the connection to Flatbush avenue with Long Island, and the only mistake that was made at that time was that this improvement was not carried to South Ferry. And I would say that, at the time the road was removed from Atlantic avenue, in 1859 or 1860, Brooklyn had a population of only 265,000 people; and at that time, from 1859 for some ten years afterward, it was the case that all the cities around New York subscribed money to raise bonds to enable the railroad companies to build railroads. But here was the City of Brooklyn, a city which has now reached a population of over a million people, afraid of having a connection by a steam railroad. There is not another case in the United States where they have driven out a connection with outlying country; they encourage them.

The Chairman—Let me call your attention to the Fourth avenue improvement in New York.

Mr. Malloy—That was done, and simply removed to Forty-second street, and that was a mistake. They are attempting now to restore rapid transit in New York. And if you take Atlantic avenue to-day, it is one of the best adapted streets in the City of Brooklyn.

The Chairman—There is no proposition to put steam in the streets of New York.

Mr. Malloy—They will do it if they depress the road. You have had more done to help your section of the city by the Nassau Company than by anything else. Mr. Flynn has done more for your section than has been done for your section for years. You have had here a corporation—the Brooklyn City Railroad—until the Nassau Company forced them to give this system of transfers, had done nothing they hadn't been compelled to do.

VIEW, MANHATTAN JUNCTION, VESTA AND ATLANTIC AVENUES IN TWENTY-SIXTH WARD, LOOKING EAST, SHOWING OCCUPATION OF STREET.

Atlantic avenue has always been on the surface of East New York, and what do you find there?

You find that lots on Atlantic avenue in the Twenty-sixth Ward bring a higher price than they do anywhere on Atlantic avenue, and it does not seem to make any difference whether it is on the north side or the south side, as it does on almost any other street. The south side has gone on and built up, but I look upon it that the reason the south side of Atlantic avenue has not been built up in other parts is that until now the streets were not cut through. Another thing that is going to help your section there is that a boulevard has been laid out, starting at Prospect Park and stopping at the City Line.

If a stranger comes here and wants to go to Jamaica or any part east of East New York he will be almost compelled to have a guide to find a street at the present time.

The remedy lies with the people, and this, I think, is the most important Commission that has been appointed in a great many years, and I think that getting a connection between Brooklyn and Long Island is next in importance to the Brooklyn Bridge. We want the business of Long Island.

You see what a city has grown up at Hunter's Point, and it has been done simply and solely by putting that railroad over to Hunter's Point.

The Chairman—What do you think ought to be done on Atlantic avenue?

Mr. Malloy—I think if this remains a surface road the company ought to ballast the road with broken stone and pave the streets right up to the track and keep the street in proper shape.

It would be better to depress the road or elevate it, but it ought to be carried back to South Ferry.

The Chairman—Do you think that would benefit the business of Brooklyn by taking the trains from South Ferry?

Mr. Malloy—I haven't any doubt of it. I crossed over South Ferry from New York one day last week, to see the condition of Atlantic avenue from South Ferry to Court street, which from 1859 to about 1870 was quite a business street, and had some fine business houses. To-day, from South Ferry to Court street there is not a business of any size to be found.

The Chairman—You are acquainted with the vicinity of the Bedford station?

Mr. Malloy—I am; yes, sir.

The Chairman—The Long Island Railroad maintains a station there at which every train, whether through trains or rapid transit, stop. Do you know whether that has improved the business at that station?

Mr. Malloy—I think it has; yes, sir—more north of the avenue than south of it.

The Chairman—But it is a fact that right in the vicinity of that station, where you would naturally expect a railroad would make an improvement, you would expect to see some activity there.

Mr. Malloy—Yes, but just at that point there is no reason for it, particularly because it would be purely a local station.

The Chairman—Is it not a fact that stores are vacant right in the immediate vicinity of that station?

Mr. Malloy—Yes.

The Chairman—Do you know anything about the values of property in this immediate vicinity?

Mr. Malloy—Not on Atlantic avenue; I haven't posted myself on that.

The Chairman—I have understood you to say that either an elevated or depressed road would be an improvement over the present condition.

Mr. Malloy—Yes, I think so.

The Chairman—In the event of its being impracticable to do either, what do you think ought to be done?

Mr. Malloy—I think the railroad ought to be ballasted with broken stone, and the street paved right up to the railroad track all the way from Bedford avenue, the latter at the expense of the city, as, at the time the avenue was improved by the Commission, the property owners paid for it, it being called Atlantic Avenue Boulevard.

Mr. Linton—Do you think it would be well for the railroad company to bring their track to the grade of Atlantic avenue?

Mr. Malloy—By all means they should.

The Chairman—It is a fact that on a large portion of the line of the railroad it does not conform to the grade, to the City Line going through the Twenty-sixth Ward.

Mr. Hobbs—What would be your idea of the city paying the expense of depressing the road?

Mr. Malloy—I think the city could well afford to pay for it. This is an improvement of the Greater New York, which will carry the city as far east as Floral Park. I think it is an improvement of great importance and one of which the city ought to bear a part of the expense.

Mr. Linton—And who will pay the other part?

Mr. Malloy—I think the railroad company should.

The Chairman—Should the depot be located at the eastern side of the Twenty-sixth Ward, and steam be stopped there, what effect do you think it would have on the property you have spoken of?

Mr. Malloy—I think it would have a very detrimental effect. Let anybody ride into Brooklyn twelve miles in a trolley car to his business, and he will see what it is. The trolley is well enough for a short distance, but for ten or twelve miles we must have something besides the trolley.

The Chairman—Doesn't the elevated afford you relief?

Mr. Malloy—In part it does, but that part of the city is not going to stop growing.

Mr. Linton—Suppose each side of the avenue, even as far as Jamaica, was improved and brought up to a condition of improvement equal to any street, even if the street were on the surface, what do you think the effect would be on property?

Mr. Malloy—It would have a very beneficial effect. I have heard gentlemen here speak about crossing the railroad. I don't know of any section or any city or village where you haven't two sides of a railroad, and if you have a railroad running through, you have to have a crossing on it. I don't see that it interferes with the growth of a city. Now, I think in the Bedford section it is more a lack of public spirit on the part of the owners than anything else that you haven't had better connections. The only route you had was the Franklin avenue road; I think that fact has had more to do toward retarding the growth of the Bedford section than anything else.

The Chairman--We have the Nostrand avenue and the Tompkins avenue lines.

Mr. Malloy--How far does the Tompkins avenue line run?

The Chairman—I cannot say now, but in the last four or five years we have had several lines opened up.

Mr. Malloy--That is what ought to have been done twenty years ago.

The Chairman--You speak of a lack of public spirit; what should have been done?

Mr. Malloy--They should have seen that those improvements were made. This should have been done some time ago. The great trouble is, the people of Brooklyn do business in New York; they go to New York in the morning and come home to sleep at night.

The Chairman--Why have you singled out this particular section?

Mr. Malloy--I think that section has suffered more than any other section in the city, and I think it has grown less than any other section in the city.

Mr. Linton--You mean it has suffered from lack of transit?

Mr. Malloy—Yes.

Mr. Linton—And people have not facilitated that, neither have they graded streets nor done anything else.

Mr. Malloy--No, sir. I don't think that from Troy avenue to Rockaway avenue there are more than a half a dozen streets that are open to the Eastern Parkway, and I think this has had a very detrimental effect on property in that section.

The Chairman—You think that people are not afraid of a steam railroad, then?

Mr. Malloy—I don't see why they should be. The trolley cars have killed more people than the steam cars, and the railroad is pretty well guarded.

The Chairman—That is a fact; it is pretty well guarded, and no lives have been lost in the last couple of years. We give them credit for taking good care of the crossings now, and they do not ring their bells and blow their whistles. I think we should give them credit for that, and it is because of the agitation of this question by public spirit that those changes were brought about.

Mr. Malloy—I have heard these gentlemen say that they did not want an elevated railroad. Why, a city is made up of nuisances; nobody wants to live on the line of a steam road or an elevated road, but we can't get along without them.

The Chairman—Is it not a fact that all cities when they get to a certain size make the railroads provide some way to bring their trains in other than on the surface?

Mr. Malloy—That may be so, but they do not attempt to drive them out. If you do as some of these gentlemen have suggested, put this road out to East New York, then the East New York people would want it put out to Jamaica; this is, of course, merely a selfish view of the question.

The Chairman—Of course all the people who come before us are looking at it from a selfish standpoint.

Mr. George H. Cook, 1097 Dean street—It seems useless, gentlemen, to take up much more of your time, but this is not a new problem.

I, personally, have lost the sale of three different houses because the people would not let their children cross the Atlantic avenue railroad tracks. We must get some relief. If we could get a depressed road, that would be well, but it doesn't seem feasible. I don't see where the money is to come from. I don't see how the Long Island Railroad can do it, and the city certainly cannot do it. If we could get the depressed road through to South Ferry it would be an ideal thing, because we could get all the advantages of the railroad and do away with all the disadvantages.

Mr. Linton—" Ideal " is rather an extensive word, and I would like to have you elaborate on it.

Mr. Cook—Because it could run to South Ferry and at the same time it would do away with the disadvantage of having to cross it and of having the trains in sight, as well as having the streets blocked every few minutes.

Mr. Linton—Wouldn't a canal or cut going along Atlantic avenue have serious disadvantages, such as locomotives going along and discharging smoke almost at a level, disturbance of light, and general unsightliness of it?

Mr. Cook—Should anthracite coal be burned there would be

very little smoke. If a stone parapet were built a few feet in height and an ornamental iron railing placed above, I don't think it would be unsightly.

The Chairman—What do you think of an elevated road?

Mr. Cook—I think it would be better than it is now. The surface steam road I regard as the worst possible thing we can have there—a great disadvantage, and it ought to be done away with. A depressed road is the best thing if it were feasible, financially. An elevated road would be better than the present system, and if we can't have either the depressed road or the elevated I would rather see it taken from the avenue.

Mr. Linton—If to-day you had the power would you take the elevated road off of Fulton street, because of the noise?

Mr. Cook—No, sir; but an elevated road such as that on Fulton street is a very light structure, and would not do for the business of the Long Island Railroad. It would be necessary to build it very much heavier, and it would be very much more of a nuisance.

Mr. Linton—If the average thickness of an iron elevated structure could be said to be one-fourth of an inch, and one-eighth of an inch were added, that would be a perceptible gain in strength, but would that affect the looks of it?

Mr. Cook—It is not likely they would do it in that way.

Mr. Linton—The thicker iron would contain the element of greater strength, and the added thickness would not be perceptible, while at the same time it would add to the strength.

Mr. Cook—An engineer would probably not do that; he would very likely make wider and deeper trusses, and put the iron in a different form.

Mr. Meserole—What is your remedy, if a depressed road is impossible and steam is intolerable?

Mr. Cook—Take it off altogether, just as they have done in New York and almost every other city. We have outgrown the system.

Mr. Linton—In New York there are two rivers running parallel with the city which afford transportation; these the City of Brooklyn has not got, and while in New York it might be effectual it wouldn't be here. So you see the question is changed by the city and the traveling facilities.

Rudolph Reimer, 2814 Atlantic avenue—It seems to me that there is a spirit of antagonism existing between the property owners and the Long Island Railroad. This is a great mistake; the interests of Greater New York and of the Long Island Railroad Company are identical.

The proper outlet for the Long Island Railroad is New York. An underground railroad in a tunnel under the river toward New York is, according to what I understand, practicable.

The underground railroads are very nice when they are properly conducted, as they are in some cities in Europe; and if we have electric motive power on an elevated structure, the nuisance of an elevated railroad will be, to a great extent, overcome. I have been doing business on Atlantic avenue for over twenty years. Freight from Jamaica down to Flatbush avenue amounts to a great deal. Some people think that the passenger traffic is the mainstay of a railroad, but I think otherwise.

The Atlantic Avenue Railroad was in existence before people lived there; all the people thought it was a good thing to have it there. The Long Island Railroad is a benefit to every man, woman and child who lives in Greater New York. We cannot do without the railroad and the railroad cannot do without the people of Greater New York. If this one point is kept in view, all questions will easily be settled.

The Chairman—You think an elevated railroad would be an improvement over existing conditions?

Mr. Reimer—Certainly.

Mr. Linton—What do you think about narrowing the sidewalks on Atlantic avenue?

Mr. Reimer—Those are questions of minor consideration.

Mr. Linton—But the sidewalks are of extraordinary width, and the railroad land is wide, and by narrowing the sidewalks you would have a wider roadbed.

Mr. Reimer—I consider that the sidewalks are too wide.

Mr. Linton—Would the narrowing of the sidewalks contribute to a larger and more valuable street?

Mr. Reimer—That is of minor consideration; that could be done to improve the general surface of the street.

Edward D. McGreal, 35 Kane place, gave as his opinion that

the Long Island Railroad should be removed from the avenue, and does not favor either an elevated or depressed railroad.

J. P. Curtis, 1075 Dean street—I think the Long Island Railroad should be compelled to vacate Atlantic avenue, and then the future occupancy could be determined.

The Chairman—What is your view of a depressed road?

Mr. Curtis—I think it would be the natural road for the Long Island Railroad. The South Brooklyn Terminal Company has already got one. They have a charter to extend to the Twenty-sixth Ward, and have an underground road to Third avenue.

Mr. Linton—You speak of the South Brooklyn Terminal Road. Of course you know a difference exists between the construction of that road and the one upon Atlantic avenue; one would be depressed in a street running its entire length, and the other through blocks where they have sloping banks.

Mr. Curtis—Well, the Park avenue improvement in New York is a fair sample of what you might do with Atlantic avenue.

The only point is that it would be much cheaper than Park avenue, because there is nothing but sand formation.

Mr. Linton—The construction of a depressed track is perfectly easy; the only problem seems to be to get the money.

It was moved and seconded that the Secretary advertise that a public hearing will be held October 26th; carried.

Adjourned.

E. F. LINTON, *Secretary.*

October 26, 1896.

A meeting of the Commission was held in their office in the Real Estate Exchange, 4 P. M.

Present—E. G. Blackford, E. F. Linton, W. M. Meserole, E. H. Hobbs, Commissioners.

Mr. Peter Milne, Chief Engineer City Works, stated that he had with him a report of the number and plans of the sewer pipes which will be affected by the consummation of a plan proposed of a depressed road on Atlantic avenue; it being the work of the Engineer of Construction, Mr. Myers.

The Chairman—What we would like to get at in a general

way is whether there are any great engineering problems in the depressing of the tracks between Flatbush avenue and the eastern extremity of the Twenty-sixth Ward.

Mr. Milne—That is as far as we go with a 28-inch main, then it diverts north by east to the Jamaica Plank Road. The only serious question in the matter is the moving of that main.

Mr. Hobbs—That lies on the east side of the street?

Mr. Milne—That lies on the north side of Atlantic avenue from Clinton street to the Manhattan Beach crossing, and then it bends and pursues its course to the Jamaica Plank Road, which is to the north and east of Atlantic avenue.

Then the other serious problem is the Ridgewood Pumping Station, where the old brick conduit passes from south to north. The bottom of that conduit is about 31 feet below the surface. Mr. Verona, the engineer of the water supply, in answer to my question, says there are two force mains, one 42 inches and the other 40 inches in diameter, and those are cast-iron. The depth of the excavation varies from 8 to 12 feet under the surface of the street. The brick conduit on the inside is 10 feet wide by 8 feet 8 inches high, and on the outside 15 feet wide by 10 feet 8 inches high. That crosses opposite the pumping station at Ridgewood. The depth of this excavation is about 31 feet below the surface. If your depth is only 16 feet you would avoid interfering with the brick conduit and necessitate interfering with the two cast-iron conduits.

The Chairman—Is that a very serious problem?

Mr. Milne—No, it is not a very serious problem. The only serious problem is the work attached to moving the 48-inch main on Atlantic avenue, between Clinton street and the Manhattan Beach crossing. The problem is throwing that size of main out of service.

It is an engineering question if the main can be moved with the water on. If we take it out of service it takes 16,000,000 gallons each twenty-four hours out of service. That main is giving us now that quantity.

The Chairman—What proportion of the total supply is that?

Mr. Milne—It is a little less than one-fifth of the daily

supply. From that main is also fed the high surface on Underhill avenue and Prospect Heights.

The Chairman—How far from the center of the street does this main lie?

(In reply to the question of the Chairman, Mr. Milne read a statement giving the distances of the main from the curb line of Atlantic avenue at different points.)

The Chairman—Are you prepared to give us any estimate of the cost of moving this pipe over?

Mr. Milne—No, sir; I am not.

The Chairman—Can you give us what you might call a guess?

Mr. Milne—I would not like to do that; it might prove misleading.

Mr. Hobbs—Can you state how much it originally cost?

Mr. Milne—No, sir.

The Chairman—Would it be a million dollars?

Mr. Milne—I think not.

The Chairman—Would it be a half million dollars?

Mr. Milne—It might cost a half million. In connection with that proposed movement, there are a number of pipes crossing Atlantic avenue; those are trifling, and mere matters of expense that can easily be calculated, but the moving of the 48-inch main would be the most expensive feature of the whole work.

The Chairman—How many sewers are there altogether that cross the line of Atlantic avenue between the points mentioned?

Mr. Milne—Thirty-nine sewers.

Mr. Linton—Does that include those recently constructed in the Twenty-sixth Ward?

Mr. Milne—Yes, sir.

The Chairman—Those lie at an average depth of over 6 feet.

Mr. Milne—The sewer at Furman street is a 36-inch sewer.

The Chairman—We are figuring only from Flatbush avenue.

(Mr. Milne then read a list of sewers crossing Atlantic avenue with their dimensions, depth and character. Mr. Milne also read a list of sewers running through Atlantic avenue east and west.)

Mr. Linton—Wouldn't there be a difficulty in depressing a sewer?

Mr. Milne—That would depend upon the depth, somewhat. Some of these are storm sewers. They will run full only in a storm, and under ordinary conditions they are only about from one-half to one-third full.

The Chairman—Do you want to name any figure as to the cost of all these undertakings?

Mr. Milne—I can't do that very well, unless your engineer has a plan pretty well defined, showing the depth at various points, and width and thickness of the retaining wall; then we could very readily determine.

The Chairman—But you could guess within a half a million dollars of it now?

Mr. Milne—Yes.

Mr. Linton—Could not there be an approximate estimate made for this Commission, within a given figure, that need not be absolutely accurate?

Mr. Milne—In conference with your engineer, I might make an approximate figure.

John B. Sabine, 569 St. Marks avenue, representing the corporation of St. Bartholomew's Church—This church owns quite a large piece of property on Atlantic avenue near Bedford, about 100 feet frontage on Atlantic and running through to Pacific street. When the church purchased the property, some eleven or more years ago, they were informed that the Atlantic Avenue Railroad would be removed from Atlantic avenue, or at least that steam would not be used there, and they have been informed ever since by our legislators that that nuisance would be removed, and for one cause or another (I presume that the Chairman is acquainted with some of the reasons) it has not been done.

We find, the church being near Bedford avenue and the station at Franklin avenue, that trains coming in from the Island, as well as those going out, are frequently stalled there; it seems to be a favorite time for them during the morning service on Sunday, about 11 o'clock or a little later.

There seems to be a train, a rapid transit, Rockaway train and Long Island train, waiting for the first to discharge passengers and another to come into the station. There is always a great commotion, puffing and roaring of locomotives, and there is enough noise to drown the voice of the most powerful preacher. We find that Atlantic avenue is quite a line of demarcation when our families remove from the south side of Atlantic avenue to the north side, and many families refuse to send their children to Sunday-school at St. Bartholomew's Church because they are afraid of accidents.

We have to rely almost wholly on families on the south side of Atlantic avenue for the support of our church. Whereas, if there were no railroad there, many of the families who have moved or reside on the north side of the avenue would still continue to attend St. Bartholomew's Church. We have been hoping and praying that something could be done to mitigate this nuisance. Of course we are in favor of the removal of the road altogether. We don't know but that a depression or an elevation of the road might help us a little; but from my communications with the wardens and the other vestrymen of the church, I am convinced that they are a unit for the removal of the road from the avenue.

Joseph O'Brien, Atlantic avenue, near Clinton street—I have had considerable experience with Atlantic avenue affairs, and my impression is that the best plan would be an elevated road, with a tunnel to New York.

The Chairman—You would prefer an elevated road to a road on the surface?

Mr. O'Brien--Yes.

The Chairman—You think it would be a benefit to the city at large?

Mr. O'Brien—I think it would be a benefit to the city at large to have an elevated railroad and tunnel to New York.

The Chairman—Do you think it would be any injury to the city at large if steam were taken off the avenue?

Mr. O'Brien—It would take life out of the city. I look upon a railroad as an aid to the city, just as a river was in ancient times. I think Atlantic avenue has been killed by taking steam off the street, and I have thought so for forty years.

Mr. Linton--You will remember, of course, as I do, that I have met you before in connection with elevated propositions. What do you think the disposition is now, as to an elevated railroad on Atlantic avenue?

Mr. O'Brien--My impression is that the kickers are all dead, or removed, or bankrupt. It has been a great misfortune that some people opposed the road. The people first opposed the Court street line coming down to South Ferry. They said stages were good enough, and when the stages went away they opposed every possible road that was tried in the street, and property is almost unsalable. The life has gone out of the street. The best business houses were on that street; grocers, tailors and dry goods merchants. There were nine dry goods houses on that street when I was a boy.

The Chairman--Do you attribute that to the railroad?

Mr. O'Brien—Yes, I think the railroad would have held it there. It would have kept life on the street, no doubt of it. The railroad had a great effect in building up the lower part of New York, and now it is getting to be better every day.

The Chairman—It wouldn't have helped lower New York if they had had a steam railroad running right down to the Battery?

Mr. O'Brien--A surface road is not so desirable as an elevated road.

The Chairman--You prefer to have a surface road?

Mr. O'Brien--Yes, I prefer to have life on the street.

Mr. Linton--The surface road has been on the street, and is there now?

Mr. O'Brien—Yes; I think I heard Mr. Linton say at one time that the most valuable lots in the Twenty-sixth Ward faced that road, and the road drew the people.

Mr. Linton--In asking the question, I excepted East New York. What I intended to ask was, to what you attributed the fact that east of Flatbush avenue until you get to the Twenty-sixth Ward there really is no life?

Mr. O'Brien—It would require a heroic effort to revive that. My impression is that an elevated railroad with a tunnel to go to New York would build up everything in that part of the city, and I can't see why it can't be done. It could be made the popular route to New York by being a quick up-to-date transit. It would be the easiest and best way to go.

The Chairman—The Twenty-third Street Ferry is the most popular route for up-town New York.

Mr. O'Brien—The Twenty-third Street Ferry wouldn't be so easy for the mass of the people. They would go on the elevated road, as it takes them in the direction they desire to go.

Mr. Linton—This Commission is appointed to consider the problem of Atlantic avenue, and your belief is that the problem can be better solved by an elevated road, and then a tunnel connecting with New York.

Mr. O'Brien—That is the idea. Now, the thing is to get it in the most practicable shape. The first thing necessary is to get quick time from New York to Brooklyn; the other questions are secondary.

Mr. Linton—And you believe it is desirable to have a railroad through the City of Brooklyn, connecting Long Island with the United States?

Mr. O'Brien—Desirable for the City of Brooklyn, Long Island and New York.

A bill was presented by the clerk for services up to October 19th, and ordered paid.

The meeting then adjourned.

E. F. LINTON, *Secretary.*

November 6, 1896.

A meeting of the Commission was held in Carson Hall, corner of Fulton street and Bedford avenue, Monday evening, November 9th, at 8 o'clock.

Present—E. G. Blackford, E. F. Linton, E. H. Hobbs, W. E. Philips, W. M. Meserole, Commissioners, and a number of members of the Atlantic Avenue Improvement Association.

The Chairman stated that the Commission was present in response to an invitation from the Atlantic Avenue Improvement Association, for the purpose of affording members of that Association an opportunity to be heard on the question of the relations of the railroad on Atlantic avenue to the avenue, and of receiving suggestions for the improvement of the present conditions of that avenue, and that the Commission would be pleased to hear from any member who might desire to make a statement.

Mr.Carpenter--Mr.Chairman and gentlemen of the Commission: This is not a new subject to us; we have been in the battle a great many years. I have lived on the line of the Atlantic Avenue Railroad about thirty years and know something of its history. I own property on the avenue, and other property that is affected by the railroad. This railroad has long been declared a nuisance by the citizens of the City of Brooklyn. Organizations along the line have sought ways to abate the nuisance. As I understand, this Commission was appointed to listen to property owners and people living along the line.

In this part of the city we have weighed both sides of this subject, knowing it is a nuisance to one part of the city and knowing it has been a convenience to some extent on the other side. I have come to the conclusion that there are only three arguments to be brought forward. One is, a depressed road; another is, an elevated road; and the third is, to entirely remove steam from the avenue. The matter of depression is entirely out of the question. We have heard the estimate of the expense of this, which runs up into four or five millions of dollars, and we know that the railroad company would not agree to pay half, and the City of Brooklyn cannot afford to depress the road, or to pay one-half of the expense of it; I believe that the Long Island Railroad can afford to do it.

They often say they will pay a certain part of it if we will take care of the pipes. Now, do not let us fall into that trap. I think that would cost more than the excavation and the building of the road. So, I think we ought to drop depression of the road; we can't afford it; it ought to be ruled out.

Now comes the question of an elevated road. The Atlantic Avenue Railroad Company have had charters for this for years past. They had one about twenty years ago for a tunnel, and they were going to do that at once. I told the people there was nothing in it; that they would simply get the charter and put it in the safe; that they could keep it for three years, and then would come a new scheme. I believe if we should get an

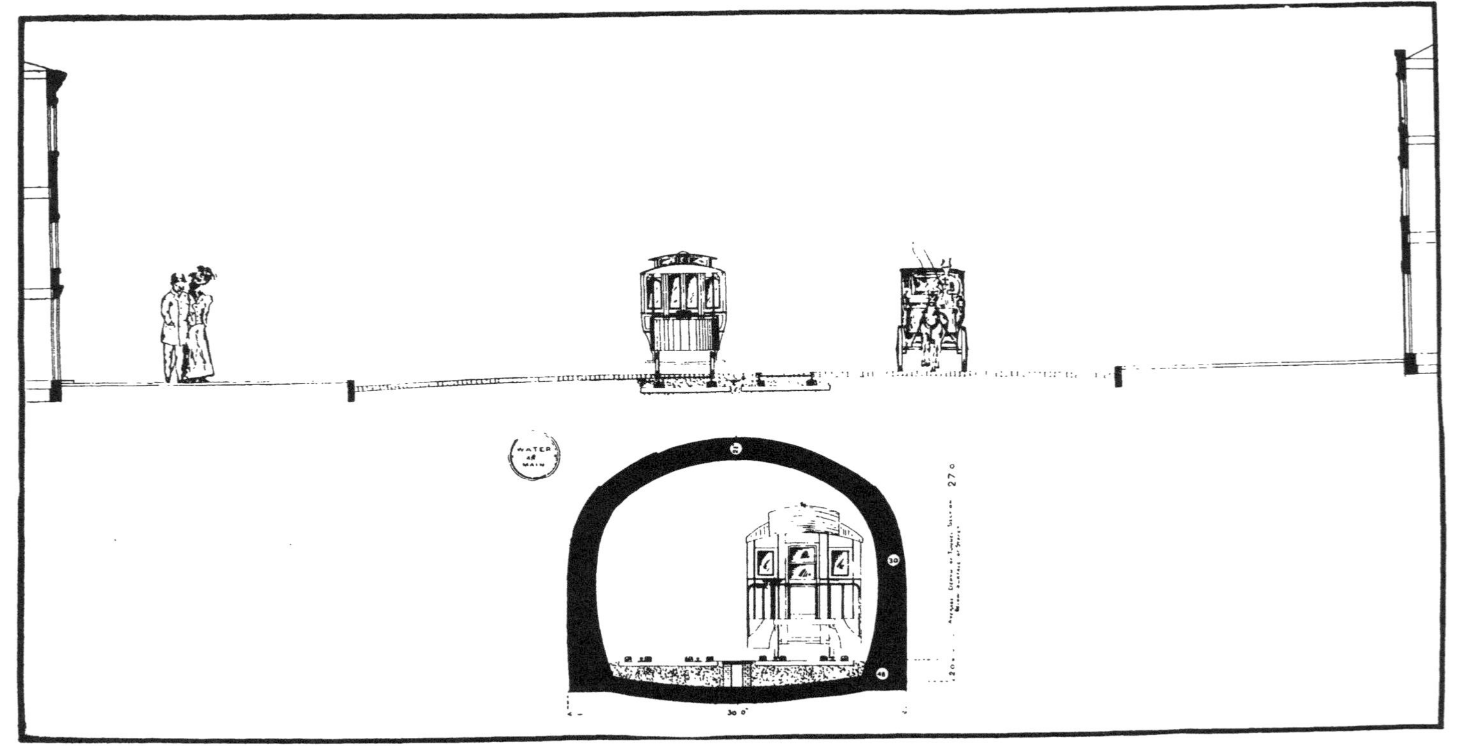

CROSS SECTION, ATLANTIC AVENUE, SHOWING TUNNEL AND SURFACE FROM HOWARD AVENUE TO STONE AVENUE, JUST WEST OF MANHATTAN CROSSING, TWENTY-SIXTH WARD.

elevated road we would have the same trouble. In fact, there was a company organized, and they were going on very happily, but when they tried to make an arrangement with Mr. Richardson, it all fell through. And we never go to Albany that they do not bring out those old blue prints of that road. I tell you, gentlemen, we have been "jollied" from year to year, and it is time for us to say we want the steam taken off Atlantic avenue by legislative act, which says that the same power that put it on can take it off. They claim to have a right to the street, but I don't believe they have any right or title. But suppose they have. I have a fee to some property, and I can run a railroad over it if I want to; but do you suppose I should be allowed to run a steam railroad over my property?

I don't think there is any trouble in going to the Legislature and getting that steam off. What would be the consequence? They could run a trolley over there. The Long Island Railroad, this side of Jamaica, is nothing but a shuttle train, barring the freight trains, which could be run down at night without any disturbance to people. Now, we have been to Albany--committees have been there time and time again. When Mr. Kelley saw the danger, he came slyly around and said, "Now we have the greatest scheme on earth!" Everybody then said, "They seem willing this time to do something;" and, if necessary, they bring up Mr. Richardson, and then they claim the problem has been solved at last. But we have been "jollied," and I believe the sentiment of this meeting ought to be to recommend taking steam off Atlantic avenue, and let whatever will follow it, whether it be trolley or other methods.

Mr. Nelson J. Gates--Mr. Chairman and Gentlemen of the Commission: I don't know that we have anything new to offer. As a taxpayer within a few hundred feet of Atlantic avenue, I am interested in a change in the management of that avenue, and as I look at it, I can see no practicable way out of it, except by demanding that steam be taken off it. I do not believe the Long Island Railroad will ever go to the expense of depressing that road; I don't believe they can afford to do it. I don't think the business is valuable enough to warrant the company in undertaking any such expense, and certainly Brooklyn is not able to go to the expense of doing it. The citizens of Brooklyn, it seems to me, including all those who go to Manhattan Beach and Coney Island and Far Rockaway on this branch of it in the summer, can be just as well accommodated by going on the trolley cars, and if they want the business, I suppose they can have an electric road on the avenue. They certainly have sufficient control to have that road there and continue the business. And as for the freight that comes down the avenue, that must be very small. Now, the people in this part of the city, and for at least two miles beginning at Flatbush avenue, where there are fine streets and fine residences, hope to be relieved of this nuisance. There is no question about it, there is great danger to small children in crossing that avenue--going through the fence and getting on the track; it is a source of great anxiety to parents who send their children to school.

A steam road running through a fine residence part of the city like this is something behind the age—something that should not be submitted to in the present stage of our civilization. I hope these Commissioners will demand that steam be taken off the avenue; I can see no other way out of it than that, and I trust the Commissioners will take that view of it.

Mr. Linton—I would like to ask you a question, and I would like to have it understood that the same question is asked of every gentleman who may speak. It is a fact that Atlantic avenue, in addition to the presence of the railroad, is uninviting in many other respects. My conception of the duties of this Commission is that they are not only to solve the problem of the Atlantic Avenue Railroad but to solve the entire problem of Atlantic avenue between the building lines, so I would like to hear expressed, not only on the line of what you have stated but carrying it a little further in regard to improving Atlantic avenue. Taking the street as it is now, it is in a deplorable condition, and I would like to have some views expressed as to the improvement of it.

Mr. Gates—My idea is that if steam were taken off that would adjust itself.

Mr. Linton—The avenue has been hoodooed by the railroad. Still it might be improved, even if the railroad were there; or without it, there is the question of how that should be done,—whether it should be done by a local assessment or otherwise.

Mr. Gates—I should suppose that if the city would not be willing to make the improvement, if steam were taken off, that property owners in the vicinity would be willing to be assessed and improve it and make it an inviting avenue. It should be one of the most inviting avenues in the city.

Mr. Carpenter—In reply to Mr. Linton's remark that he would like our views on the improvement of the avenue itself, I would say it is in a deplorable condition to-day. In front of my different properties on Atlantic avenue I know the mud is from eight to ten inches deep. It should be paved and put in good condition.

Mr. Cranford—When my father bought property on Atlantic avenue in 1863 it belonged to a lady, and upon searching the title it was found that the property had been sold for the taxes for removing steam, and she was obliged to pay $500 to make that title good. I think Mr. Carpenter has covered the whole ground.

Mr. Linton—I think there is a misapprehension of what I requested, and I will make it clear. My conception of the duties of the Commission under the act is that they are to take into consideration the problem of Atlantic avenue in its entirety, whatever they may find that problem to be. My judgment is that there is a problem in addition to the railroad, and I want you gentlemen to get that idea,—that the avenue is to be considered from every standpoint of anything that constitutes a problem. I wish to hear, with my fellow Commissioners, views upon the subject of Atlantic avenue, not only with relation to the existence of a railroad, and whatever may be done with that, but also what shall be done with Atlantic avenue besides considering the railroad. I want to hear views of people on that. I make no suggestions of improvements, no suggestions of anything that is to be done. We are here to get suggestions.

Mr. Adams—The railroad company is answerable for the present condition of Atlantic avenue. This would have been one of the finest boulevards in the country if the railroad had been kept off.

Mr. Carpenter—I understand now that it is the whole problem of Atlantic avenue that is before the Commission. I would suggest that in case steam should be removed from Atlantic avenue, that you recommend that the avenue have a good pavement—an asphalt pavement—half at the expense of the city and half at the expense of the property owners. But unless steam be removed, I object to any pavement or any assessment on property, because a steam road ruins it. Should a recommendation be sent up to have steam removed, let it include a recommendation that it be paved equally as good as any street in the city. In case steam be not removed, then we object to any kind of pavement, because we think the property would not stand it.

Alderman Leich—I represent the Fifth Aldermanic District, on the northern side of Atlantic avenue, and ever since my first election I have had under thoughtful consideration the condition of that street. From time to time I have introduced resolutions and tried to have the northern side repaved. I finally put through, however, a resolution for the northern side of Atlantic avenue between Troy and Albany avenues. I have succeeded in having that passed, and the city has advertised for bids to pave that section. I think steam should be removed from the avenue. It has been removed once, but a few years after it appeared again, and despoiled the street all the way through.

John F. Anderson—Now, in regard to the matter of repaving the street: We have a mud hole in wet weather and a perfect whirl of dust in dry weather, and the street is intolerably dirty and nasty. A bill was drawn, and in the last contest of the Legislature it was killed by somebody from East New York. Word was sent to me that unless we should extend it through the Twenty-sixth Ward it would be killed. I submitted it to Mr. Schieren, and he said, "Let it be killed." The only thing for this Commission to recommend is that, after the removal of steam, the street shall be paved.

Mr. Linton—I would like to ask Mr. Anderson a question. I understood you to say that that proposed bill was to pave Atlantic avenue, in sections, to Vesta?

Mr. Anderson—Yes; at the expense of the city at large.

Mr. Linton—That would include the Twenty-sixth Ward in paying their part?

Mr. Anderson—Yes.

Mr. Linton—And the opposition came from East New York?

Mr. Anderson—The opposition came from East New York. My neighbor, Mr. Felix Campbell, gave me that information.

Mr. Linton—It is true. But I want to state that East New York would gladly have joined in for a pavement to the City Line, but was not enthusiastic for a pavement, no part of which came within the Ward at all.

Captain Hayes—I am here to represent one of the largest property owners on the avenue, and he is positive as to what he wants done: he wishes steam removed from the street. This has been discussed, and it has been to Albany; I have been there several times myself, and we are just where we started four years ago. Some are in favor of a depressed road, and an elevated road has been mentioned. I should rather see the nuisance remain just where it is rather than have an elevated road there, for if an elevated road be put up, it will be permanent.

At any time they could repeal the bill for the removal of steam from the avenue, and that is what we want. We want these Commissioners to go to Albany with a bill to remove steam from the street.

Mr. Linton wants to know about the street,—what they are going to do with it. In my opinion, that will adjust itself. First take the steam off, and then we will fix the street up. I think the same rule applies to this street as in others—that it be paved properly, and the entire city pay half the expense and the property owners the other half.

Mr. Rae—Some of those whom I represent on the south side and the north side of Atlantic avenue, not on the street itself but south of it, have felt that there has been a lack of improvement south of Atlantic avenue for years past, because of the steam road there. I think we are all agreed that it should be taken off. I am not familiar with the manner in which we should proceed, but if a meeting were called for the purpose of hearing their protests against the steam road on the surface, I do not think you would have a hall sufficiently large to hold the people. I have been in the real estate business twenty years in this section. We have been unable to develop the property south of Atlantic avenue.

The main objection seems to be based upon the children having to cross the avenue; they fear they may be run over. That is a question of large importance. I don't know of a section of the city that so lacks improvements as that between Franklin avenue and East New York south of Atlantic avenue. It is desirable in height and elevation. It is within reach of the bridge to come and the present bridge.

I am not opposed to railroads—I believe they build up a city; we require all the properly conducted railroads that we can get. I think if steam were removed and an elevated road substituted, the increase in values which would result on all the property south of Atlantic avenue would bring to the city a sufficient amount of money to allow the city to pay for the improvement of Atlantic avenue. I enter my protest against steam on Atlantic avenue.

F. L. Green—I have lived on Vanderbilt avenue, near Atlantic, for many years, and own property there. I wish to speak about facts which have not been brought forward. Vanderbilt avenue is an important traffic avenue. The crossing at Vanderbilt and Atlantic avenues is dangerous. The traffic on Vanderbilt avenue has trebled within the last eight years. I have seen one woman killed at that crossing and many narrow escapes.

Since the paving and improvement of Atlantic avenue a few months ago, I think the traffic has doubled. Vanderbilt is a wide street running to the Park. You would be surprised to see the people crossing Atlantic avenue at Vanderbilt. I had thought, until recently, that depressing the road would be the ideal method; that seems now to be out of the question, and the only means left is to remove the steam.

Granville W. Harman—I would like to see steam taken off of Atlantic avenue, that is all. I think the only way to take it off is to go to the Legislature. I think the Commissioners should so report. No elevated road or depressed road; steam off the avenue, and a grand boulevard.

Nelson G. Gates—I would like to know how many of our citizens are opposed to taking steam off of Atlantic avenue. I would like to know how many business men on Flatbush avenue and Fulton street are opposed to removing steam.

I think you could not do a better thing than to show the Legislature that nobody is asking for the continuance of steam on Atlantic avenue. I don't believe anybody is asking for it, and it certainly would be a very important thing to know if anybody does favor it.

Mr. Green—I wish it were possible to get at some figures showing the traffic at Vanderbilt avenue crossing. I think it would be very striking, especially in summer. Thousands of people are obstructed by the gates there.

Isaac Howland—Everybody who knows anything about this section, knows there are thousands of building sites as good as any in the city of Brooklyn. With proper improvements we might extend the city south of Atlantic avenue. I am unalterably opposed to an elevated road, because everybody knows it would destroy the avenue, and it is the widest in the city.

It would prevent it becoming a residence avenue; therefore, I don't see any other course but to take steam off the avenue.

Howard M. Smith—The discussion so far seems to be confined mostly to property owners on Atlantic avenue, and particularly the nuisance to them. Now, I think it has a very much wider scope. I think the Atlantic avenue railroad is a nuisance to the entire city. A gentleman spoke a few minutes ago about Vanderbilt avenue becoming a great cross thoroughfare. Take any of the avenues parallel to that—Classon avenue, Bedford avenue, Nostrand avenue, Utica, Franklin and other avenues—and you will find that the closing of gates there, especially in the summer time, is an annoyance to thousands of people. This afternoon I saw Bedford avenue blocked with carriages, from Atlantic avenue to Pacific street. Business people, merchants with delivery wagons have to wait from five to ten minutes to cross the avenue, and the same thing is true as to other cross thoroughfares; the drivers from the Eastern District have to wait the passage of Atlantic avenue trains.

I have timed the gates for nine minutes when they were closed;

business wagons, truckmen with building materials, all standing there waiting the passage of trains. It is a great loss to the business public, and no steam railroad should be allowed for a moment to interfere with the public business as that road does. It takes a very much wider scope than simply the interests of those who are property owners along the line of the road. I think the citizens all through the city would be delighted to see steam taken from that road. I don't know where it was learned, but a gentleman said to me to-day that he understood that the new president of the Long Island Railroad was contemplating to make Jamaica the terminus of the road, and to run electric cars from there to Flatbush avenue and to the Bridge. It seems to me that it is time to have steam taken from the road.

Mr. Hayes—It has been figured by good judges that if steam could be removed from Atlantic avenue it would increase the value of property south of Atlantic avenue and between Franklin and Albany avenues to the amount of $20,000,000.

Mr. Morse wanted steam removed from Atlantic avenue.

Mr. Seamans—I fully agree with Mr. Smith and the gentlemen who spoke before him – it is a much broader question than the effect upon the property holders upon Atlantic avenue. I believe for every one who is accommodated by riding in the cars, fifteen or twenty are held waiting to cross.

Mr. Morse—What can be done for the future improvement of Atlantic avenue? That is of course a very important question. It seems, however, to be a little like a man whose house was burning to begin to question what the repairs should be; I think we had better put out the fire first and then question about repairs. I went out through the Back Bay region in Boston and along the boulevard they have there; I saw the system of trolley cars combined with the boulevards. My admiration is almost unbounded for that city with its beautiful boulevards. On Election Day I went to the upper part of New York on the Riverside drive and out to St. Nicholas avenue; we can rival any of them on Atlantic avenue if we have the right public spirit, and get rid of that nuisance. This avenue is the most magnificent thoroughfare reaching to beautiful Long Island.

Mr. Linton—How would Atlantic avenue in Brooklyn compare

with Commonwealth avenue in Boston, if you removed steam only and did nothing more to improve it?

Mr. Morse—Of course there is an immense amount of work to be done, but I believe the people will be willing to do it. If this Commission will get steam off Atlantic avenue it will do Brooklyn the greatest benefit that any commission ever did this city, and the city will take care of the rest.

The President of the Atlantic Avenue Improvement Society—Some years ago the street was improved at a cost of eight or nine hundred thousand dollars; and the property owners were assessed, and they paid it most cheerfully.

It was decided to hold an informal meeting Wednesday evening, November 11th, at the Union League Club, at which Mr. Baldwin, President of the Long Island Railroad Company, was to be invited to be present. On the following Saturday evening, at the same time and place, Mr. Johnson, President of the Nassau Railroad Company, was to be invited to a similiar conference.

The next regular meeting, at which the public, and especially Mr. Henry W. Maxwell and Mr. Peter Milne, will be heard, will be held at the rooms of the Commission, Monday evening, November 16th, at 8 o'clock.

Adjourned.

E. F. LINTON, *Secretary.*

November 16, 1896.

A meeting of the Commission was held in their rooms in the Real Estate Exchange on the above evening.

Present—E. G. Blackford, E. F. Linton, E. H. Hobbs, W. E. Philips, W. M. Meserole, Commissioners.

Mr. Alexander Campbell—I represent specifically Mr. and Mrs. Wells, who own 160 feet on Atlantic avenue, between Nostrand and Bedford avenues. I live on Pacific street, and I know I represent the sentiment of all my neighbors.

I think the community is of the opinion that something ought to be done. What is the best thing to be done? There is a large section there which is absolutely retarded in its improvement by its inaccessibility, owing to the Long Island Railroad.

We have a large avenue, a direct line from South Ferry to East New York. It is unimproved, and has been at the mercy of this corporation ever since it got possession of it. There is no reason why Atlantic avenue should not be almost as valuable as Fulton street.

Now, I am not opposed to corporations. I regard them as a good thing, except when honorable gentlemen use the corporate cloak to cover actions which they would not be guilty of as business men. I think that the largest stockholder of the Long Island Railroad would not, as an individual, stand in the position in which he places his corporation.

It seems to me there is only one thing that can be done to relieve the situation, and that is to remove steam entirely from the avenue as far as East New York.

Mr. Linton—To what point?

Mr. Campbell—To such point where the main line branches off; I have not considered that feature at all.

Mr. Linton—Have you considered the question of having it go to the Howard House? That would mean they could come by steam from Long Island to the Howard House and not west of it.

Mr. Campbell—The question is how that can be accomplished. I suppose the only thing that remains is that another assessment be laid and the Long Island road be repaid what they have already been paid for; they were paid $125,000.

Mr. Linton—That would mean paid twice?

Mr. Campbell—Yes.

The Chairman—Let me understand your proposition. The road having already been paid $125,000, you would propose to pay them another $125,000?

Mr. Campbell—As the cheapest way out of it, or whatever sum might be agreed upon. It is simply buying over again what we have already paid for.

The Chairman—How would you raise that $125,000?

Mr. Campbell—By assessment.

The Chairman—On the property holders?

Mr. Campbell—Yes; I think it should be a charge against the city at large. There is no reason in the world why this city should suffer the inconvenience, the depression, and retarding of improvements simply to furnish the Long Island Railroad means of doing business. We give up a beautiful avenue in order that they may do business. You know that under the statutes they get a larger rate of fare than any other road in the State. Whatever will be done, I hope it will be done in such a way that if we buy them out they will be unable to do it a third time. I am often cheated twice, but am never caught the third time. I have not seen any reference to that $125,000.

Mr. Linton—It has been referred to about five hundred times.

Mr. Campbell—I am glad of it, and I hope if you have any more sessions it will be referred to again.

Mr. Linton--Are you acquainted in the Twenty-sixth Ward east of the Howard House?

Mr. Campbell—No, I do not know its character. I live between Kingston and Albany avenues.

Mr. Linton--You suggest that steam be removed from Flatbush avenue to East New York. I would like to ask you whether it should be removed west of the Howard House in East New York and continued east of the Howard House. What equity would there be in that, so far as the Twenty-sixth Ward is concerned?

Mr. Campbell—I simply carried it as far as I knew; I would be perfectly content if you would remove it to Jamaica.

The Chairman—We will now consider the plans of Mr. Strong and his estimate.

Bills were presented and approved as follows: Stationery and printing, $8.50; rent for months of August, September, October and November, $83.34; stenographic and typewriting work connected with report of Mr. Hobbs on the history of the Long Island Railroad Company, $50.40.

The Commission decided to wait on the Mayor the following Friday to submit a preliminary report, and to ask his Honor for more time to prepare their final report; also to make a personal inspection of the condition of Atlantic avenue during the following week, and to make a trip to Boston to inspect the system of tunneling under construction there.

Adjourned. E. F. LINTON, *Secretary.*

December 14, 1896.

A meeting of the Commission was held in its rooms in the Real Estate Exchange at 4 o'clock.

Present—E. G. Blackford, E. F. Linton, E. H. Hobbs, W. E. Philips, W. M. Meserole, Commissioners.

On motion of Commissioner Philips, seconded by Secretary Linton, Commissioner Meserole was appointed a committee of one to have the estimate of cost of proposed improvement, suggested by the Long Island Railroad Company, verified.

On motion of Commissioner Hobbs, seconded by Commissioner Philips, it was voted that the President address a communication to the President of the Long Island Railroad Company asking him to furnish plans and specifications for an elevated structure from Snediker avenue to some point east of Elton street.

The following bills were presented and ordered paid:

For advertising in Brooklyn *Citizen*..................	$14 85
" " " " *Freie Presse*.............	20 25
" " " " *Standard Union*..........	16 80
" " " " *Eagle*.................	15 30
" " " " *Times*.................	9 24
Mrs. Pettingill, stenographer..........................	120 80
For rent of rooms for month of December.............	20 84
" expenses of Commission to Boston................	74 45

Adjourned.

E. F. LINTON, *Secretary*.

ROOM 200 REAL ESTATE EXCHANGE.

December 23, 1896.

The Commission met pursuant to adjournment.

Present—E. G. Blackford, E. F. Linton, W. M. Meserole, W. E. Philips, Commissioners.

A lengthy discussion of plans was had. Upon motion of Mr. Philips, seconded by Mr. Meserole, the following preamble and resolution were adopted:

WHEREAS, There has been prepared, under the direction of

this Commission, a series of plans for the improvement of Atlantic avenue,

Resolved, That this Commission favors the general idea for the improvement of said avenue shown by said plans, which contemplates starting from some point in the city of New York, thence by tunnel under the East River and various streets in Brooklyn, coming to the surface at or near Bedford and Atlantic avenues; thence by elevated road to or near Howard avenue; thence by tunnel to Sackman street; thence on the surface to Snediker avenue; thence by elevated road to or near Atkins avenue; thence on the surface to the City Line. Carried; all the Commissioners voting in the affirmative.

Adjourned subject to the call of the President.

E. F. LINTON, *Secretary.*

OFFICE OF THE COMMISSION.

December 31, 1896.

The Commission met pursuant to the call of the President.

Present—E. G. Blackford, E. F. Linton, W. E. Philips, E. H. Hobbs, W. M. Meserole, Commissioners.

Mr. W. H. Baldwin, President of the Long Island Railroad, was present by invitation, and a lengthy discussion of matters pertaining to the work of the Commission was had. It was determined that the time had come for making public, through a preliminary report to the Mayor, the plans and general conclusions of the Commission. Provision was made for the preparation of copies of the plans and of the preliminary report for the use of the press.

Mr. Philips moved that the President be instructed to consult with his Honor, Mayor Wurster, and fix a time and place for the making of the preliminary report of the Commission. Carried.

The Commission was informed that the rooms occupied by them were rented to other parties after January 1st, and Mr. Meserole was instructed to procure other rooms in the same building for the use of the Commission.

The Secretary reported that the Mayor had communicated with the Commission requesting a synopsis of the work of the

Commission to date, to be used by him in the preparation of his annual message, and that the request had been complied with by sending to him the appended communication, signed by the President and Secretary. The action of the President and Secretary was approved by the Commission.

BROOKLYN, December 28, 1896.

To His Honor, the Mayor :

Complying with your communication of the 23d inst., we beg leave to submit a synopsis of the work of the Atlantic Avenue Commission to date.

The Commission was appointed under authority conferred by the Legislature of the State of New York. Chapter 394, Laws of 1896, entitled "An Act to authorize the appointment of a Commission to examine and report a plan for the relief and improvement of Atlantic avenue in the city of Brooklyn."

The following gentlemen were appointed by your Honor, May 28, 1896: Eugene G. Blackford, Edward F. Linton, Edward H. Hobbs, William E. Philips, Walter M. Meserole. The Commission organized by electing Eugene G. Blackford President and Edward F. Linton Secretary. Rooms were secured in the Real Estate Exchange, 189 Montague street, wherein public meetings have been held from time to time. Said meetings have been advertised in the Brooklyn papers. Ten hearings in all have been had.

A number of people have appeared, the interest having been quite marked. A large number of those who appeared before the Commission were strongly opposed to a surface railroad operated by steam upon any part of Atlantic avenue.

The general condition of Atlantic avenue, aside from the operation of a steam railroad thereon, was condemned in emphatic terms. Arguments looking to a remedy for existing ills largely took the form of depressing the tracks from Flatbush avenue to the City Line. Very many desired the tracks removed altogether; some suggested an elevated railroad ; the majority, however, favoring depressing the tracks. Estimates were submitted by disinterested engineers and others, varying from three million to five million dollars cost. No practical plan for providing such cost has been submitted by any one. The Commission have personally visited and carefully inspected the physical condition of Atlantic avenue from Flatbush avenue to Woodhaven, and found the conditions deplorable, worse than an average country road and unworthy of a prosperous city of one million inhabitants. The circumstances that have contributed to this condition are too well known to comment upon further here.

A committee from the Commission visited the City of Boston, Mass., for the purpose of examining the work connected with the subway now being carried on there. The Commissioners were received with marked courtesy by the Boston authorities, and conducted by the engineer through the work in progress.

Valuable knowledge of new construction was obtained, and the visit is regarded as of advantage.

The Commission has given the matter committed to their care much thought and study. They were embarrassed somewhat in the progress of their work by the sad and untimely death of Austin Corbin, President of the Long Island Railroad, and the consequent delay in consultation with authorized representatives of that corporation. Immediately after the appointment of Mr. W. H. Baldwin as president several interviews were had with him. We found him to be a gentleman of progressive, broad-minded views, disposed to co-operate in the work of the Commission in every way. These interviews have resulted in formulating plans comprehensive in character, treating the whole subject of transportation on Atlantic avenue, having regard for the importance of communication throughout Long Island as well as the interests of the City of Brooklyn.

The Commission have been mindful of certain rights of the railroads, as well as the imperative need of radical change of present conditions. The problems involved have been especially difficult of solution, yet the Commission feel that they have found a practical plan that will meet with almost universal approval, certainly one that will meet nearly every demand along reasonable lines of financial and engineering possibilities, at the same time affording permanent relief from past and present inconveniences of a most serious and annoying character. The Commission will, at an early date, submit a more elaborate report, embodying fully detailed plans, estimates of cost, suggestions of

VIEW, PENNSYLVANIA AND ATLANTIC AVENUES, TWENTY-SIXTH WARD, SHOWING OCCUPATION OF STREET.

improvement, needed legislation, etc. The Commission feel sanguine of the acceptance by all parties in interest of the result of their labors, which will accomplish real rapid transit, not only from Brooklyn to all parts of Long Island but ultimately reaching the central business portions of New York City, and this, too, at a cost very greatly less than any sum heretofore mentioned in connection with the subject.

In closing, the Commission desires to express its appreciation of the uniform courtesy and valuable aid by the various city departments during its work.

Respectfully submitted,

E. G. BLACKFORD, *President.* E. F. LINTON, *Secretary.*

Adjourned subject to the call of the Chair.

E. F. LINTON, *Secretary.*

MAYOR'S OFFICE, January 8, 1897.

Present—E. G. Blackford, E. F. Linton, E. H. Hobbs, W. E. Philips and W. M. Meserole, Commissioners.

The Commission presented its first report to his Honor, the Mayor.

Adjourned subject to the call of the Chair.

E. F. LINTON, *Secretary.*

UNION LEAGUE CLUB, January 20, 1897.

Present—E. G. Blackford, E. F. Linton, E. H. Hobbs, W. E. Philips, W. M. Meserole, Commissioners.

A general discussion was had with reference to the preparation of a bill to be submitted to his Honor, the Mayor, and the Corporation Counsel for their approval.

After an exchange of opinion, Mr. Philips moved that it be the sense of this Commission that the City of Brooklyn should pay one-half of such expenses connected with the work outlined in the Commissioners' report of January 8, 1897, in which the Commissioners may hereafter determine that it is proper for the city to participate. Carried.

The Chairman appointed Messrs. Meserole and Philips a committee to consult with the Mayor and Corporation Counsel in reference to the bill.

Adjourned to meet at the same place on the call of the Chair.

E. F. LINTON, *Secretary*.

UNION LEAGUE CLUB, February 8, 1897.

Present—E. G. Blackford, E. F. Linton, E. H. Hobbs, W. E. Philips, W. M. Meserole, Commissioners.

Corporation Counsel Burr was also present. The bill drafted by the Corporation Counsel was read and discussed at length. Some changes were made in the phraseology. No definite action was taken, and the Commission adjourned subject to the call of the Chair.

E. F. LINTON, *Secretary*.

UNION LEAGUE CLUB, February 10, 1897.

Present—E. G. Blackford, E. F. Linton, E. H. Hobbs, W. E. Philips, W. M. Meserole, Commissioners.

The President of the Long Island Railroad Company and Corporation Counsel Burr were also present.

The proposed bill was discussed at length, and further changes made, looking to perfecting the measure.

At a late hour the Commission adjourned.

E. F. LINTON, *Secretary*.

February 16, 1897.

The Commission met at the rooms of the Commission in the Real Estate Exchange at 4 P. M.

Present—E. G. Blackford, E. F. Linton, E. H. Hobbs, W. E. Philips, W. M. Meserole, Commissioners, and a number of property owners of the Twenty-third and Twenty-fourth Wards, who desired a hearing.

W. G. Hoople—Mr. President and Gentlemen of the Commission: We appear before you representing a meeting held in

Kings County Hall about a week ago, in regard to the proposed construction of an elevated structure on Atlantic avenue.

The meeting that we represent was opposed to having an elevated structure on that street on the part proposed by this Commission. It was the opinion that if anything were done with Atlantic avenue to change its present status, the thing to do was to have it underground from the place where it starts out to the City Line.

It was discussed in the meeting as to an elevated structure on part of the street and underground on part; some gentlemen were willing to have it elevated a portion of the way, and underground a portion of the way in order to get some relief on Atlantic avenue. It was agreed at that meeting that Atlantic avenue for railroad purposes was a very valuable franchise to be connected with the Long Island Railroad system, knowing that they favor a tunnel under the East River to Church street, New York, thus touching the most populous part of that city. It will give the Atlantic Avenue Railroad Company an enormous travel not many years hence; therefore, we contend that the Long Island Railroad people could well afford to give us an underground railroad from one end of the avenue to the other.

An elevated structure on a part of the street and an underground structure on another part of the street would not only be an unseemly looking affair and injure property, but would be something you could not get rid of. It would be a permanent structure, and it would blight all that portion of the avenue; it would affect its future to such a degree that no improvement could be made on that street where the elevated structure was erected.

And it was for that purpose we appear before you to-day to protest against an elevated structure on that portion of Atlantic avenue. We ask that they will give us this underground railroad. That is all I have to say in regard to this matter.

The Chairman—You speak about an elevated road being a blight on Atlantic avenue. We have a pretty bad blight there now, I think. The one common object that we have is to get rid of the nuisance from a steam railroad.

Mr. Hoople—We agree on that.

The Chairman—And that if we could have a subway all the way from Flatbush avenue to the City Line that that would certainly be much more desirable than this plan which has been proposed?

Mr. Hoople—We all agree on that.

The Chairman—Now, of course, all of you gentlemen know that in the last eight years I have been fighting on those lines—to get rid of steam on the surface. We have been beaten in every effort we have made in the Legislature through our Citizens' Association there—the Atlantic Avenue Improvement Association—because we could not agree upon a plan that the railroad would accept. One was to stop steam—the use of steam on Atlantic avenue—this side of the City Line. We have been beaten on that in the Legislature, and all the schemes we have had have come to naught up to the present time. You speak about this being a valuable franchise. That franchise the Long Island Railroad own now; you can't take it away from them.

Mr. Hoople—The Atlantic Avenue Company, I believe.

The Chairman—The Atlantic Avenue Company, by its lease, so that the two are as one factor in the matter. That lease is for ninety-nine years.

Mr. Hoople—Is there anything in the fact that the Atlantic Avenue Railroad is willing to release the Long Island Company from this lease, if they are permitted to put a trolley on Atlantic avenue?

The Chairman—No, sir; the Atlantic Avenue Company receives a fixed rental of $60,000 a year for the use of that property on Atlantic avenue which the Atlantic Avenue Company claims to own the fee of, and which they have fenced in and which the city itself cannot take away from them without paying for it.

Mr. Hoople—Isn't there some question about that?

The Chairman—As to certain parts there is; as to others there is not.

Mr. Meserole—They are in possession and must stay in possession.

The Chairman—I have 165 feet on Atlantic avenue just east of Bedford avenue, where this thing begins to open. The cars come out, and before they get away they are pretty well up; in addition to that, there is a trolley car on each side, and they have to go around that opening. There are four tracks in front of my entire property. After considering the whole thing, I calculate that the conditions will be very much better than they are now, and that my property will be improved in value way beyond what it is now, because of the rapid transit feature which is linked up with this rapid transit under the tunnel to East New York.

Mr. Hoople—That might be at that point, where there is a depot.

The Chairman—It will be at any point on the avenue. They have only one station proposed, and that is at Nostrand avenue. They have a trolley service, which they calculate to operate in connection, and a man who lives a good way from the depot will get on a trolley car, and the fare they will charge him from the point where he gets on the trolley to the point in New York won't be greater than if he started from the Nostrand avenue depot.

Mr. Hoople—It is proposed to run the trolley through the tunnel?

The Chairman—No, sir; on the surface.

Mr. Hoople—They will have to transfer at some point?

The Chairman—At Flatbush, or Nostrand avenue, or the East New York stations; the whole scheme, take it all together, with all the benefits that we will get from it, over-balances entirely the short section on which you gentlemen are located. We have studied it in the interest not only of the whole of the property owners but of all the property owners, and we have tried and done our best; we have disposed of a great many difficulties that first came to us, but this part of it we don't seem able to overcome. As Chairman of this Commission, and familiar of course with the whole subject, and all the ramifications of it, and all the capital that is expected to be brought into it, I tell you now, that if this Commission were to say to the Long Island Railroad Company that we will not approve of anything except a railroad which will run beneath the surface in a cut or tunnel, that it would be the end of this thing for the time being—for this year, for next year or several years, and we don't know when we will get anything better. You speak about the franchise being so valuable that the questions are involved and so large, and of the benefits they expect to get out of it. They have other resources. They have a bridge started to go across Blackwell's Island. It is like a great many of Mr. Corbin's schemes which were started and then stopped. Mr. Baldwin has been brought here by the Long Island Railroad people to study these problems, and he has been brought here for the purpose of building that bridge and finishing it up, and in that way give them a traffic into New York City. Mr. Baldwin thinks this is a great deal better. It means a great benefit to the Long Island Railroad Company; it means, also, a great benefit to the city of Brooklyn as a whole; it means, also, a great benefit to every man or every property owner on the line of Atlantic avenue, as well as those who live north or south.

Mr. Hoople—I think, Mr. Blackford, that the people who would get the benefit of that road, as it is going to be a rapid road, would be the people beyond the city.

The Chairman—We have a very large section of the city to the south of Atlantic avenue and further east, the Twenty-sixth Ward, and all through there—we have room for a vast increase in our population, which a scheme like this is sure to bring.

There never was a scheme of this kind but that some point was a disadvantage to some property owners, compared with some others along the line. Of course it goes without saying, that a greater amount of benefit can be had where the subway is than with an elevated structure in front of you.

In all the experiences of Brooklyn, we see what they have done and what they have sacrificed to get rapid transit. Every property owner on the line of Fulton street has a continual reminder of the railroad. There is no question that there are disadvantages of the elevated on Fulton street, but stores and property on Fulton street are worth more to-day than before that elevated was put there.

Mr. Hoople—Would that apply to living apartments over the stores?

The Chairman—I don't know that it would. You could buy property on Fulton street at a great deal less price before that elevated was put on it, and when that elevated was built up through Fulton street, all the property in the section where I live had a big boom and nearly doubled in value.

Mr. Hoople—Do you attribute that to the railroad?

The Chairman—To the railroad, because the railroad brought the business. It did not exist before the railroad, but it came after the railroad was built, and it is the history of all these enterprises. By this proposed rapid transit a man will be carried from the heart of the business section of New York in twelve or fifteen minutes to a place where he can get a home a great deal less than in New Jersey.

Mr. Hoople—I think a portion of that change in values can be attributed to the fact that the whole business center of Brooklyn was changed from lower Fulton street to where it is at present; that drove the small trader further out on account of advanced rents.

Mr. Linton—How about Rockaway avenue? What are the conditions there now; Rockaway and Fulton street?

Mr. Hoople—It has moved the whole business of Brooklyn from the fact that this part has been changed. The lower part of Fulton street has been killed. I guess property has gone down from 50 to 100 per cent.

The Chairman—This is not a serious matter. It was serious when Fulton street dominated everything pertaining to the City of Brooklyn, but it was not serious when Brooklyn got a little freedom of thought and action.

Mr. Hoople—No doubt the elevated had something to do with it, because the whole business center was changed.

The Chairman—The section between Howard avenue and Bedford avenue is not the only portion to be covered by an elevated structure; they get an elevated from Manhattan Crossing to Atkins avenue. So far as this Commission has heard from that section they are all pleased with it.

Mr. Hoople—I think perhaps those people would put up with anything. The hubbub in that part of Atlantic avenue is terrible.

The Chairman—There is not going to be any great viaduct as you speak of in Jersey City. This work, if finally decided upon, will be done probably by a commission on which the present members of this Commission naturally expect to be, and we propose to supervise and control the whole matter so as to get the best possible results for the city and for the property owners along the line.

Mr. Hoople—We have heard, and maybe it is only made-up stories, that the idea was to have this elevated structure so that they might have places to unload freight.

The Chairman—There is nothing in that at all. There is nothing in that stretch of elevated road from Bedford avenue to Howard avenue in which a single pound of freight is intended to be side-tracked.

Mr. Linton—On the contrary, there is a freight yard at Carlton avenue, and they will go in there from a depressed track. What number were present at the meeting you speak of?

Mr. Hoople—About thirty.

Mr. Linton—Was there nobody there to take any affirmative side of this question, and who could have explained to the meeting?

Mr. Hoople—I think not.

Mr. Linton—It would have been interesting at that meeting to have had somebody there who would have given information?

Mr. Hoople—I had nothing to do with the calling of the meeting; I don't know that Mr. Blackford was invited.

The Chairman—No.

Mr. Hoople—I was only an invited guest myself.

Mr. Linton—You came here representing an important body of property owners, and as much in earnest in your relations as this Commission is (we simply are an organized body for a purpose, and your people are an interested body organized in your way and had your own methods of ascertaining opinions), but in the sense that we are all citizens, we must be regarded in the same light.

Mr. Hoople—We got our information from the newspapers.

Mr. Linton—You get a general knowledge from that. I, as one of this Commission, have a very strong desire that you shall learn quite a little that is not in that report, in order that you may convey to your associates the knowledge so gained. Knowledge is better than error.

Mr. Hoople—We suppose you gentlemen put the best face on it you could in order to please the people?

Mr. Linton—I want to call your attention to a little past history, without going too broadly into it, that preceded the coming into existence of this Commission. The conditions of the avenue you are familiar with, and the history of the railroad, etc., for the past thirty years. But until now there has been no organized, systematic body of men created by law to give their attention to the great problem, or to arrive at the very best conclusions they were capable of.

I speak of this Commission being the only organized body of men appointed through legislation to examine into a great problem; that was the purpose of this Commission, and the problem is not confined to railroad tracks and the operation of a railroad. There is a problem outside of that almost as important, in regard to what may be done with Atlantic avenue beyond that. It is a sad and dreary avenue now in some of its parts. The problem is what shall be done with it in its entirety. We do find a railroad there, and we deal with that first. Mr. Blackford has gone over that very thoroughly. We have studied this question with thoroughness; we have not been governed by any body of men or any particular interests. The financial problem was a very serious one; the question of cost came into it, and where was the money coming from? We have never had any one state where the money was to come from for a depressed road. If some one could tell where to get it, you would not be here pressing us for a depressed road.

Mr. Hoople—Mr. Kelley said at a meeting held in Carson's Hall that the Long Island Railroad at that time was willing to bear half the expense of depressing the road if the city was willing to bear the other half.

Mr. Linton—If to-day they would do that, you will find by going into the financial possibilities, that that would be the only half in sight.

The Chairman—The railroad company hasn't got the money to pay that one-half now in this business, and the only way they get their share of this expense for this improvement is by the connection of the tunnel scheme to New York.

Mr. A. J. Bassett—The city should spend half and the railroad half.

The Chairman—The city hasn't the money now; it has not any in sight and the only fear this Commission has, and one of the things we have been working on, is to bring this thing down to where the financial question could be handled; we believe we have it where the city will not be called upon to exceed $1,000,000 as their share. I am not hopeful of getting that $1,000,000. It is the thing needful to carry this thing out. If we can't get it, and can't agree upon a practical scheme, you will have the present condition indefinitely.

Mr. Linton—You made a remark which I want to speak of, as to the heavy structure of the elevated road, and the heavy trains on it. I wish to disabuse your minds regarding the character of it. The difference between it and those we see in the city now will be so slight, that, standing on the sidewalk, you will find it very difficult to discover with the naked eye.

Iron ⅛ of an inch thicker will add vastly to its strength, but no one would notice that the railroad iron structure, which is usually ½ an inch thick, was ⅝, but it would give a vastly increased strength. Therefore, it does not follow, because this elevated structure will be built that way, that it is going to be more unsightly than the present ones. The elevated seems to be a part of modern progress. In the Twenty-sixth Ward the property along Atlantic avenue, for a mile east of Manhattan Crossing, is more valuable for commercial purposes than almost any point between Manhattan Crossing and Flatbush avenue. Notwithstanding we have in that section many more inconveniences, yet the condition of the avenue and the traffic there has not been a bar to the enhancement of value. I own about 1,000 feet on Atlantic avenue which this elevated structure will be in front of and I hold, personally, a peculiar position about that. I was asked years ago about a two-track or a four-track road there. I took this position, because I was a property owner, that I would like to have the business traffic require ten tracks, and if two tracks would enhance it five per cent. I would take the chances of the property if ten tracks were there.

Mr. J. H. Burroughs—Has the Atlantic Avenue Railroad a right to build an elevated road?

The Chairman—The people who own the Long Island Railroad own a contract for an elevated road from South Ferry.

Mr. Burroughs—If this scheme should fail, do you suppose that the railroad company would want to go to the extra expense ?

The Chairman—I don't think so.

Mr. Burroughs—If the present conditions were to remain for five or ten years when we are Greater New York, don't you think the problem could be easily solved with the additional borrowing ability of the city, and the expense which stopped the completion of the plan would be an easy factor?

The Chairman—There is only one factor, and that at the present time, the greatest.

Mr. Burroughs—In five years you could have a subway all the way out. Isn't it better to wait five years and have something for all time?

The Chairman—I don't think we shall ever require that, because I think we shall get such substantial returns out of this. The people who are interested in the tunnel scheme will not build a tunnel from New York to Flatbush avenue to connect with the Long Island Railroad tracks, if the Long Island Railroad tracks are to go in a subway or tunnel clear to East New York without coming to the light.

That is one of their conditions, they say the distance is too great to carry people under ground ; it would impair the value of the whole scheme so much so that that would be a detrimental factor with them.

Mr. Burroughs—If there is going to be an electric motor to carry the train, I don't see where the objection is.

The Chairman—There is no difference in the aims of the gentlemen composing this Commission and yourselves, as to what we would like to get, and the question is as to whether we will take a part or not. Are you all prepared to say that, if you can't have a subway all the way out, you would rather have the existing conditions continue?

Mr. Hoople—That was the sentiment of the meeting.

Mr. Skelley—I would like to say, as an individual owning sixty feet on Atlantic avenue, and also in behalf of the neighbors whom

I represent, that we are unanimous in preferring the present conditions to an elevated structure.

I own property in the Fifth Ward, also on Fulton street, and find that rents are very much lower now than they were before the elevated railroad was built. People will not pay the same rent for property on the line of an elevated road that they would if the road were not there; even if it were operated by electricity the noise would be terrific. Rapid transit is good for the Twenty-sixth Ward; rents are going down there. We are positive that our property will be injured by an elevated road. We are decidedly opposed to it; we would like an underground road, but if we cannot have that, don't give us anything that will not be an improvement. We have had enough nuisances on Atlantic avenue.

Mr. Linton--The history of Brooklyn shows that in every large undertaking that has ever been proposed it has been bitterly opposed. The building of the Brooklyn Bridge was opposed for years; also granting of the right of horse cars to take the place of stages; the trolley system instead of horse cars was opposed; even the introduction of water in pipes met with opposition.

Notwithstanding this fact, all those things which were so strongly opposed have been really a benefit in the largest sense.

I would like to ask you in the matter of rents; is it not true that property values are down all over the city?

Mr.——— —We are all agreed on that.

Mr. Linton—Is it not hard to get fair rents anywhere?

Mr.——— —In that regard, it is not a fair question. Immediately after the elevated road was built on Fulton street the rents were reduced.

Mr. Linton—I want to know in a large sense, is it not a fact that property owners find difficulty in getting rentals where a man will receive a fair income?

Mr. ——— —That is owing to the times.

Mr. Linton—It does appear inevitable that in the case of large numbers, some will be benefited and some not; we must be guided by the largest advantage of all. One of the rights that Long Island has, is the right to reach New York City and the rest of this continent, notwithstanding the fact that Brooklyn is built across the end of it.

Mr. ——— —Every man's rights should be preserved ; I say condemn the property and take it.

Mr. Linton—Condemn what property ?

Mr. ——— —Condemn Atlantic avenue and pay us for it ; that is the only just way out of it.

Mr. Linton—We don't want to injure anybody.

Mr. ——— —But you will if you pass this bill.

Mr. Tilley—Have you considered a continuous tunnel to Albany avenue ?

The Chairman—Yes. I did not like this thing to come up in front of my property on the corner of Bedford avenue. I would like it the way it is below, or the way it will be above Howard avenue, with a trolley line, and I asked the engineer to make a plan of what it would be to carry it to Kingston avenue. We found we would have a grade crossing at Brooklyn avenue, and at Kingston avenue there is only 5 feet 6 inches clearance. We would get up to the proper height at Albany avenue.

Mr. Meserole—There is no place where they can get out as they can at Bedford avenue. Nostrand avenue is 10 feet lower than Bedford avenue. Troy avenue is only 4 feet 7 inches lower than Albany avenue; the block is only 700 feet long.

Mr. Hoople—How high can they climb in 100 feet ?

Mr. Meserole--Two feet in 100 is their limit.

The Chairman—They won't consider anything where it is greater than two per cent. If anybody can show us how we can attain the end we all want in any other way, we are open to conviction. It will have to be done quickly, though. I consider it the best plan obtainable.

Mr. Linton—He is speaking the sentiments of the whole Commission.

The Chairman--The Commission has been a unit and worked in harmony to get an improvement upon the present condition. The thing is immensely popular with everybody who hasn't the sore right in front of them, and you gentlemen, unfortunately, have the sorest spot. I think you are overrating the consequences and unpleasantness of it. I think if you will take the

VIEW, VAN SICLEN AND ATLANTIC AVENUES, TWENTY-SIXTH WARD, SHOWING DANGEROUS GRADE CROSSING.

matter up and study it with regard to distances, as we have, you will be satisfied that it is not going to be so bad a thing. It is not as pleasant as a covered road; nobody tries to convince you of that. We only say that is the situation, and we can't get away from it, and it is not going to be anything like the nuisance that exists on any other elevated road in this city, for the reason that you have a street wider than any of the others.

Adjourned.

E. F. LINTON, *Secretary.*

OFFICE OF THE ATLANTIC AVENUE COMMISSION.

February 17, 1897.

Present—E. G. Blackford, E. F. Linton, E. H. Hobbs, W. E. Philips, W. M. Meserole, Commissioners, and President Baldwin and Counselor Kelley of the Long Island Railroad Company.

The proposed bill was read and further amendments were made.

Mr. Philips moved that the bill as read be submitted to the Corporation Counsel by President Blackford. Carried.

Adjourned.

E. F. LINTON, *Secretary.*

UNION LEAGUE CLUB, February 20, 1897.

Present—E. G. Blackford, E. F. Linton, E. H. Hobbs, W. E. Philips, W. M. Meserole, Commissioners.

The improvement bill was further discussed and regarded as complete.

It was moved by Mr. Philips that the President submit the bill as read to the Corporation Counsel, as embodying the ideas of the Commission.

Adjourned.

E. F. LINTON, *Secretary.*

UNION LEAGUE CLUB, February 24, 1897.

Present—E. G. Blackford, E. F. Linton, E. H. Hobbs, W. E. Philips, W. M. Meserole, Commissioners.

The subject of the condition of Atlantic avenue, as distinguished from the question of the presence of the railroad, was taken up and discussed at length.

The sense of the Commission was that it was within the province of the Commission to take action looking to the improvement of the avenue's roadbed. Questions of the plan of improvement, character of material, paving and the financial problems were gone over. After a free discussion of the various matters the Commission adjourned.

E. F. LINTON, *Secretary.*

UNION LEAGUE CLUB, March 6, 1897.

Present--E. G. Blackford, E. F. Linton, E. H. Hobbs, W. E. Philips, W. M. Meserole, Commissioners.

Further discussion was had with regard to the improvement of Atlantic avenue. Mr. Meserole submitted a partial plan of suggested improvements. After further discussion Mr. Linton moved that Mr. Meserole be directed to complete the plan shown for improvement of Atlantic avenue, and report it at the next meeting, with estimate of cost, etc. Carried.

Adjourned to meet on Friday, March 12.

E. F. LINTON, *Secretary.*

UNION LEAGUE CLUB, March 12, 1897.

Present—E. G. Blackford, E. F. Linton, E. H. Hobbs, W. E. Philips, W. M. Meserole, Commissioners.

Mr. Meserole reported further with reference to the plan of improvement of Atlantic avenue.

The report was discussed at length.

Mr. Philips offered the following resolution:

Resolved, That the Secretary be directed to prepare a report covering the improvement and paving of Atlantic avenue, for the consideration of the Commission at the next meeting, said report to provide that the improvement be under the proposed Commission for altering the railroad grade, provided for in the bill formulated by the Corporation Counsel; that the Commission be empowered to fix on the character and distribution of the proposed work, subject to the approval of the Mayor; that the Commission shall be empowered, with the approval of the Mayor, to enter into contracts for such work and thereafter to superintend the work; that the funds to pay for the work and attendant expenses shall be furnished, one-third by the city, one-third by the railroad and the balance by an assessment of the property within the usual district of assessment for local improvement; that the report contain reasons why this work could be done more economically by the said Commission and in connection with the railroad work. Carried.

It was moved by Mr. Philips that the counsel of the Commission, Mr. Hobbs, be directed to prepare, with such assistance as he may require, a bill embodying the views of the Commission to be submitted to the Corporation Counsel.

Adjourned.

E. F. LINTON, *Secretary.*

UNION LEAGUE CLUB, March 16, 1897.

Present—E. G. Blackford, E. F. Linton, E. H. Hobbs, W. E. Philips, W. M. Meserole, Commissioners.

The Secretary, Mr. Linton, submitted a report embodying the views as expressed at the last meeting, looking to the further improvement of the avenue.

Mr. Hobbs submitted a bill which had been drafted by the co-operation of Almet F. Jenks, formerly Corporation Counsel. The bill was read, discussed at length, approved, and directed to be submitted to the Corporation Counsel as embodying the views of the Commission on the subject.

It was resolved that the Commission go to Albany to attend a hearing on March 23.

Adjourned.

E. F. LINTON, *Secretary.*

MAYOR'S OFFICE, March 20, 1897.

Present—E. G. Blackford, E. F. Linton, E. H. Hobbs, W. E. Philips, W. M. Meserole, Commissioners.

The Commission submitted its second report to his Honor, the Mayor. Copies of it were furnished the press.

Adjourned.

E. F. LINTON, *Secretary*.

UNION LEAGUE CLUB, March 25, 1897.

Present—E. G. Blackford, E. F. Linton, E. H. Hobbs, W. E. Philips, W. M. Meserole, Commissioners.

The bill of Almet F. Jenks for drafting the Improvement Bill was read. It was moved by Mr. Meserole that the bill, as read, be paid. Carried.

The Commission, since the last meeting, had attended a hearing at Albany, and appeared before the Assembly Committee on Cities, and advocated the passage of the bill then pending in the Legislature providing for a change in the grade on Atlantic avenue and an improvement of the same.

Adjourned.

E. F. LINTON, *Secretary*.

UNION LEAGUE CLUB, April 10, 1897.

Present—E. G. Blackford, E. F. Linton, E. H. Hobbs, W. E. Philips, W. M. Meserole, Commissioners.

This meeting was called for the purpose of a hearing and consultation between the Commission and Senator Weiman, Assistant Corporation Counsel Sperry, Dr. Wells and Paul E. DeFere, Esq. The bill pending at Albany was the subject of discussion. By reason of an amendment introduced at Albany, after its introduction, the gentlemen present expressed their views at length. Explanations were had which modified the views of those opposing the bill, and a final agreement was arrived at, that the amendment should be stricken out of the bill and the bill restored to its original phraseology. The discussion was entirely friendly and very gratifying, in its results, to the Commission.

It was resolved that the Commission again go to Albany to attend a hearing before the Senate Cities Committee in reference to the bill.

Adjourned.

E. F. LINTON, *Secretary*.

UNION LEAGUE CLUB, April 20, 1897.

Present—E. G. Blackford, E. F. Linton, E. H. Hobbs, W. E. Philips, W. M. Meserole, Commissioners.

The meeting was called for the purpose of discussing the situation at Albany, with a view of determining if any further steps were needed to be taken to promote the passage of the Commission's bill. No action was taken, and the Commission adjourned.

E. F. LINTON, *Secretary.*

UNION LEAGUE CLUB, May 4, 1897.

Present—E. G. Blackford, E. F. Linton, E. H. Hobbs, W. E. Philips, W. M. Meserole, Commissioners.

The expenses of the Commission in their journeys to Albany were ordered paid.

Mr. Philips moved that the Secretary be directed to prepare a full and final report of the Commission's work, and to employ such help as he needed, it being understood the said report is to be printed and become a public document for distribution and filing in the archives of the city. Carried.

Mr. Meserole moved that photographs of various places on Atlantic avenue be made for illustrating the proposed report, the work to be done under the direction of President Blackford. Carried.

It was resolved to give up the rooms heretofore occupied by the Commission in the Real Estate Exchange on May 1.

Adjourned.

E. F. LINTON, *Secretary.*

UNION LEAGUE CLUB, May 10, 1897.

Present—E. G. Blackford, E. F. Linton, E. H. Hobbs, W. M. Meserole, Commissioners.

The Commission discussed general matters pertaining to the relation of the old Commission to the new Commission. Also, the final report of the old Commission, in preparation.

Adjourned subject to the call of the Chair.

E. F. LINTON, *Secretary.*

UNION LEAGUE CLUB, September 24, 1897.

Present—E. G. Blackford, E. F. Linton, E. H. Hobbs, W. M. Meserole, Commissioners.

The Secretary's report was considered.

Mr. Meserole moved that:

WHEREAS, The Secretary has requested that he should be instructed as to whether the final report should contain in extenso the statements made by the citizens who appeared at the public hearings;

Resolved, That the Commission decides that the report should contain a brief statement only of the remarks of each person. Carried.

Mr. Hobbs moved that the Secretary prepare the final report as outlined in his memoranda, except as modified by the motion of Mr. Meserole. Carried.

Adjourned subject to the call of the Chair.

E. F. LINTON, *Secretary*.

UNION LEAGUE CLUB, October 1, 1897.

Present—E. G. Blackford, E. F. Linton, W. E. Philips, W. M. Meserole, Commissioners.

The Commission discussed the Secretary's progress report at length.

Adjourned subject to the call of the Chair.

E. F. LINTON, *Secretary*.

OFFICE OF THE ATLANTIC AVENUE COMMISSION.

November 16, 1897.

Present—E. G. Blackford, E. F. Linton, W. E. Philips, W. M. Meserole, Commissioners.

The Secretary submitted his final report.

Mr. Philips moved that the report as read by the Secretary, be approved and adopted. Carried.

Mr. Philips moved that the report presented by the Secretary, together with the Laws relating to the Long Island Railroad, as prepared by Mr. E. H. Hobbs—and certain plates showing portions of the proposed improvements—be adopted as the report of the Commission. Carried.

Mr. Philips moved that the matter of securing bids for the printing and publishing of the report of the Commission be referred to a Committee consisting of the President and Secretary to report their findings to the Commission. Carried.

Adjourned subject to the call of the Chair.

E. F. LINTON, *Secretary.*

OFFICE OF THE ATLANTIC AVENUE COMMISSION,

November 22, 1897.

Present—E. G. Blackford, E. F. Linton, W. E. Philips, E. H. Hobbs, Commissioners.

Minutes of last and all previous meetings read and approved.

The Secretary submitted bids for printing the Commission's report.

Mr. Philips moved that the matter of printing be referred to the President and Secretary with full power. Carried.

Adjourned subject to the call of the Chair.

E. F. LINTON, *Secretary.*

FINANCIAL STATEMENT.

Amount available for expenses of Commission under Chapter 394 Laws of 1896		$5,000

EXPENDITURES.

Rent	$225 02	
Stationery	11 40	
Furniture	43 00	
Advertising	95 33	
Traveling—Boston and Albany	143 50	
Clerical Services	1,454 71	
Preparing and printing 1,000 illustrated copies final report	1,257 90	
Incidentals—Postage, etc	25 90	
Total	$3,256 76	
Balance unexpended	1,743 24	
	$5,000 00	$5,000

Brooklyn, N. Y., December 31, 1897.

EDWARD F. LINTON,
Secretary.

A HISTORY OF TRANSIT

ON

ATLANTIC AVENUE.

BEING A COMPILATION OF LEGISLATIVE ENACTMENTS, AGREEMENTS, JUDICIAL DECISIONS, AND OTHER PROCEEDINGS THROUGH WHICH THE LONG ISLAND RAILROAD COMPANY NOW CLAIMS THE RIGHT TO OPERATE ITS ROAD BY STEAM POWER.

Prepared expressly for the Atlantic Avenue Commission by
EDWARD H. HOBBS.

THE BROOKLYN AND JAMAICA RAILROAD COMPANY.

The first railroad authorized to be constructed and operated within the "village of Brooklyn" was that of the Brooklyn and Jamaica Railroad company in 1832, the act incorporating that company being as follows:

CHAPTER 256, LAWS OF 1832.

AN ACT to incorporate the Brooklyn and Jamaica Railroad company.

Passed April 25, 1832.

The People of the State of New York, represented in Senate and Assembly, do enact as follows:

SECTION 1. James Foster Fanning C. Tucker, William R. Gracie, Abraham Vanderveer, Philip Brasher, Joshua Sands, David Lamberson, John C. Smith, David Anderson, Obadiah Jackson, Van Wyck Wickes, Nathaniel F. Waring, John Johnson and Samuel Smith, and all such other persons as shall become stockholders agreeably to the provisions of this act, in the corporation hereby created, shall be, and for the term of fifty years from the passage of this act, shall continue to be a body corporate and politic, by the name of "The Brooklyn and Jamaica Railroad company,"

§ 2. The said corporation shall have the right to construct, and during its existence to maintain and continue a railroad, with a single or double track, and with such appendages as may be deemed necessary for the convenient use of the same, commencing at any eligible point within the village of Brooklyn, in the county of Kings, and extending to any point within the village of Jamaica, in the county of Queens; and also of extending, constructing and using a single or double lateral railroad or ways to the villages of Flushing or Flatbush, as the one or the other shall be rendered expedient by the line which shall be adopted for the main road, on the north or south side of the ridge of hills which lie between Brooklyn and Jamaica.

§ 3. The capital stock of the corporation shall be three hundred thousand dollars; and it shall be deemed personal property, and shall be divided into shares of fifty dollars.

§ 4, Eliphalet Wickes, James B. Clarke, Nathan Shelton, Samuel A. Willoughby, Peter Conover, James Herriman, and George Hall, shall be Commissioners for receiving subscriptions to the capital stock of the corporation, and for apportioning the same among the subscribers agreeably to the provisions of this act.

§ 5. It shall be the duty of the Commissioners, within six months after the passage of this act, to give notice once a week for three successive weeks, in a newspaper printed and published in each of the counties of Kings and Queens, of the time when the books will be opened, at some convenient place in each of the villages of Brooklyn and Jamaica, for receiving subscriptions to the capital stock of the said corporation.

§ 6. One or more of the said commissioners shall attend at the time and at the places appointed by the said notice for the opening of the said books, and for three days successively, and during at least six hours of each day, shall continue to receive subscriptions to the capital stock of the said corporation, from all persons who will subscribe thereto, in conformity with the provisions of this act.

§ 7. Each subscriber, at the time he subscribes, shall pay to the commissioners five dollars on each share of the stock subscribed by him.

§ 8. If, at the expiration of the time mentioned in the sixth section of this act, it shall appear that more than the requisite number of shares has been subscribed, it shall be the duty of the commissioners forthwith to apportion the shares among the subscribers in such a manner as they shall deem most for the interest of said company, and to issue certificates to each subscriber, stating the number of shares which have been apportioned to him.

§ 9. In case the capital stock shall not be fully taken up during the time specified in the preceding sixth section, it shall be the duty of the commissioners, from time to time, to take such further measures as they may deem necessary, in order to fill up the subscription for the stock.

§ 10. The concerns of the corporation shall be managed by a board of thirteen directors, to be chosen annually by and from among the stockholders.

§ 11. As soon as may be after the stock has been thus apportioned, the commissioners shall give a notice of the time and place at which a meeting of the stockholders will be held for the choice of directors; such notice shall be published once in each week for three successive weeks prior to the time therein appointed for such election, in a newspaper printed and published in each of the counties of Kings and Queens.

§ 12. At the time and place appointed for that purpose, the commissioners, or a majority of them, shall attend, and the stockholders present, or their proxies duly appointed in writing, shall proceed to elect by ballot the requisite number of directors; the commissioners present shall preside at the election, and shall certify the result under their hands; which certificate shall be recorded in the books of the corporation, and shall be sufficient evidence of the election of the directors therein named; all future elections shall be conducted in the manner prescribed in the by-laws of the corporation.

§ 13. Each stockholder shall be allowed as many votes as he owns shares of stock at the commencement of any such election, and a plurality of votes shall determine the choice; but no stockholder shall be allowed to vote at any election after the first, for any stock that shall have been assigned to him at any time within thirty days prior to the time at which such election shall be held.

§ 14. The directors shall hold their office for one year following their election, and until others are elected in their places; they shall appoint one of their number as president, and some suitable person a secretary of the corporation; they may also appoint such other officers as the interest of the corporation may require, who shall hold their offices at the pleasure of the directors.

§ 15. In addition to the general powers given by the Revised Statutes to corporations, the corporation hereby created shall have power to prescribe the manner in which the said railroad shall be used; by what force the carriages to be used thereon may be propelled, and the rates of toll for the transportation of persons or property thereon: it shall have power also, by its officers, agents and servants, to enter upon any of the lands lying within the contemplated range of the said railroad, for the purpose of examining, surveying and establishing its lines.

§ 16. In case the corporation shall not be able to acquire the title to the lands through which the said railroad shall be laid, by purchase or voluntary cession, it shall be lawful for the said corporation to appropriate so much of such lands as may be necessary to its own use for the purposes contemplated by this act, on complying with the provisions of the six following sections.

§ 17. The directors may present a petition to the vice-chancellor of the first circuit, setting forth, by some proper description, the lands which are wanted for the construction of the said railroad, or the appendages thereto, and the names of the owners thereof, if known; distinguishing with convenient certainty, if it can be done, the parcels claimed in severalty by the respective owners, and praying for the appointment of appraisers to assess the damages which the owners of such lands will severally sustain, by reason of the appropriation thereof by the said corporation to its own use.

§ 18. On the presentment of such petition, the said vice-chancellor shall appoint a day for the hearing of the parties in interest, and shall direct such notice as he shall deem reasonable to be given of the time and place of hearing; and in case it shall appear that any of the owners of the said lands is a *femme couverte*, an infant or insane, or otherwise incompetent to take proper care of his or her interest, it shall be the duty of the said vice-chancellor to appoint some discreet and responsible person to act in the premises in his or her behalf.

§ 19. At the time appointed for such hearing, the said vice-chancellor shall appoint three disinterested freeholders, residents of the county of Kings or of the county of Queens, for the purpose of assessing such damages; and in the order for their appointment shall direct as to what lands are to be appropriated by the said corporation for the purposes aforesaid.

§ 20. The said appraisers, after being sworn before some officer authorized to administer oaths, honestly and impartially to assess such damages, shall proceed by viewing the said lands, and by such other evidence as the parties may produce before them, to ascertain and assess the damages which each individual owner will sustain by the appropriation of his land for the use or accommodation of such railroad or its appendages.

§ 21. The said appraisers shall make a report to the said vice-chancellor in writing, under their hands and seals, reciting the order for their appointment, and specifying the several parcels of land described therein, with all necessary certainty; the names of the owners of the respective parcels, if known, and if not known, stating that fact; and specifying also the damages which the owners of the said respective parcels will sustain by reason of the appropriation of the same for the purposes aforesaid; and in case either of the parties are dissatisfied with the assessment, the said vice-chancellor may, on the hearing of the parties in interest, modify the assessment as shall appear to be just.

§ 22. On payment of the damages thus assessed, together with the expenses of assessment, as the same shall be settled by the said vice-chancellor, or on depositing the amount thereof for the use of such owners in either of the banks of the village of Brooklyn, as the said vice-chancellor shall direct, the said corporation shall immediately become entitled to the use of the said lands, for the purpose aforesaid; and the report of the said appraisers, with the order of the said vice-chancellor modifying the same, in case the same shall have been modified, may be recorded in the proper office, in the same manner and with the like effect as deeds are recorded, without any other proof than the certificate of the said vice-chancellor, that the report is genuine.

§ 23. The corporation shall be bound to repair all public highways, bridges and water courses, which may be injured in constructing the said railroad or its appendages, and shall restore them, as far as practicable, to as good a condition as they were in before they became injured.

§ 24. The said corporation may establish such by-laws, not inconsistent with the laws of the state, respecting the calling in of the capitalstock, and prescribing the duties of its officers and servants, and for the regulation of its affairs, as may be deemed expedient.

§ 25. The said corporation shall be allowed three years from the passage of this act for the commencement of the construction of the said railroad; and in case the same shall not be completed within five years thereafter, the privileges herein granted shall be forfeited.

§ 26. Every person who shall wilfully injure the said railroad, or any of its appendages, shall forfeit to the use of the said corporation a sum equal to three times the amount of damages occasioned by such injury, to be recovered with costs of suit, in the name of such corporation, in an action of debt, before any court having cognizance thereof.

§ 27. The railroad company hereby created shall, on the fifteenth day of May next, or as soon thereafter as the necessary arrangements for that purpose can be made, purchase the stock of the Brooklyn, Jamaica and Flatbush Turnpike Company at the rate of twenty-six dollars per share in cash, or shall pay them for said stock at the rate of twenty-three dollars a share in railroad stock of the said company at par, at the option of each stockholder; and the said turnpike company shall be at liberty to divide previous to such sale all the surplus money then on hand, and money due the said turnpike company, and shall transfer to the said railroad company all their lands and all other property, (except the said surplus money) now belonging to them, and money due the said turnpike company; and, also, from the said fifteenth day of May, or as soon thereafter as the necessary arrangements for that purpose can be made, the directors of the said railroad company shall be the directors of the said turnpike company, if the said railroad company shall go into operation.

§ 28. No street or lane in the village of Brooklyn shall be made use of by the said railroad company for the said railroad, nor shall steam power be used on any part of the railroad within the said village without the permission of the corporation of Brooklyn first had and obtained.

§ 29. The directors of the said corporation for the time being, if required to do so by the Legislature, shall, at the end of every year after the construction of the said railroad shall have been commenced, and for the term of fifteen years after the same shall have been completed, cause to be filed in the office of the Secretary of State, a detailed account of all the moneys expended during the year in constructing the said railroad and its appendages, and in superintending and keeping the same in repair; and a similar account of the income derived by tolls or otherwise from the use of the said railroad; to the end that a just estimate may be made of the profits received by the said corporation therefrom; such accounts shall be verified by the oaths of at least two of the directors or other officers of the said corporation.

§ 30. If the Legislature of this State shall, at the expiration of ten, and within fifteen years, from the completion of said road, make provision by law for the repayment to the said corporation of the amount expended by them in the construction of said railroad, together with all moneys expended by them for permanent fixtures for the use of said railroad, with interest on said sums from the time of their expenditure, at the rate of fourteen per centum per annum, together with all moneys expended by said company for repairs or otherwise, for the purposes of said road, after deducting the amount of tolls received on said road, then the said railroad, with all its fixtures and appurtenances, shall vest in and become the property of the people of this State.

§ 31. The said corporation shall be subject to the restrictions and liabilities imposed by such parts of the eighteenth chapter of the first part of the Revised Statutes as are not repealed.

§ 32. The legislature may at any time alter, modify or repeal this act.

THE LONG ISLAND RAILROAD COMPANY.

The Long Island Railroad company was organized and incorporated in 1834, by the following act:

CHAPTER 178.

An Act to incorporate the Long Island Railroad company.

Passed April 24, 1834.

The People of the State of New York, represented in Senate and Assembly, do enact as follows:

Section 1. Valentine Hicks, William Wicks, Edmund Frost, Timothy Clews, Selah B. Strong, John Lawrence, Joseph C. Albertson, Robert W.

Mott, Joshua Fanning, Alden Spooner, William F. Blydenburgh, Singleton Mitchell, Gabriel Furman, Daniel E. Smith, James Hallock, William Rockwell and Joshua B. Smith, and all such other persons as shall become stockholders agreeably to the provisions of this act in the corporation hereby created, shall be and continue for the term of fifty years from the passage of this act, a body corporate and politic, by the name of "The Long Island Railroad company."

§ 2. The said corporation shall have the right to construct, and during its existence to maintain and continue a railroad or railroads, with a single or double track, and with such appendages as may be deemed necessary for the convenient use of the same, commencing at any eligible point adjoining Southold bay, in or near the village of Greenport, in the county of Suffolk, and extending from thence on the most practicable route, through or near the middle of Long Island, to a point on the water's edge in the village of Brooklyn, in the county of Kings, to be designated by the trustees of that village, and to a point on the water's edge in the village of Williamsburgh, in the said county of Kings, to be designated by the trustees of that village, and in like manner to construct, maintain and continue a branch railroad from the said main road to Sag Harbor.

§ 3. The capital stock of the corporation hereby created shall be one million and five hundred thousand dollars; it shall be deemed personal property, and shall be divided into shares of fifty dollars.

§ 4. Samuel Hicks, Benjamin Strong, John L. Graham, Joseph Moser, Edwin Hicks, Edmund Frost, Valentine Hicks, Singleton Mitchell, Nicholas Wyckoff, William F. Blydenburgh, James H. Weeks and Joseph H. Goldsmith, shall be commissioners for receiving subscriptions to the capital stock of the said corporation, and for apportioning the same among the subscribers, agreeably to the provisions of this act.

§ 5. It shall be the duty of the commissioners within one year after the passage of this act, to give notice once a week for four successive weeks, in a newspaper published in the city of New York, and in each of the counties of Kings, Queens and Suffolk, of the time when the books will be opened at some convenient place in the said city, and in each of the said counties, for receiving subscriptions to the capital stock of the said corporation.

§ 6. One or more of the said commissioners shall attend at the time and places mentioned in the said notices, and for three days successively, and during at least six hours of each day, shall receive subscriptions to the capital stock of the said corporation, in conformity with the provisions of this act.

§ 7. The president and directors of the Brooklyn and Jamaica Railroad company may, at the time so appointed, subscribe for six thousand shares of the capital stock of the corporation created by this act; and the said commissioners shall thereupon allot the same to the stockholders of the said Brooklyn and Jamaica Railroad company, apportioning to each stockholder the same number of shares as were held by such stockholder in the said last-mentioned company.

§ 8. If the said president and directors of the Brooklyn and Jamaica railroad company shall subscribe to the stock of the corporation hereby created pursuant to the provisions of the last preceding section, and the residue of the stock of

CROSS SECTION, ATLANTIC AVENUE, SHOWING TUNNEL FROM FLATBUSH AVENUE TO TUNNEL ENTRANCE AT EAST RIVER; SAME CONSTRUCTION IN NEW YORK CITY.

the said last mentioned corporation shall be taken pursuant to the provisions of this act, within two years from the passage of the same, it shall be the duty of the said president and directors of the Brooklyn and Jamaica railroad company, within three months after being notified by the said commissioners that such stock has been taken, to assign, transfer and convey to the corporation hereby created, all the property, rights, privileges and immunities of the said Brooklyn and Jamaica railroad company, first deducting their surplus fund, if any there should be, and the same shall thereupon vest in the corporation hereby created, and the said Brooklyn and Jamaica railroad company shall thereupon cease to exist as a separate corporation.

§ 9. If the said Brooklyn and Jamaica railroad company shall be united with the corporation hereby created pursuant to the provisions of this act, the stockholders of the said Brooklyn and Jamaica railroad company shall be stockholders of the corporation hereby created The amount paid in by them respectively for their shares, with interest at seven per cent. from the date of such payments and the further sum of five dollars on each share, deducting any dividends which they may have respectively received, shall be deemed and taken as paid to the corporation hereby created, at the date of the conveyance mentioned in the last preceding section.

§ 10. If the amount allowed to the stockholders of the Brooklyn and Jamaica railroad company, as paid by them respectively on each share, pursuant to the provisions of the last preceding section, shall exceed the amount then paid by the stockholders of the corporation hereby created respectively on each share, the stockholders of the Brooklyn and Jamaica railroad company shall be allowed interest on the excess thus paid on their respective shares at the rate of seven per cent. per annum in any future payments.

§ 11. If any stockholder or stockholders of the Brooklyn and Jamaica railroad company shall signify his or their determination not to become a stockholder of the corporation hereby created, to the commissioners, or either of them, at the time first appointed by them to receive subscriptions to the said capital stock, the share or shares of such stockholders shall be deducted from the number of shares allotted to the stockholders of the said Brooklyn and Jamaica railroad company; and when such company shall transfer their property and rights to the corporation hereby created pursuant to the provisions of the eighth section of this act, the stockholder or stockholders so signifying such determination, shall be entitled to demand and receive from the corporation hereby created, the sums of money previously paid by him or them on his or their shares, with interest thereon at the rate of seven per cent. per annum, and the further sum of five dollars on each share, deducting therefrom the amount of dividends thereon previously received by him or them.

§ 12. Each subscriber for stock, at the time he subscribes, shall pay to the commissioners five dollars on each share of the stock subscribed for by him.

§ 13. If at the expiration of the time mentioned in the sixth section of this act, it shall appear that more than the requisite number of shares has been subscribed, it shall be the duty of the commissioners forthwith to apportion the shares not taken by the Brooklyn and Jamaica railroad company, among the subscribers, in such manner as they shall deem most for the interest of said corporation.

§ 14. If the capital stock shall not be fully taken up during the time specified in the sixth section, it shall be the duty of the commissioners from time to time to take such further measures as they may deem necessary to fill the subscriptions for the stock.

§ 15. The concerns of the said corporation shall be managed by a board of thirteen directors, who shall be chosen annually by and from among the stockholders.

§ 16. As soon as may be after the stock has been thus apportioned, the commissioners shall give a notice of the time and place at which a meeting of the stockholders will be held for the choice of thirteen directors. Such notice shall be published once in each week for three weeks successively, prior to the time therein appointed for such election, in a newspaper printed and published in the city of New York, and in the counties of Suffolk, Queens and Kings.

§ 17. At the time and place appointed for the purpose, the commissioners, or a majority of them, shall attend, and the stockholders present, or their proxies duly appointed in writing, shall proceed to elect, by ballot, thirteen directors; the commissioners present shall preside at the election, and shall certify the result under their hands; which certificate shall be recorded in the books of the corporation, and shall be sufficient evidence of the election of the directors therein named. All future elections of such directors shall be conducted in the manner prescribed in the by-laws of the corporation.

§ 18. Each stockholder shall be allowed as many votes as he owns shares of stock at the commencement of any such election, and a plurality of votes shall determine the choice; but no stockholder shall be allowed to vote at any election after the first, for any stock that shall have been assigned to him at any time within thirty days prior to the time at which such election shall be held.

§ 19. The directors shall hold their offices for one year following their election or appointment, and until others are elected or appointed in their places; they shall appoint one of their number as president, and some suitable person secretary of the corporation.

§ 20. In addition to the general powers given by the Revised Statutes to corporations, the corporation hereby created shall have power to prescribe the manner in which the said roads shall be used; by what force the carriages to be used thereon may be propelled, and the rates of toll for the transportation of persons or property thereon; it shall have power, also, by its officers, agents and servants, to enter upon any of the lands lying within the contemplated range of the said railroad, for the purpose of examining, surveying and establishing its lines.

§ 21. The said corporation may also construct, purchase or hire docks or wharves at the easterly termination of the said road, for the convenient use of the same. And the title of this state to any land covered with water, which may be requisite for the construction of such docks or wharves, and which may be taken for that purpose without injury to the navigation of the waters thereof, shall be conveyed to the said corporation by the commissioners of the land office.

§ 22. The said corporation may, also, either separately or in conjunction with any other railroad company incorporated by the laws of this or any other state, purchase or employ one or more steamboats for the conveyance of passengers and goods between the eastern termination of the said railroad and any other railroad incorporated by the legislatures of Connecticut or Rhode Island.

§ 23. The said corporation may acquire title to the lands through which the said railroads shall be laid by purchase or voluntary cession. If any of the owners of the said lands is an infant or insane, and such infant has a guardian, or such insane person a committee, it shall be lawful for such guardian or committee to agree to convey the land of such infant or insane person to the said corporation, and on such agreement being reported by such guardian or committee to the vice-chancellor of the first circuit, and approved by him as conducive to the interests of such infant or insane person, the said vice-chancellor may authorize the said guardian or committee to, and such guardian or committee may thereupon, convey to the said corporation the right, title and interest of such infant or insane person in and to such lands.

§ 24. In case the corporation shall not be able to acquire the title to such lands as may be requisite for the said railroads, or the use thereof, by purchase or voluntary cession, it shall be lawful for the said corporation to appropriate so much of such lands as may be necessary to its own use for the purposes contemplated by this act, on complying with the provisions of the six following sections:

§ 25. The directors of the corporation hereby created may present a petition to the said vice-chancellor, setting forth by some proper description the lands which are wanted for the construction of the said railroads, or the appendages thereto, and the names of the owners (or if the title thereto is in dispute, of the claimants) thereof, if known; distinguishing with convenient certainty, if it can be done, the parcels claimed in severalty by the respective owners or claimants, and their title or claim to the same, whether as tenants, reversioners or remaindermen, and praying for the appointment of appraisers to assess the damages which the owners of such lands will severally sustain by reason of the appropriation thereof by the said corporation to its own use.

§ 26. On the presentment of such petition, the said vice-chancellor shall appoint a day for the hearing of the parties, and direct such notice as he shall deem reasonable to be given of the time and place of hearing; and in case it shall appear that any of the owners or claimants of the said lands is a *femme couverte*, an infant, or insane, or otherwise incompetent to take proper care of his or her interest, it shall be the duty of the said vice-chancellor to appoint some discreet and responsible person to act in the premises in his or her behalf.

§ 27. At the time appointed for such hearing, the said vice-chancellor shall appoint three disinterested freeholders, residents on Long Island, for the purpose of assessing such damages; and in the order for their appointment shall direct what lands are to be appropriated by the said corporation for the purposes aforesaid.

§ 28. The said appraisers, after being sworn before some officer authorized to administer oaths, honestly and impartially to assess such damages, shall proceed by viewing the said lands, and by such other evidence as the parties may produce before them, to ascertain and assess the damages which each individual owner, whether his estate be in possession, reversion or remainder, (or in case of a disputed title, which the true owner, naming all the claimants) will sustain by the appropriation of his or her land for the use or accommodation of such railroad or its appendages.

§ 29. The said appraisers shall make a report to the said vice-chancellor in writing, under their hands and seals, reciting the order for their appointment, and specifying the several parcels of land described therein, with requisite certainty, the names of the owners or claimants of the respective parcels if known, and if not known, stating that fact, and specifying also the damages which the owners of the said respective parcels will sustain, by reason of the appropriation of the same for the purposes aforesaid; and in case either of the parties is dissatisfied with the assessment, the said vice-chancellor may, on the hearing of the parties in interest, modify the assessment as shall appear to be just.

§ 30. The rights of any future claimants to any of the lands which may be taken by the said corporation for the use of the said railroads, or any of their appendages, shall at any future time be ascertained, valued and acquired for the use of the said corporation, in the manner directed in the six preceding sections.

§ 31. On payment of the damages thus assessed, together with the expenses of assessment, as the same shall be settled by the said vice-chancellor, or on depositing the amount thereof for the use of such owners in either of the banks of the village of Brooklyn as the said vice-chancellor shall direct, the said corporation shall immediately become entitled to the use of the said lands for the purposes aforesaid; and the report of the said appraisers, with the order of the said vice-chancellor modifying the same,in case the same shall have been modified, may be recorded in the proper office, in the same manner and with the like effect as deeds are recorded, without any other proof than the certificate of the said vice-chancellor that the report is genuine.

§ 32. The corporation shall be bound to repair all public highways, bridges, railroads, and water courses which may be injured in constructing the said railroads or their appendages, and shall restore them, as far as practicable, to as good a condition as they were in before they become injured.

§ 33. The said corporation shall be allowed two years from the passage of this act for the commencement of the construction of the said railroad; and in case the said railroad from Greenport to Brooklyn and Williamsburgh, shall not be completed within six years thereafter, the privileges herein granted shall be forfeited.

§ 34. The said corporation shall construct the said road to both Brooklyn and Williamsburgh, and the said branch to Sag Harbor, at the same time with the main road, if it shall appear to the directors from the report of the engineers or surveyors employed to survey the route of the main road and the said branch, that the capital stock of the said corporation subscribed will be sufficient for the purpose.

§ 35. Every person who shall wilfully injure the said railroad or any of its appendages, shall forfeit to the use of the said corporation a sum equal to three times the amount of damages occasioned by such injury, to be recovered with costs of suit, in the name of such corporation, in an action of debt.

§ 36. No street or lane in Brooklyn or Williamsburgh shall be taken by the said corporation for the said railroads without the previous permission of their respective corporations; nor shall steam power be used on any part of the railroads within either of the said places without such permission.

§ 37. The directors of the said corporation shall, at the end of every year after the construction of the said railroad shall have been commenced, and for the term of fifteen years after the same shall have been completed, cause to be filed in the office of the secretary of state a detailed account of all the moneys expended during the year, in constructing the said railroad and its appendages, and in superintending and keeping the same in repair; and a similar account of the income derived by tolls or otherwise from the use of the said railroad, to the end that a just estimate may be made of the profits received by the said corporation therefrom; such account shall be verified by the oaths of at least two of the directors, or other officers of the said corporation.

§ 38. If the legislature of this state shall, at the expiration of ten and within fifteen years from the completion of said road, make provision by law for the repayment to the said corporation of the amount expended by them in the construction of their railroads, together with all moneys expended by them for permanent fixtures for the use of the said railroads, with interest on the said sums from the time of their expenditure, at the rate of ten per centum per annum, together with all moneys expended by said company for repairs or other necessary expenses for the purposes of said roads, after deducting the amount of tolls received on said roads, then the said railroads, with all their fixtures and appurtenances, shall vest in and become the property of the people of this state.

§ 39. The said corporation shall be subject to the restrictions and liabilities imposed by such parts of the eighteenth chapter of the first part of the Revised Statutes as are not repealed.

§ 40. The legislature may at any time alter, modify or repeal this act.

LEASE OF THE BROOKLYN AND JAMAICA ROAD TO THE LONG ISLAND RAILROAD COMPANY.

Four years subsequent to its incorporation, the Brooklyn and Jamaica Railroad Company leased its road to The Long Island Company, under authority of a legislative act subjoined.

CHAPTER 94.

AN ACT to authorize the demise of the Brooklyn and Jamaica railroad to the Long Island railroad company.

Passed April 2, 1836.

The People of the State of New York, represented in Senate and Assembly, do enact as follows:

SECTION 1. It shall and may be lawful for the Brooklyn and Jamaica railroad company to demise or lease the railroad from Brooklyn to Jamaica, on Long Island, with its appurtenances, to the Long Island railroad company, for such term or terms of years, and at such rent, and upon such conditions, as shall be agreed upon between the said companies; and it shall be lawful for the said Long Island railroad company, to take and hold such railroad and its appurtenances agreeably to the terms of such demise or lease.

§ 2. It shall be lawful for said railroad companies, at any time hereafter to enter into an agreement for the absolute sale and purchase of said Brooklyn and Jamaica railroad and such sale and purchase shall be binding and legal on both of the aforesaid corporations.

§ 3. It shall be lawful for the said Brooklyn and Jamaica railroad company to take and hold, and for the Long Island railroad company to give and execute, under its corporate seal, such securities, leases, deeds and other evidences of transfer as shall be deemed by said companies sufficient for the object of this act; and that such securities, leases, deeds and other evidences shall and may be enforced in law or equity.

§ 4. The said Long Island railroad company are hereby authorized to construct a branch railroad to lead from the said Brooklyn and Jamaica railroad to any suitable point on the East river in the village of Williamsburgh, and the construction of such branch, and the use of the said Brooklyn and Jamaica railroad, under any demise or purchase of the same, as hereinbefore sanctioned, shall be deemed and taken as a performance of the obligation on the part of the said Long Island railroad company to make their road from Greenport to Brooklyn and Williamsburgh.

§ 5. The legislature may at any time alter, modify or repeal this act.

Pursuant to the authority granted by the foregoing statute, The Brooklyn and Jamaica Railroad Company, by an instrument executed on the 1st day of December, 1836, leased its roads to The Long Island Railroad Company. The lease follows:—

THIS INDENTURE, made this first day of December, in the year of our Lord one thousand eight hundred and thirty-six, between the Brooklyn and Jamaica Railroad Company, of the first part, and the Long Island Railroad Company, of the second part, witnesseth, that the said parties of the first part, for and in consideration of the rents, covenants and agreements hereinafter mentioned, reserved and contained, on the part and behalf of the said parties of the second part, their successors and assigns, to be paid, kept and performed, and by virtue and in pursuance of the power and authority contained in a certain act of the Legislature of the State of New York, entitled: "An Act to authorize the demise of the Brooklyn and Jamaica Railroad to the Long Island Railroad Company," passed 2d April, 1836, and by virtue of all and every other power and authority for that purpose vested in the said parties of the first part, have demised, granted and to farm letten, and by these presents do demise, grant, and to farm let, unto the said parties of the second part, their successors and assigns: All and singular the railroad of the said parties of the first part, extending from its commencement at the ferry at the foot of Atlantic street, in the City of Brooklyn, in Kings County, to its termination in the village and town of Jamaica, in the County of Queens, including all its appendages and the depot lots at the village of Jamaica aforesaid, and at Bedford, and the right to construct branches, at the expense, however, of the said parties of the second part, to Flushing or Flatbush, as secured to the said parties of the first part by their act of incorporation; and also all and singular the real estate of the said parties of the first part upon which their said railroad is constructed and built, and which is used, reputed and taken as part and parcel thereof, together with all and singular the liberties, privileges and franchises of the said railroad, but not including as part and parcel of this demise the turnpike road of the said parties of the first part, or any of its rights, privileges or appurtenances. To have and to hold the said above mentioned and described premises hereby demised, with the appurtenances, unto the said parties of the second part, their successors or assigns, from the day of the date of these presents, for and during and until the full end and term of forty-four years and six calendar months thence next ensuing, and fully to be complete and ended, yielding and paying therefor unto the said parties of the first part, their successors and assigns, yearly and every year during the said term hereby granted, the yearly rent or sum of thirty-three thousand three hundred dollars, lawful money of the United States of America, in two equal semi-payments, to wit: on the first day of June and the first day of December in each and every of the said years. Provided, always, nevertheless, that if the yearly rent above reserved, or any part thereof, shall be behind or unpaid on any day of payment whereon the same ought to be paid as aforesaid, or if default shall be made in any of the covenants, clauses or agreements herein contained, on the part and behalf of the said parties of the second part, their successors and assigns, to be paid, kept and performed, then and thenceforth it shall and may be lawful for the said parties of the first part, their successors and assigns, into and upon the said demised premises, and every part thereof, wholly to re-enter and the same to have again, re-possess and enjoy as in first and former estate, or to distrain for any rent that may remain due thereon, anything hereinbefore contained to the contrary thereof in anywise notwithstanding. And the said parties of the second part, for themselves and their successors, do covenant, promise, and agree, to and with the said parties of the first part, their successors and assigns, by these presents in manner and form following, that is to say, that the said parties of the second part, their successors or assigns, shall and will yearly and every year during said term hereby granted, well and truly pay or cause to be paid unto the said parties of the first part, their successors or assigns, the said yearly rent above reserved, on the days and in the manner limited and prescribed as aforesaid for the payment thereof without any deduction, fraud or delay, according to the true intent and meaning of these presents; and that they, the said parties of the second part, their successors or assigns, shall and will, at their own proper costs and charges, bear, pay and discharge all such taxes, duties, assessments and impositions of every nature or kind, both ordinary and extraordinary, as shall or may, during the said term hereby granted, be charged, assessed, or imposed upon the said demised premises, or any part or parts thereof, and that they, the said parties of the second part, their successors or assigns, shall and will, at their own proper cost and charges, maintain, keep and preserve the said demised premises, and every part thereof, with its appendages, fences and enclosures, depot houses, and all other appurtenances, in the state and condition of good and sufficient repair and preservation for all the uses and purposes of a railroad; and that neither the said parties of the second part, nor their successors, shall or will assign, transfer, or set over these presents for the whole or any part of the said term hereby demised, nor underlet the said demised premises, or any part or parts thereof, to any person or persons whomsoever, or any body or bodies corporate or politic whatsoever, without the previous consent and approbation of the said parties of the first part, their successors or assigns, for that purpose first had and obtained in writing under their corporate seal, except as to the depot building and the land attached thereto, at Bedford, which the parties of the second part may assign or underlet at their pleasure. And also, that they, the said parties of the second part, their successors or assigns, shall and will, without delay, at their own proper costs and charges, erect and build a depot house on the lot fixed upon for that purpose at the village of Jamaica aforesaid, and use the same as the stopping and starting place for their train and cars, and keep and maintain the same in good and sufficient repair and preservation, and that on the last day of the said term, or other sooner determination of the estate and demise hereby granted, they, the said parties of the second part, their successors or assigns, shall and will peaceably and quietly leave, surrender and yield up, unto the said parties of the first part, their successors or assigns, all and singular the said demised premises, including fences, inclosures, depot houses, and all other appendages and appurtenances, in a state and condition of good and sufficient repair and preservation, fit and proper in all respects for the immediate and continued uses and purposes of a railroad, and the said parties of the first part, for themselves and their successors, do, by these presents, covenant, promise and agree to, and with the said parties of the second part, their successors or assigns, in manner and form following, that is to say, that the said parties of the second part, their successors and assigns, paying the said yearly rent, above reserved, and keeping, performing and fulfilling all and singular the covenants, clauses and agreements herein contained, on the part and behalf of the said parties of the second part, their successors or assigns, to be kept, performed and fulfilled, that the said parties of the second part, their successors or assigns, shall and may, at all times during their said term hereby granted, peaceably and quietly have, hold, use, occupy, possess and enjoy, all and singular the said demised premises, and the fare, freight, income, revenue and profits thereof, without any manner of let, suit, trouble, molestation or hindrance, of or from the said parties of the first part, their successors or assigns, or any other person or persons whomsoever lawfully claiming or to claim the same. And that the said parties of the first part, their successors or assigns, shall not, and will not, during any part of the said term, use or in any manner employ their said railroad, as a railroad, or any part thereof, or take the profits avails, or other proceeds thereof, except only the rent aforesaid, and that at the expiration of the said term, by the efflux of time, the said parties of the first part, their successors or assigns, shall and will pay, or cause to be paid to the said parties of the second part, their successors or assigns, the fair value at that time of any depot houses which the said parties of the second part, their successors or assigns, shall have theretofore erected for the use and benefit of the said demised railroad, such value to be ascertained and affixed upon by two judicious and disinterested persons, one to be chosen by each of the said parties, who shall be sworn honestly and faithfully to estimate and fix upon the said value, and whose award, to be made in writing and signed by them, shall be final and conclusive on both of the said parties to these presents. with power to those two, in case of their disagreement, to choose a third person as umpire, whose umpirage in the premises shall be conclusive and final, and who shall in like manner be sworn, and make his umpirage in writing, and sign the same. Provided always, nevertheless, and these presents are executed and accepted by both of the said parties hereto, upon the following terms and conditions, that is to say, should the Legislature of this State, within the time for that purpose limited by the respective acts of incorporation of the said parties, respectively, make provisions by law for the repayment to the said parties, respectively or either of them, for the amount expended by them, or either of them, in the construction of their railroads, together with all moneys expended by them for permanent fixtures, for the use of the said railroads, or either of them, whereby the said railroads, or either of them, with all their fixtures and appurtenances, should vest in and become the property of the people of this State, then and in either of such cases, these presents shall cease, and the term hereby granted terminate, except as to any aliquot portion of six months' rent, which may be due at the time of such cessation, which shall be recoverable in like manner as a full half year's rent, but in case of such termination of these presents by the people of this State becoming invested with the said demised railroad, all interest payable by the Legislature, on account thereof, beyond nine per centum per annum, shall belong to the said parties of the first part, their successors or assigns, and the said nine per cent. shall belong to the said parties of the second part, their successors or assigns, and that should the said parties of the second part, their successors or assigns, at any time during the said term become insolvent, or should any judgment or decree pass against them for the recovery or payment of money, and should the same not be paid before any execution issued thereon, then and immediately upon the issuing of any such execution, these presents shall at the option of the said parties of the first part, their successors or assigns, cease, and the said term terminate, except as to any rent or any aliquot portion of rent then due, and except further as to any breach of covenant previously incurred as to all which these presents shall continue in full force, effect and operation, but for no other purpose whatsoever, and that the contract, agreement and understanding heretofore made or had by and between the said parties of the first part and the Mayor, Aldermen and Commonalty of the city of Brooklyn, to the effect following, that is to say, that if, at the end of five years, a majority of owners of property on Atlantic street should declare the rails of the said parties of the first part, and which are hereby demised to be a nuisance, and should petition the said Mayor, Aldermen and Commonalty of the city of Brooklyn, to have them removed, the said parties of the first part would, in that case, remove the said rails and repair all damages, upon condition that the cost of grading and finishing said street should be refunded to them, shall be obligatory upon, and the same are by these presents adopted by the said parties of the second part, their successors and assigns; but in case the said contract, agreement or understanding shall be enforced by the said Mayor, Aldermen and Commonalty of the city of Brooklyn, whereby the said parties of the second part, their successors or assigns, shall be deprived of the use and enjoyment of that part of the said demised premises, known and distinguished as Atlantic street, then, and in that case, there shall be thenceforth an abatement of nine per cent. per annum of the said rent, to be computed upon the sum to be allowed, and which shall have been paid to the said parties of the first part, their successors or assigns, for the cost of grading and finishing Atlantic street aforesaid, so long as the said parties of the second part, their successors or assigns, shall be deprived of the use and enjoyment of the said street for the said railroad, and that all and singular the provisions and requirements contained in the respective charters of both of the said parties, shall, by each of them, their respective successors and assigns, be at all times during the said term, well, and faithfully kept, observed, performed and fulfilled according to the true intent and meaning thereof, respectively. And that should the said rent hereinabove reserved, or any part thereof remain due and unpaid for the space of ten days beyond any day whereon the same is above made payable, then, and in every such case, it shall and may be lawful for the said parties of the first part, their successors or assigns, immediately upon, or at any time after such any default, to appoint a receiver of all the income, profits and avails of the said demised premises, at every place where such income, profits or avails may be receivable, which receivers shall thenceforth exclusively receive all and singular the said income, profits and avails, for the use and benefit of the said parties of the first part, their successors or assigns, till out of the net proceeds thereof all such arrearage of rent be fully paid off, and satisfied.

In witness whereof, the said parties to these presents have hereunto interchangeably set their respective corporate seals, and caused the same to be subscribed by their respective presidents, the day and year first above written,

[Long Island Railroad Co.,] Seal.

W. F. BLYDENBURGH,
Vice-President and Acting President, Long Island Railroad Company.

[Brooklyn and Jamaica Railroad Co., Seal,]

JOHN A. KING,
President of the Brooklyn and Jamaica Railroad Co.

Sealed and delivered in the presence of
GEORGE W. STRONG.

THE ATLANTIC AVENUE TUNNEL.

In the year 1844, in the process of extending its traffic, the Long Island Railroad Company desired to construct a tunnel through Atlantic avenue, and the Brooklyn Common Council granted authority for it in the appended ordinance.

IN COMMON COUNCIL, March 29, 1844.

The following was adopted:

An ordinance granting permission to the Long Island Railroad Company to construct a tunnel through Atlantic street.

The Mayor and Aldermen of the city of Brooklyn, in Common Council convened, do ordain as follows:

I. The Long Island Railroad Company are hereby permitted to construct a tunnel through Atlantic street for the passage of their cars and locomotive engines upon the following conditions, viz.:

1. The excavation of Atlantic street, on the westerly end thereof, shall be made from a point on said street where a line drawn on the easterly side of Columbia street will intersect said street; and the excavation on the easterly part of said street shall commence at a point on said street where a line drawn on the westerly side of Boerum street will cross the same.

2. The work forming the open approach to said tunnel on the easterly end shall be constructed within the space between Boerum and Court streets, and on the westerly end within the space between Columbia and Hicks streets; and the said entrances shall not exceed fourteen feet in width between the walls, and the walls of said entrances shall be constructed of solid and durable materials, and surmounted both at the sides and ends with a good and sufficient coping, with an iron railing thereon at least four feet in height, with suitable lamp posts and lamps on each side of said entrances.

3. The said tunnel shall be constructed of good materials, with sides having good and substantial stone wells, to be arched with brick or stone, laid in good mortar of lime or cement; to have iron gates at each end, and the whole to be done in a safe and workmanlike manner.

4. The Long Island Railroad Company shall be permitted to construct openings over said tunnel on Atlantic street for the admission of light at different points, such openings not to exceed four feet in diameter, and to be constructed with suitable iron railing at least four feet in height, and surmounted by lamps; but no opening to be constructed on any of the intersecting streets.

5. The said company are to indemnify and save harmless the city of Brooklyn from all damages, costs and injury whatsoever, which the city may incur or sustain in consequence of the granting of the permission and the carrying of the same, in whole or in part, into effect; such indemnity shall be by a bond to

the Mayor and Common Council of the city of Brooklyn, in the penalty of fifty thousand dollars, in such form as shall be approved by the said Common Council, and with such additional security as they shall prescribe; and until such bond and security shall be given, the said company shall do no act towards the construction of the said tunnel.

II. And be it further ordained, that whenever the said company shall have constructed a tunnel in accordance with the foregoing sections, they shall remove all the iron rails, machinery and fixtures of the Brooklyn and Jamaica Railroad Company between the points on said street described in the first subdivision of the first section of this ordinance.

III. And be it further ordained, that the said Long Island Railroad Company shall, on completion of said tunnel, remove all their trains of passenger or burden cars, locomotive engines and other machinery and fixtures now used or permanently fixed on Atlantic street, between Court and Hicks streets, to a wharf or wharves adjoining or in the neighborhood of said street, by means of a single or double track, and all the operations of said company in the lading or unlading of freight shall be conducted beyond the limi's of said street.

IV. And be it further ordained, that on the approach from the west of every train or locomotive engine to the easterly end of the tunnel on said street, due notice shall be given by the ringing of a bell permanently and suitably placed for that purpose; and on the approach of each and every train or locomotive engine to the said street from the depot or wharf, or from the said street to the said depot or wharf. the same notice shall be also given of such approach, under the penalty of five dollars for every omission.

V. And be it further ordained, that the trains of cars and locomotive engines, in their passage from the mouth of the tunnel at the western end to the wharf, or from the said wharf to the tunnel, shall not exceed a speed of four miles per hour, under the penalty of five dollars for each offense.

VI. And be it further ordained, that on the compliance on the part of the Long Island Railroad Company with the provisions of the foregoing sections, and with the provisions of so much of the law of this corporation passed November 2, 1839, as is not repealed, they, the said Long Island Railroad Company, shall be allowed and authorized to use steam-power upon the said road within the city of Brooklyn and through the said tunnel to their depot beyond the limits of said street.

VII. This ordinance may be at any time altered or amended.

TRANSFER OF RAILROAD BED AND WIDENING OF ATLANTIC AVENUE.

The growth of the city and the increase of business demanded certain changes and improvements along Atlantic avenue, which are described in full in the subjoined acts and agreements:

CHAPTER 220.

AN ACT relative to railroads on Long Island, in this State.

Passed April 13, 1853.

The People of the State of New York, represented in Senate and Assembly, do enact as follows:

SECTION 1. Every railroad corporation on Long Island, formed pursuant to the provisions of the general railroad act, or under under any act of the Legislature of this State heretofore passed, whose railroad has been constructed and is now in use, shall have the right to use their said road in the same manner, and to propel their cars over the same, throughout its entire length, with the like motive power as that used by them thereon at the time of the passing of this act, and also to regulate the time and manner in which passengers and property shall be transported over the same; provided, however, that the Supreme Court of this State, upon the application of any person or persons, or bodies corporate, conceiving themselves aggrieved by the manner in which any such corporation use their road, and upon notice of such application served upon such corporation, together with copies of all papers upon which the same is founded, not less than thirty days previously thereto. may, at a general term thereof, held in the district where such road or some part thereof is located, for good cause shown, make an order regulating and directing the manner in which the motive power of such road shall be used.

§ 2. This act shall take effect upon condition that the strip of land owned by the Brooklyn and Jamaica Railroad Company, on the south side of Atlantic avenue, between the Gowanus lane and Classon avenue, shall be ceded to the city of Brooklyn as and for a public street, on such terms and conditions as shall be agreed on by and between the said company and the city of Brooklyn, and said company are hereby authorized to cede the same; and said city to agree as aforesaid, and such agreement shall be in writing and be recorded in the office of the register of the county of Kings.

Under the authority of the foregoing act, a tripartite agreement was made between the Brooklyn and Jamaica Railroad

CROSS SECTION, SHOWING DOUBLE TUNNEL SYSTEM UNDER EAST RIVER.

Company, the Long Island Railroad Company and the City of Brooklyn, in terms as follows:

THIS AGREEMENT, tripartite, made the 10th day of April, in the year one thousand eight hundred and fifty-five, between the Brooklyn and Jamaica Railroad Company, party of the first part, The Long Island Railroad Company, party of the second part, and the City of Brooklyn, party of the third part, witnesseth:

That in pursuance of the authority conferred upon the party of the first part, by virtue of a certain act of the Legislature of the State of New York, entitled "An Act relative to Railroads on Long Island," passed April the thirteenth, eighteen hundred and fifty-three, and by virtue of other existing rights and powers, independent of said act, the party of the first part, in consideration of the covenants, grants and agreements of the party of the third part, hereby agrees to cede and convey by proper deed of conveyance, free of all incumbrance, except the pending assessment for grading Atlantic avenue, to the party of the third part, the strip of land particularly described in said act owned by the Brooklyn and Jamaica Railroad Company, on the south side of Atlantic avenue, between Gowanus lane and Classon avenue, for the purpose of a public street forever, and for no other use or purpose whatsoever. Provided, however, and upon this express condition, that the party of the third part shall cause to be graded and paved the said strip of land in such manner as is or shall be provided by law under the charter of said city, and shall forever maintain the same as a public street in addition to the present width of Atlantic avenue, and upon this further condition that the party of the first part, and its lessees, successors and assigns, shall have, from and after this date, the right to use and occupy a space of thirty feet in width in the center of said Atlantic avenue after it shall have been so widened, for the purpose of railroad tracks, to be used by the parties of the first and second parts and their respective successors and assigns so long as said street shall be maintained as a public street, in the same manner and for the like purpose that they or either of them now use and occupy the said strip of land so to be ceded. The party of the second part hereby agrees, at its own proper costs and expense (the party of the first part assenting thereto), to remove the railroad tracks now on said strip of land so to be ceded, and to relay the same in the center of said Atlantic avenue as so widened, so as to conform to the grades thereof as now established, after the same shall have been graveled and become well and compactly settled; the northerly track to be graveled first, so that the rails may be laid thereon before the present tracks shall be removed; the graveling of said strip so to be ceded to be done in such manner as best to facilitate the moving of the said track without interrupting the business of the railroad.

The party of the third part, for itself and its successors, hereby agrees to accept the cession of said strip of land pursuant to said act, and in the exercise of its other corporate powers, and to grant to the party of the first part and its lessees, successors and assigns, the right to occupy and use a strip of land thirty feet wide, in the middle of Atlantic avenue (as the same shall be widened by the addition of the said strip of land so ceded), for the purpose of railroad tracks and turnouts, to be used, traveled over, and employed by cars, carriages and locomotives, and otherwise, in the same manner as the railroad tracks on the said ceded strip of land is now in use by the party of the second part, and also with like rights and powers as if the said railroad track had been originally constructed and in use upon said strip of land, thirty feet in width, on said avenue, at the time of passing said act. The parties of the first part and second part, in consideration of the covenants and agreements herein, hereby, for themselves severally, expressly waive all right to require an application to the Supreme Court, for the purpose mentioned in said act, and they severally agree that the common council of said city may, by ordinance, make all prudential and reasonable orders, regulating the rate of speed of trains over said Atlantic avenue and Atlantic street; and also over said avenue when extended, and over Schuyler street, when widened as hereinafter mentioned, east of Classon avenue and within the city limits, as soon as the said avenue and street shall have been actually extended and widened, and the railroad tracks and rails removed to the center thereof, as hereinafter mentioned. And in consideration of the foregoing agreements of the parties of the first and second parts, the party of the third part, for itself and its successors, hereby covenants and agrees with the parties of the first and second parts, and each of them, that the party of the first part and its lessees, successors and assigns, shall have the right to use locomotives and steam power within the limits of said city, during the continuation of their respective charters and the renewals thereof under general acts or otherwise, without interruption or molestation by the party of the third part or their successors, and subject only to the right of the party of the third part, its successors, to regulate the rate of speed as before mentioned. And it is further agreed by and between these parties respectively, that they will mutually assist each other in procuring to be passed by the Legislature of this State such an act or acts, as may serve to ratify and confirm the foregoing acts and covenants, and such acts and deeds as shall be done and executed pursuant thereto, or to these presents.

And inasmuch as the party of the third part proposes to obtain from the Legislature the requisite power and authority to enable it to alter the commissioner's map of said city by extending Atlantic avenue of the width of one hundred and twenty feet from Classon avenue to Schuyler street, and also by widening Schuyler street as now laid down on said map, by adding thereto a strip of land fifty feet in width on the northerly side of said Schuyler street, so as to make the same of the width of one hundred and twenty feet from its intersection with Atlantic avenue, as extending to the easterly line of the city limits, and assess and apportion the expenses of the purchase hereinafter mentioned, and the cost and expense of grading Atlantic avenue between Gowanus lane and Classon avenue, heretofore assessed, upon the strip hereinbefore agreed to be ceded, together with any interest or default that may be due thereon, and all other costs and expenses incurred in pursuance of this agreement, as a local assessment upon the property to be benefited thereby. Now, therefore, in case such power and authority shall be obtained, and in case the said party of the third part shall, by ordinance or resolution, passed within one year from the passage of such act, determine to make such improvement in conformity with an act so to be passed, and in case said Atlantic avenue be so extended, and Schuyler street be so widened, and in case both of them shall be opened, graded and graveled, and all necessary legal proceedings taken and completed for this purpose within a reasonable time from this date, the parties of the first and second part do, in such case and cases, but not otherwise, hereby severally agree with the party of the third part as follows, viz.:

First. That the parties of the first and second parts shall sell and convey to the party of the third part such portion of the lands owned by them respectively, between Classon avenue and Franklin avenue, as shall be required for the purpose of extending Atlantic avenue of the width of one hundred and twenty feet, as herein mentioned, in consideration of the payment of the full and fair value thereof, to be appraised and fixed by three appraisers, one to be chosen by the party of the third part, one by the parties of the first and second parts, and the two others chosen to select the third, and said payment to be made before removal therefrom by the parties of the first and second parts; provided, however, that the parties of the first and second parts shall have the right of occupying a space in the center of said avenue, as thus extended, of the width of thirty feet, for the purpose of railroad tracks and turn-outs without interruption or molestation.

Second. That the parties of the first and second parts will also cede and convey to the party of the third, if authorized to do so by the Legislature, the strip of land of fifty feet in width, now owned by the parties of the first part and occupied by the railroad tracks, extending from the westerly side of Franklin avenue to the easterly line of the present city limits, provided, however, and upon this express condition, that the parties of the first and second parts shall forever have the exclusive right to use and occupy a strip or space of the width of thirty feet in the center of said Atlantic avenue as so extended, and in the center of Schuyler street as thus widened, from the intersection of Atlantic avenue to the easterly line of the city as thus widened, for the purpose of railroad tracks and turnouts and the running of locomotives and cars thereon, without interruption or molestation. And in the like manner, with the like powers and the like effect, as hereinbefore provided in reference to that part of Atlantic avenue as hereinbefore proposed to be widened, which lies west of Classon avenue, and provided, also, that such rights shall be well and securely assured, and made over to them, together with the right to make turnouts from said tracks into the depots of the said parties of the first and second parts, on the line of said railroad at any point within the city limits, both east and west of Gowanus lane; and provided further, that the grade and grades of said avenue so extended, and Schuyler street so widened, shall not, any time or times, be made any greater than ten inches in any one hundred feet, or such other grades as may be agreed upon between the said parties, and that the curvatures of the track shall not be required to be of a less radius than those now existing in said roads within the city limits, and that the road of the parties of the first and second parts shall not be chargeable with any portion of the expenses of extending said Atlantic avenue, or widening Schuyler street, or opening, grading, regulating and paving said avenue and street; and provided, further, that the party of the third part, and its successors, shall forever keep open and maintain the said extension of Atlantic avenue and Schuyler street, as so widened, as public streets, subject to the use thereof by the parties of the first and second parts as hereinabove and hereinafter mentioned; and provided, further, that the sidewalks on said street and Atlantic avenue shall not be of a greater width than fifteen feet; and provided, further, that the said parties of the first and second parts may use rails and lay the tracks in such manner as they are now laid on the strip so to be ceded.

Third. That upon the cession and conveyance mentioned in the second clause by the parties of the first and second parts, and when said Atlantic avenue as so extended, and also Schuyler street as so widened, shall have been laid out, graded and graveled, and such grading and graveling well and compactly settled, the parties of the second part shall proceed to remove the rails from the strip of land so to be ceded, and to lay the necessary tracks in that portion of Atlantic avenue so extended, and in Schuyler street as so widened, with the usual and proper timbers and supports, within the limits of said strip of land, thirty feet in width; but the tracks shall be removed and relaid at such time or times and in such manner as shall fully enable the parties of the first and second parts to continue the use of and travel over their road daily and without interruption or intermission; and such parties of the first and second parts shall be allowed to lay temporary tracks where the same may be conveniently required for the purpose of insuring the continuance of such travel while said tracks are being removed. And the party of the third part shall immediately after said tracks and turnouts shall be laid pay to the party of the second part the cost or expense of removing and laying the same on that part of said tracks which lies east of Classon avenue, not, however, to exceed twenty-five cents per running foot of said tracks and turnouts, also the cost and expense of removing the buildings, fixtures, etc., required to be removed from the depot lots and replacing the same, not, however, to exceed the sum of four hundred dollars: and it is hereby expressly agreed by and between the parties that they shall and will respectively sign, seal, execute and deliver all such deeds, writings and instruments as may be reasonably proper or requisite for the more fully expressing or effectuating the true intent and meaning of these presents.

No part of this agreement to be binding on either party until an act of the Legislature be passed pursuant to the terms and conditions herein expressed and contained. Nothing herein contained shall be construed to make the city of Brooklyn chargeable out of its general treasury for any portion of the costs and expenses of the aforesaid unpaid assessment, or of the purchase of the aforesaid lands, or the removal of the buildings or tracks aforesaid, or any other expenses to be incurred under or by virtue of this agreement, nor shall the same nor any portion thereof be demanded of the said party of the third part until the same shall be levied by local assessment, and the moneys so levied shall be collected and paid into the City Treasury, and nothing herein contained shall authorize the parties of the first and second parts, or either of them, to run cars or locomotives within the limits of the city of Brooklyn on Sundays; the parties of the first and second parts hereto do hereby mutually agree with each other that the lease of the Brooklyn and Jamaica Railroad, heretofore executed between them, shall be extended to those parts of the said road which are to be altered and made under this agreement, and nothing herein contained is to be taken or construed so as in any manner to alter or affect said lease, or any clause thereof, or any existing agreement between said companies in regard to the rent to be paid under said lease. Also that the Long Island Railroad Company shall save harmless the said Brooklyn and Jamaica Railroad Company against costs and expenses of the alterations and removals provided for herein, also that the said Brooklyn and Jamaica Railroad Company shall apply the proceeds of the land sold to said city under these presents in or toward the purchase of other lands which may be used and occupied by the Long Island Railroad Company as part and parcel of the premises demised by said lease in lieu of the lands so sold.

In witness whereof the said parties have caused their respective corporate seals to be hereunto affixed.

JOHN A. KING, [L. S.]
President of the Brooklyn and Jamaica Railroad Company.

As a part of the general plan of improvement is here cited an act passed April 13, 1855, to authorize the Common Council to widen Atlantic avenue, and ratifying and confirming the agreement last above inserted.

CHAPTER 475.

AN ACT authorizing the common council of the city of Brooklyn to widen and extend Atlantic avenue, and to widen Schuyler street in the city of Brooklyn, and to ratify and confirm an agreement therein mentioned, between the said city and the Long Island Railroad Company and the Brooklyn and Jamaica Railroad Company.

Passed April 13, 1855, three-fifths being present.

The People of the State of New York, represented in Senate and Assembly, do enact as follows:

SECTION 1. The Common Council of the city of Brooklyn is hereby authorized to lay out, open and extend Atlantic avenue, of the width of one hundred and twenty feet from the easterly side of Classon avenue to Schuyler street, and also to widen Schuyler street as heretofore laid down on the commissioner's map of said city, by adding thereto on its northerly side, a strip of land of the uniform width of fifty feet, extending from the point where Atlantic avenue, as so extended and widened, shall intersect said Schuyler street, to the easterly line of the said city limits; the northerly line of said Schuyler street, as so widened, shall be parallel with the present northerly line of said street, as laid down on said map, and at the distances of fifty feet therefrom.

§ 2. The common council of the city of Brooklyn may cause application to be made to the county court of the county of Kings, or to the Supreme Court, at a special term thereof, held in said county, for the appointment of three commissioners, to estimate and assess the expenses of said improvements, and the amount of damages and benefit to be sustained and derived therefrom by the owners of such lands and premises as may be affected thereby, and the powers of the said courts in the premises, and of the said commissioners when appointed, shall be the same as those now provided by law in reference to commissioners for opening streets in said city.

§ 3. All the provisions of law relating to the opening of streets in said city, after the appointment of commissioners therefor, and to the imposition and collection of assessments for opening and laying out streets, shall, upon the appointment of the commissioners under this act, be applicable to the improvements hereby authorized, and the same proceedings shall be had after such appointment, in relation to such improvements and to the imposition and collection of the assessments to be laid therefor, as if the said street and avenue had been originally laid out on said commissioner's map, as extended and widened under this act, and as if said improvements were commenced under the existing laws for the opening of streets in said city, excepting only so far as the same are modified or varied by this act.

§ 4. The agreement made between the Brooklyn and Jamaica Railroad Company and Long Island Railroad Company and the city of Brooklyn, on the tenth day of April, in the year eighteen hundred and fifty-five, respecting the agreed cession to said city of the strip of land on the southerly side of Atlantic avenue, between Gowanus lane and Classon avenue, and the strip of land of fifty feet in width, now occupied by said companies, extending from the westerly side of Franklin avenue to the easterly line of the city limits, is hereby ratified and confirmed, together with all the clauses and covenants therein contained; and the said companies and the city of Brooklyn are hereby respectively and fully authorized to do and execute all such further acts and deeds, matters and things, as may be necessary or requisite for fully carrying out and effectuating the true meaning and intent thereof; and the said improvements are to be made, and the proceedings of the commissioners under this act are to be had, subject to the terms of said agreement and in conformity thereto.

§ 5. The costs and expenses of grading Atlantic avenue, between Gowanus lane and Classon avenue, heretofore assessed, together with any interest or default that may be due thereon, by or under the direction of the common council of said city, shall be included in and added to the amount to be assessed by the commissioners appointed under this act for said improvement, and the aggregate amount shall be re-assessed and re-apportioned by said commissioners; provided, however, that the owners of these lots and lands who have already paid any portion of said costs and expenses, shall be allowed and credited upon such re-assessments, with all sums so paid by them respectively.

§ 6. The said city is authorized to accept from the Brooklyn and Jamaica Railroad Company, the cession of the strip of land of fifty feet in width, owned by said company, extending from the westerly side of Franklin avenue to the easterly line of said city, and when so ceded, the said city shall own and hold said strip of land in fee simple absolute, subject only to the terms of said agreement and the provisions of this act. And the commissioners appointed under this act shall allot said strip of land into parcels, with reference to the ownership of the separate parcels of land adjoining the southerly line of said strip of land, and extending therefrom to Schuyler street, and said commissioners shall separately value said several pieces of land at their fair value respectively which allotments and valuations shall for the purposes of this act be final; and after the said strip of land shall be so allotted and valued, and the report of said commissioners shall have been confirmed and ratified, the respective owners of the several parcels of land adjoining the same, shall be entitled to a conveyance from the said city, in fee simple, of the separate portion or portions of said ceded strip, which shall be allotted by said commissioners to the said parcels of land owned by them respectively, upon payment of the amount at which the same shall have been so valued; provided, however, that such owners shall apply in writing for such conveyance to the said commissioners, and bind themselves to accept the same at such valuations, before they shall have made their report, and within a certain time to be fixed by said commissioners, by a notice for the purpose, published in two or more public newspapers printed in said city, at least once in each week for three successive weeks; and provided, further, that the amount, if any, which shall be awarded by such commissioners to said owners for benefit, shall be set off against the value or consideration of the lands so to be conveyed to them; and in case the said commissioners shall not be so applied to by such owner, or any of them, that portion of said ceded strip shall be sold at public auction by said city, and the proceeds thereof shall be applied towards the cost and expense of said improvements.

§ 7. The said city is authorized to accept from the Brooklyn and Jamaica Railroad Company the cession of the strip of land owned by said company, of the width of fifty feet, and extending from the westerly side of Franklin avenue to the easterly limits of said city, and for the purpose of the said improvements, the said city is authorized to purchase from said company, and from the Long Island Railroad Company, the strip of land one hundred and twenty feet in width, extending from the easterly side of Classon avenue to the westerly side of Franklin avenue, or so much thereof as belongs to said companies respectively, and as is required for the purpose of extending Atlantic avenue, as hereinbefore directed; and the city shall hold and own the said strip of land of fifty feet in width so to be ceded, in fee simple absolute, subject to the provisions of this act, and to the terms of said agreement, and the said strip of land so to be purchased by said city, shall form part of Atlantic avenue as so extended.

§ 8. The Brooklyn and Jamaica Railroad Company, and the Long Island Railroad Company, are respectively authorized to cede, sell and dispose of the lands belonging to them as stated in the aforesaid agreement; and the said city is authorized to make the purchase contemplated in said agreement, and the expense of such purchase, and the other costs and expenses agreed to be incurred by the said city in or by said agreement, shall be assessed and apportioned by the said commissioners as part and parcel of the expense of the said improvements. The said companies are severally authorized to acquire in fee simple, or otherwise, such lands and real estate as may be required by them for the purpose of depot lots, depot accommodations, and turnouts, in the manner and by the special proceedings prescribed in the "Act to authorize the formation of railroad corporations, and to regulate the same," passed April second, eighteen hundred and fifty.

§ 9. The act entitled "An act relative to railroads on Long Island, passed April thirteenth, eighteen hundred and fifty, so far as the same is inconsistent with this present act, and all or any other acts inconsistent herewith, are hereby repealed; and after the said avenue and street shall be actually laid out, extended and widened, as hereinbefore provided, and the report of said commissioners finally confirmed, the street now known as Atlantic street in said city, together with said avenue as so extended, and Schuyler street, as so widened, shall be known and distinguished by the name of Atlantic avenue.

§ 10. This act shall take effect immediately.

REMOVAL OF STEAM POWER FROM THE AVENUE.

It is important to reproduce here Chapter 444 of the Laws of 1859, for the reason that the last section of the act relates to the subject treated in Chapter 484 of the Laws of 1859, which is the act under which the tunnel was closed, and steam removed from the avenue. It is as follows:

CHAPTER 444.

AN ACT supplementary to the charter of the Long Island Railroad Company.

Passed April 18, 1859.

The People of the State of New York, represented in Senate and Assembly, do enact as follows:

SECTION 1. The Long Island Railroad Company are hereby authorized to take and accept a lease of any railroad on Long Island now connecting with said Long Island Railroad, or that may hereafter be connected therewith, and to run and operate and hold the same, under the general powers, and subject to the liabilities of the charter of the said Long Island Railroad Company.

§ 2. And said Long Island Railroad Company are further authorized to become the purchasers, in whole or in part, of the stock or bonds issued or to be issued by said connecting road or roads, built or to be built, or to guarantee the payment of said bonds, principal and interest; provided the giving said guarantee shall have been first authorized and approved at a meeting of the stockholders of said Long Island Railroad Company, by a majority of two-thirds in interest of the stockholders attending said meeting.

§ 3. The general railroad act of this State, passed April second, eighteen hundred and fifty, is so amended as to allow the Long Island Railroad Company to use upon their road, or any of the branches used by them, rails of fifty pounds in weight to the lineal yard; provided said rails be of American manufacture.

§ 4. That the law authorizing land to be purchased and taken for the prevention of snow-drifts along the route of the Long Island Railroad Company, passed March twenty-third, eighteen hundred and fifty-seven, be and the same is hereby amended so as to extend along the lengths of the several branches constructed or leased, or which may be constructed or leased, by said Long Island Railroad Company, except along the Brooklyn and Jamaica Railroad, from Jamaica to Brooklyn and within the limits of any incorporated village.

§ 5. The said Long Island Railroad Company may also purchase or employ one or more steamboats or lighters for the conveyance of their passengers and freight between the steam terminus of their road at Hunter's Point and the city of New York; provided, that the same shall in no manner interfere with the rights of the mayor, aldermen and commonalty of the city of New York.

§ 6. The said The Long Island Railroad Company shall not be authorized to make any change of its present running termination at the South Ferry, Brooklyn, until such company shall have complied with the provisions of an act entitled, "An act to provide for the closing of the entrances of the tunnel of the Long Island Railroad Company in Atlantic street, in the city of Brooklyn, and restoring said street to its proper grade, and for the relinquishing by said company of its right to use steam power within said city;" and this act is passed upon condition that all the provisions of the contract authorized to be made with said company, or its assigns, in and by said act shall be well and truly kept and performed; and this act is to take effect, so far as the allowance of the change of terminus, only upon the passage of said act, and upon a compliance with the terms thereof.

CHAPTER 484.

An act to provide for the closing of the entrance of the tunnel of the Long Island Railroad Company in Atlantic street, in the city of Brooklyn, and restoring said street to its proper grade, and for the relinquishment by said company of its right to use steam power within said city.

Passed April 19, 1859; three-fifths being present.

The People of the State of New York, represented in Senate and Assembly, do enact as follows:

Section 1. The common council of the city of Brooklyn shall, upon petition or application of a majority of the owners of land, at the time of the passage of this act, in the district proposed to be assessed by this act, make application to the Supreme Court, at a special term in the county of Kings for the appointment of three commissioners, as provided under the act passed April seventeenth, of the Laws of eighteen hundred and fifty-four, entitled

"An act to consolidate the cities of Brooklyn and Williamsburgh and the town of Bushwick into one municipal government, and to incorporate the same," and in title four of the said act.

§ 2. Each of the said commissioners shall, within a reasonable time after their appointment, before entering upon the discharge of their duties, qualify before the clerk of the county of Kings, and file in said office a bond in the penalty of fifty thousand dollars, with sufficient sureties, executed to the people of the State of New York, conditioned to the faithful performance of their duties as commissioners under this act. But said bond and sureties shall first have been approved by one of the justices of the Supreme Court of the second judicial district of this State; and in case of any default, neglect of duty or breach of trust, the district attorney of the county of Kings shall, upon proper information, proceed without delay to sue for and recover upon the bond aforesaid, for any damage or injury which may be done by reason of such default, neglect or breach of trust. Any neglect or refusal on the part of the commissioners, or either of them, to comply with the requirements of this section, shall vacate their appointment, and in case of any vacancy occurring by death, resignation or otherwise, it shall be filled in the same manner as hereinbefore mentioned. The concurrence of a majority of the said commissioners shall be sufficient to legalize all acts and things done by them required by this act.

§ 3. The said commissioners so appointed are hereby authorized and empowered to enter into a contract, in writing, with the Long Island Railroad Company, or its assigns, that they shall close the entrances of the tunnel in Atlantic street, in the city of Brooklyn, and restore and pave and regulate the same to its proper grade, and also for the relinquishment, by said company and its assigns, of the right to use steam power within said city, and also that the said company, or its assigns, shall lay rails upon the surface of said street in a proper manner, and shall so keep and continue the same, and also that the said company, or its assigns, shall run horse cars for freight and passengers from the South Ferry to the city line, in such numbers and as often as may be required for the accommodation of the public; said cars to connect at the city line, or East New York, with steam power to the village of Jamaica, and the trains to be run from Jamaica and East New York each way as often as once every half hour, between six o'clock A. M. and eight o'clock P. M., and one night train after ten o'clock P. M., each way, at such hours as shall accommodate the citizens of Jamaica; way trains to be run as often and make the same stoppages they now do, and so many of such trains as may be necessary shall be run through from the South Ferry, Brooklyn, and from Jamaica, at such times and in such manner as to make connections with the trains of the Long Island Railroad Company at Jamaica, and that such passengers and freight shall be carried at a rate not exceeding that charged by the Long Island Railroad as the average rate over the road of said company, and also to provide suitable and sufficient accommodations for receiving and delivering the freight drawn upon the said road, at Jamaica, East New York, and also at some convenient point between Fifth avenue and the South Ferry, Brooklyn, and to carry all proper merchantable freight upon said road from the South Ferry to

Jamaica, any freight which may be declared a nuisance by the common council of the city of Brooklyn. And that the said Long Island Railroad Company, or its assigns, shall receive as compensation for the compliance with such contract, and the surrender of the right of the said company and the Brooklyn and Jamaica Railroad Company to use steam within the city limits, the sum of not exceeding one hundred and twenty-five thousand dollars, to be paid in pursuance of the terms and provisions of this act, which sum, together with an amount sufficient to cover all the expenses of collecting the same and executing this commission, and not exceeding five thousand dollars, shall be assessed upon the lots of land and premises (excepting from said assessment, however, all the lands owned and occupied by any religious denominations) within the following described district and limits, viz.: Commencing at the East River at the foot of Atlantic street and including the lots upon each side of Atlantic street and Atlantic avenue or Schuyler street to the city line, and commencing at the city line at the end of Pacific and Dean streets, and including the lots upon each side of Pacific and Dean streets to Smith street. Lots fronting on all streets and avenues crossing said Atlantic street and avenue or Schuyler street, comprised in the foregoing limits, shall be included in said assessment district.

§ 4. The said Long Island Railroad Company and their assigns shall also in their said contract stipulate and agree to cause the streets now used or authorized to be used by said company, within the said city, to be conformed to the grade lines which shall have been or may hereafter be fixed and determined upon by the common council of said city for the grade of any street or avenue upon which said road may now or hereafter run; and that the said common council may fix and regulate the rate of fare upon the said horse railroad within the limits of said city, and which shall be the same as charged by the Brooklyn City Railroad Company, and shall have a municipal control and regulation over said road within the limits of such corporation; and the said common council shall, from time of the compliance with the terms of such contract made by the commissioners, have and possess the powers over the said road within said city, as to grade, rate of fare, and control, and regulation specified in this section; and the said commissioners shall not make their said contract with the said Long Island Railroad Company, or its assigns- until the Brooklyn and Jamaica Railroad Company shall signify their assent to the provisions of this act by a stipulation, in writing, under their corporate seal, duly executed and acknowledged, and which shall be duly recorded in the office of the register of the county of Kings, and which shall contain a full relinquishment of the right of said company to use steam within the corporate limits of said city, pursuant to the provisions of and upon the conditions specified in this act.

§ 5. The said contract shall, when duly executed and acknowledged on the part of said company or its assigns, be recorded in the office of the register of the county of Kings, and thereupon it shall be the duty of said commissioners to determine the amount for which an assessment shall be levied, not exceeding, however, in the whole, the sum of one hundred and thirty thousand dollars, and to estimate and determine the amount of benefit to be derived therefrom by the owners of the land within the limits in the preceding section specified, and to assess the same upon such lands.

§ 6. Unless in this act otherwise provided, said commissioners shall be clothed with the same powers and duties, and shall proceed in the same manner, and be subject to the same rules and regulations, and receive the same compensation as commissioners whose appointment is provided for by section three of title four of Chapter three hundred and eighty-four of the Laws of eighteen hundred and fifty-four, passed April seventeenth, and vacancies occurring in the commission hereby appointed shall be filled in this manner, provided by said section. All the provisions of titles four and five of said act, applicable to the improvement and assessment hereby provided for, and not inconsistent with this act, shall regulate and govern said commissioners in the discharge of their duties as such, except that the commissioners under this act are hereby substituted for the common council and their clerk in said act mentioned, and all the acts and things required to be done by said commissioners under this act may be done by a majority of them. Said commissioners shall be allowed to use any of the maps now in use upon said district, for the purpose of making the assessment, and to employ such assistants as may be necessary, but shall not be required to make searches for title; and upon the confirmation of the report of the said commissioners, the right to use steam by the said Long Island Railroad Company, and their assigns, and by the Brooklyn and Jamaica Railroad Company within the limits of said city, shall cease; and all laws allowing the use of steam by either of said companies within the corporate limits of said city of Brooklyn, are, as from the time of such confirmation, hereby repealed.

§ 7. Upon the compliance on the part of the said Long Island Railroad Company, or their assigns, and of the said Brooklyn and Jamaica Railroad Company, with the provisions of the said contract, the said commissioners shall appoint a collector to collect said assessment, and shall take from him a bond, in a penalty of fifty thousand dollars, executed to the people of the State of New York, with sureties, who shall justify in the aggregate in the sum of fifty thousand dollars, conditioned for the faithful performance of his duties as such collector, which bond shall be approved by said commissioners; and in case of any default or breach of his trust by said collector, said commissioners shall prosecute the same in the name of the people of said State. Said collector, before he enters into the discharge of his duties as such, shall take the oath of office before an officer authorized to administer oaths, and said commissioners shall thereupon certify and deliver to said collector their assessment list, with a warrant under their hands and seals, authorizing him to levy and collect the same, and thereupon, unless herein otherwise provided, said collector shall levy and collect the amount of the several assessments therein mentioned in the same manner as the county tax is levied and collected, and the same measures taken to enforce the collection thereof as are provided by law in regard to the county tax. Unless in this act otherwise provided, said collector shall be clothed with the same powers and duties, and be subject to the same rules and regulations in the discharge thereof as are possessed by and govern the collectors in the city of Brooklyn.

§ 8. During thirty days after the confirmation of their report, said assessment may be paid to said commissioners without any interest, and a deduction of one per cent. shall be allowed upon all assessments so paid. After the expiration of said thirty days said collector may add to said assessments then unpaid, and collect therewith interest at the same rate as collected by the collector of the city of Brooklyn, until paid, from the confirmation of said report, and two per cent. thereon for collection and disbursement fees; and after the expiration of sixty days, the collection and disbursement fees so to be added and collected, as aforesaid, shall be three per cent.; which collection and disbursement fees shall belong to the collector, for his fees, under this act. As fast as such assessment and interest shall be collected, they shall be paid over by said collector to the said commissioners, whose duty it shall be immediately to deposit the same in some solvent bank in the city of Brooklyn, to be drawn out by said commissioners upon their warrant, for the purposes in this act provided.

§ 9. It shall be the duty of said commissioners to enforce the fulfillment by the Long Island Railroad Company, or its assigns, of the contract, then entered into. in accordance with the terms thereof, and to take all necessary and legal measures for that purpose, and they shall cause the said company, or its assigns, or any company or individual running such road, to run the same agreeably to such contract, and prevent the running of the same contrary thereto: but this shall not be construed to affect the rights and remedies of any individual, or of the municipal corporation.

§ 10. This act shall take effect immediately.

THE COST OF THE REMOVAL.

This act to provide for the closing of the tunnel and removing steam from Atlantic avenue was amended by Chapter 100 of the Laws of 1860; but the change related mainly to the method of the collection of the assessments to be laid on the adjoining property, and is not particularly important in this connection.

It is not necessary to reproduce the proceedings in full which were taken under the acts for the closing of the tunnel and the removal of steam from Atlantic avenue.

It is enough to say that in accordance with the act the common council of the city of Brooklyn, on the first day of August, 1859, presented a petition to the Supreme Court, asking for the appointment of commissioners as provided by the act, and that an order was made on that day naming such commissioners; that the commissioners made their report on the 28th day of July, 1860, determining what amount should be paid to the Long

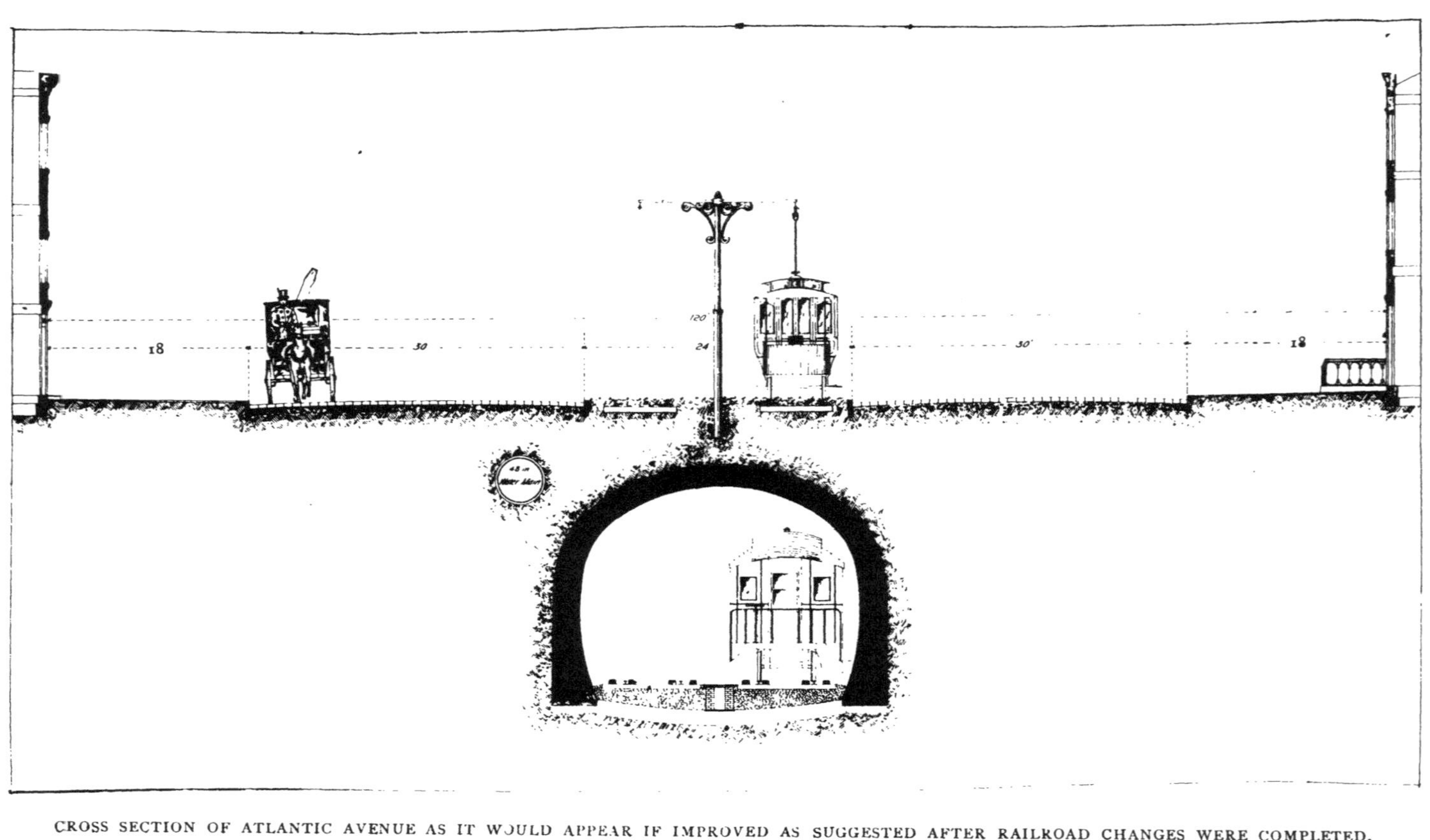

CROSS SECTION OF ATLANTIC AVENUE AS IT WOULD APPEAR IF IMPROVED AS SUGGESTED AFTER RAILROAD CHANGES WERE COMPLETED.

Island Railroad Company as compensation, fixing such amount at the sum of $125,000, which, together with the expenses of the commission, amounting in the aggregate to the sum of $129,801.80, was assessed upon the property lying along the avenue; that on the 27th day of September, 1861, the court made an order duly confirming the report of the commissioners, and that thereafter this amount was collected from the owners of the adjoining property; the amount so collected was paid to the Brooklyn and Jamaica Railroad Company, which had then become the assignee of the Long Island Railroad Company in respect to that fund; and that the tunnel was thereafter closed and steam was removed from Atlantic avenue as provided by the act in question.

THE HUNTER'S POINT TERMINUS.

The charter of the Long Island Railroad Company was amended by an act passed March 12, 1860, entitled: "An Act to amend the charter of the Long Island Railroad Company," and is Chapter 65 of the Laws of 1860.

Section 1 provides that the Long Island Railroad Company is authorized to construct or extend its railroad from Jamaica to the East River, at or near Hunter's Point in Queens County, and to maintain, operate and hold the same under the provisions of its charter, and under the provisions of the General Railroad Law, which had before this time been enacted.

Section 2 provides that the Long Island Railroad Company might, at its option, purchase the New York and Jamaica Railroad, then in course of construction between the points named in the first section of the act, on such terms and conditions as might be mutually agreed upon between the two railroad companies.

On March 21, 1860, an act was passed which is Chapter 92 of the Laws of that year, and entitled: "An Act to provide for the widening of Atlantic avenue in the city of Brooklyn, and to establish a public drive and promenade on said avenue."

Section 2 of that act provides that Atlantic avenue as established by an act of the Legislature passed April 13, 1855, entitled: "An Act authorizing the common council of the city of Brooklyn to widen and extend Schuyler street in the city of Brooklyn, and to ratify and confirm an agreement therein mentioned between the said city of Brooklyn and the Long Island Railroad Company and the Brooklyn and Jamaica Railroad Company," is hereby widened so as to be of the uniform width of 160 feet from its intersection with Atlantic avenue, as heretofore laid down on the commissioners' map of the city of Brooklyn, to its easterly termination at the city line; and the same as so widened shall be known and distinguished by the name of Atlantic avenue; and that, for the purpose of such widening, there shall be added to the said Atlantic avenue, as established by the said act of April 13, 1855, a strip of land of the uniform width of 40 feet upon the northerly side of said avenue, so that when said avenue shall be so widened, as directed, the northerly line thereof shall be 160 feet distant northerly from the southerly line of said avenue, as prescribed by said above recited act of the Legislature, and 160 feet distant northerly from the southerly line of said Schuyler street, as heretofore laid down on said commissioners' map, and running parallel with said southerly line of Atlantic avenue and Schuyler street.

The sections of the act from the first to the sixth relate merely to the method of effecting such widening, and the collection of the assessments therefor, and is not of sufficient importance to be here reproduced.

Section 6 provides that nothing in the act shall be deemed to repeal any of the provisions of the act of April 13, 1855, entitled: "An Act authorizing the common council of the city of Brooklyn to widen and extend Schuyler street, and to ratify and confirm an agreement therein mentioned between the said city, the Long Island Railroad Company, and the Brooklyn and Jamaica Railroad Company," nor of an act of the Legislature, passed April 19, 1859, entitled: "An Act to provide for the closing of the entrance of the tunnel of the Long Island Railroad Company in said Atlantic street in the city of Brooklyn, restoring said street to its proper grade, and for the relinquishment by said company of its right to use steam power within said city,"

Section 7 provides that no proceedings shall be taken under this act until the Brooklyn and Jamaica and Long Island Railroad Companies shall have executed and delivered the agreement referred to in said act of April 19, 1859, relinquishing their right to use steam on said avenue.

THE BROOKLYN CENTRAL AND BROOKLYN AND JAMAICA CONSOLIDATION.

On April 16, 1860, an act was passed, known as Chapter 460 of the Laws of 1860, entitled "An Act authorizing the Brooklyn Central and the Brooklyn and Jamaica Railroad Companies to consolidate and continue their roads."

Section 1 provides that the Brooklyn Central Railroad Company and the Brooklyn and Jamaica Railroad Company, upon obtaining the written consent of the holders of three-quarters of the stock of each of said companies may consolidate their stock, interests and property, assuming the name of the Brooklyn Central and Jamaica Railroad Company, and be entitled to all the privileges after consolidation enjoyed by the respective corporations at the time of consolidation, and be fully authorized to finish, complete and operate such lines of roads not finished at the time of consolidation as are designated or provided for in the articles of association of the former and the charter of the latter company, upon the petition of the majority of the owners of property in interest upon each of said streets and avenues in the city of Brooklyn upon the line of said roads.

Section 4 provides that any agreement made with the Long Island Railroad Company, or its assigns, or by the Brooklyn and Jamaica Railroad Company, or the said consolidated company with the commissioners appointed under an act passed April 19, 1859, to provide for the closing of the tunnel in Atlantic street, Brooklyn, which shall release or prohibit the use of steam power upon said road or roads within the limits of the city of Brooklyn shall be binding upon each of said companies, their successors or assigns, or any other party or corporation using said road or roads within said limits; and after the discontinuance by the Long Island Railroad Company of the use of steam upon said road, all laws authorizing the use of steam upon the same or any other road in said city are hereby repealed.

THE CONTRACT UNDER WHICH REMOVAL WAS COMPLETED.

Subsequently, on the 26th of April, 1860, a contract was made between the Long Island Railroad Company and the Brooklyn and Jamaica Railroad Company, which is recorded in the office of the Clerk of the County of Kings, in Liber 525 of Conveyances, April 26, 1860. It follows:—

Whereas, The Brooklyn and Jamaica Railroad Company has heretofore executed and delivered to the Long Island Railroad Company a certain lease, dated the first day of December, in the year of our Lord one thousand eight hundred and thirty-six, demising the railroad then of the Brooklyn and Jamaica Railroad Company for the term of forty-four years and six months, at the yearly rent therein reserved, which lease was modified by certain agreements between the same parties, dated, respectively the first day of June, in the year of our Lord one thousand eight hundred and forty-seven, and the 13th day of April, in the year of our Lord one thousand eight hundred and fifty-three, under which lease and modifications the said Long Island Railroad Company is now in the possession of the demised premises.

And Whereas, The said Long Island Railroad Company proposes to remove the terminus from the East River at Brooklyn, and to locate the same at or near Hunter's Point, and is about to communicate its arrangements for this purpose, but before taking further steps to accomplish such change of terminus, requires to have its rights determined by these presents.

And Whereas, The Brooklyn and Jamaica Railroad Company has procured, or is about to procure, from the city of Brooklyn, certain rights to run city cars, and is, therefore, and for other reasons, desirous to have the lease aforesaid surrendered, and the rights of the Long Island Railroad thereunder extinguished.

Now, therefore, these presents, between the Long Island Railroad Company, party of the first part, and the Brooklyn and Jamaica Railroad Company, party of the second part, witness as follows: That in consideration of the premises, and the mutual covenants and agreements herein contained, the said parties do hereby, for themselves and their successors, mutually grant, covenant and agree as follows, namely:

First.—That the Long Island Railroad Company hereby yields up and surrenders the said lease and the estate and term of years therein mentioned unto the Brooklyn and Jamaica Railroad Company, in consideration of the agreements of the latter company hereinafter contained, and the Brooklyn and Jamaica Railroad Company hereby accepts such surrender, and fully releases and discharges the Long Island Railroad Company and its successors from all and singular the rents, conditions and covenants contained in said lease, or in any of the modifications thereof.

Second.—The Long Island Railroad Company, for the like considerations, grants and assigns to the Brooklyn and Jamaica Railroad Company, its right, title and interest, whatever the same may be, of, in, and to the tunnel in Atlantic street, in the city of Brooklyn, and the opening and approaches to said tunnel, and the track and roadway therein, and of, in and to any easements in or under Atlantic street, through or under said tunnel, and also any right of the Long Island Railroad Company and its successors to use steam-power within the limits of the city of Brooklyn, and it is expressly understood and agreed by and between the parties hereto, that the grant and assignment contained in the second clause of these presents are to take effect on the completion of the new road mentioned in the second section of said act of March twenty-third, 1860, and are so made in order that among other things, to enable the Brooklyn and Jamaica Railroad Company to yield up, surrender and extinguish all right to said tunnel, and all rights to use steam-power within the limits of the city of Brooklyn, under the general powers and by virtue of the provisions of the act of the Legislature of the State of New York, one passed on the nineteenth day of April, 1859, and known as the Tunnel Act, and the other passed the twenty-third day of March, 1860, mandatory thereof, or if for any cause such rights should not be extinguished under said acts, that the extinguishment thereof shall be accomplished in some other manner satisfactory to the Long Island Railroad Company.

Third.—The Brooklyn and Jamaica Railroad Company, in consideration of the surrender of the aforesaid lease by the Long Island Railroad Company, hereby covenants and agrees with the latter company as follows: That it will, upon demand, convey or cause to be conveyed to the Long Island Railroad Company, its successors or assigns, by a good and sufficient title in fee simple, a portion of the premises described in said lease, namely: a parcel of land and premises situate at Jamaica, being twenty-five feet in width on the north side of the Brooklyn and Jamaica Railroad, with one track along the south side thereof, extending from a point on said Brooklyn and Jamaica Railroad, designated by a locust post west of Jamaica, eastwardly to the westerly side of the depot at Jamaica at the old Rockaway road, and also all the lands, depot grounds, roadbeds, tracks, machine shop and appurtenances of the Brooklyn and Jamaica Railroad Company, situate east of the old Rockaway road at Jamaica; said premises are covered by the mortgage made by the Brooklyn and Jamaica Railroad Company to secure certain bonds now outstanding, but the Brooklyn and Jamaica Railroad Company agrees to indemnify the Long Island Railroad Company against any demands on account of the said mortgage and bonds; and inasmuch as it is one of the inducements to the Long Island Railroad Company in removing from Brooklyn to Hunter's Point, to prevent the use of steam power within the said city, as and for the benefit of property owners in Atlantic street, and other persons objecting to the use of steam, as, also, for the private interests of the Long Island Railroad Company, connected with its change of location, the Brooklyn and Jamaica Railroad Company hereby further covenants and agrees that from and after the time when the Long Island Railroad Company shall remove to Hunter's Point, the use of steam power shall cease upon the present or any future track of the Brooklyn and Jamaica Railroad Company, its successors or assigns, or any persons or corporations claiming under it, or using its tracks or lands, within the limits of the said city, and that no steam engine or locomotive shall be at any time hereafter used, or suffered or permitted by the Brooklyn and Jamaica Railroad Company within the said city limits, or by its successors or assigns, or any persons or corporations claiming under them, and that the said Brooklyn and Jamaica Railroad Company, its successors and assigns, shall and will insert in any conveyance, grant or demise of their said road or franchises, a covenant to the same effect by the grantee, in such form that it shall inure to the benefit of the Long Island Railroad Company, its successors or assigns, and it is expressly understood that the said Long Island Railroad Company shall, in case of any attempt to use steam, in violation of the agreements herein contained, be entitled, in its own name, to have an injunction against its use, and to have the covenants of the Brooklyn and Jamaica Railroad Company herein contained, specifically.

Fourth.—The Long Island Railroad Company agrees, upon the completion of the railroad now being constructed between Jamaica and Hunter's Point, to assign to the Brooklyn and Jamaica Railroad Company the lease now held by the former, from Mulford Martin, of the wharf and water lots of the South Ferry in Brooklyn; and the Brooklyn and Jamaica Railroad Company agrees that it will pay to said Martin all rents that shall accrue upon said lease, after the Long Island Railroad Company vacate said wharf, to remove to Hunter's Point, and will indemnify the Long Island Railroad Company against all its covenants contained in said lease, and will assume the same as if made originally by the Brooklyn and Jamaica Railroad Company. The Brooklyn and Jamaica Railroad Company also agrees that the Long Island Railroad Company shall have as and for its own property, and that it may remove the wood sheds and hay sheds, and water tanks and pipes, at Bedford Station and South Ferry, and the turn-tables at South Ferry, and also all the tracks and switches on any part of the railroad now in use by the latter company, between the East River and Jamaica, excepting a single track from the end of the dock on the East River, to the westerly end of the tunnel, and excepting also a double track through the tunnel to Bedford avenue, excepting a single track from Bedford avenue to the old Rockaway road at Jamaica and excepting the turn-out erected at East New York prior to the first day of December, 1858, and also excepting one of the turn-outs at Jamaica, west of the old Rockaway road.

Fifth.—Each of said parties shall, upon the reasonable request of the others, execute all such further acts and instruments as may be reasonably required for the purpose of carrying out and effectuating the intents of these presents.

In witness whereof, the said parties to these presents have hereunto interchangeably set their respective corporate seals, and caused the same to be subscribed by their respective Presidents, the 26th day of April, in the year of our Lord one thousand eight hundred and sixty.

Signed, sealed and delivered by the Long Island Railroad Company, in presence of

WILLIAM E. MORRIS,
Pres. of L. I. R.R. Co. [L. S.]

Signed, sealed and delivered by the Brooklyn and Jamaica R.R. Co., in the presence of

E. B. LITCHFIELD,
Pres. of Brooklyn and Jamaica R.R. Co. [L. S.]

The following agreement was made April 28th, 1860, between the Brooklyn and Jamaica Railroad Company, the Long Island Railroad Company, and the Commissioners appointed under the act providing for the removal of steam from Atlantic avenue, and was recorded April 28th, 1860, as follows:

KNOW ALL MEN BY THESE PRESENTS: Whereas, An act of the Legislature of the State of New York was passed April nineteenth, 1859, entitled: "An Act to provide for the closing the entrance of the tunnel of the Long Island Railroad Company, in Atlantic street, in the city of Brooklyn, and restoring said street to its proper grade, and for the relinquishment by said company of its rights to use steam within said city," under which act Theodore F. King, John D. Lawrence and John Winslow have been appointed commissioners; and whereas, a certain other act of said Legislature was passed on the 23d of March, 1860, entitled: "An Act in relation to the collection, payment and application of certain assessments in the city of Brooklyn;" and whereas, the Long Island Railroad Company has executed and delivered to the Brooklyn and Jamaica

Railroad Company a grant and assignment of all its rights, title and interest in the tunnel in Atlantic street, in the city of Brooklyn, and also all of its right to have and receive the compensation payable under said acts, and all moneys assessed and payable thereunder, and by virtue of which grant and assignment the said Brooklyn and Jamaica Railroad Company are the assignees of the Long Island Railroad Company, within the true meaning and intent of both the said acts; now, therefore, this agreement, made between the Brooklyn and Jamaica Railroad Company, party of the first part, and the said Theodore F. King, John D. Lawrence and John Winslow, commissioners, appointed under the first mentioned act, parties of the second part, witnesseth, that in consideration of the premises, and of the sum of one dollar lawful money, duly in hand paid to the party of the first part by the parties of the second part, and the consideration to be secured for the compliance with this agreement, as provided for in said acts, and for the purpose of carrying out and effectuating the closing of said tunnel, and the abolition of steam power within the limits of the city of Brooklyn, the party of the first part doth hereby, for itself, its successors and assigns, contract and covenant as follows:

First—That the said party of the first part shall and will close the entrance of said tunnel in Atlantic street, in the city of Brooklyn, and restore and pave and regulate the same to its proper grade. And also, that the party of the first part shall and will relinquish all right to use steam power within said city, and also, that the party of the first part shall and will do and perform all the other acts and things provided to be done by the Long Island Railroad Company or its assigns, in the third section, or the other sections of said first-mentioned act, and in the said act of March twenty-third, 1860, and that it will not do the acts, or any of the acts, provided against in the same sections, it being intended that it shall be bound to the performance of all and singular such acts, and to such omissions, as if the same were herein particularly set forth.

Second—That the party of the first part shall cause the streets used by the Long Island Railroad Company at the time of the passage of the first mentioned act, or authorized to be used by said company within said city, to be conformed to the grade line, which, at that time, or at any other time since then, or at any time hereafter, were, have been, or shall be fixed and determined upon by the common council of said city, for the grade of any street or avenue upon which said road may now or hereafter run. And that the said common council may fix and regulate the rate of fare upon the horse railroad, mentioned in said act, within the limits of said city, and which shall be the same as charged by the Brooklyn City Railroad Company, and that said common council shall have a municipal control and regulation over said road within the limits of the corporation; and that the said common council shall, from the time of the compliance with the terms of this contract made by the commissioners, have and possess the powers over the said road, within the city, as to grade, rate of fare, and the control and regulation specified in the fourth section of the first mentioned act.

Third—The party of the first part hereby also fully yields up and relinquishes all its right to use steam within the corporation limits of the city of Brooklyn, pursuant to the provisions of, and upon the conditions specified in said acts, and the discontinuance of steam to take effect upon the completion of the new road between Jamaica and Hunter's Point, mentioned in the second section of said act of March 23d, 1860, and the said party of the first part fully assent to all the provisions of said act and each of them, and binds itself to perform all the acts and things therein required to be done or contracted for by the Long Island Railroad Company, or its assigns, and the party of the first part also agrees that the steam power shall not be used or permitted upon its road, or any part thereof within the limits of the city of Brooklyn, at any time or times after the completion of said new road between Jamaica and Hunter's Point.

Fourth—The party of the first part also agrees to accept from said commissioners the assignment of the assessment list, and of the right of the said commissioners to receive payment of the assessment, as provided for in the said act secondly above mentioned, in lieu of the moneys to be paid, and also to discontinue the use of steam within the limits of the said city upon completion of the new road, from Jamaica to Hunter's Point.

Fifth—The said commissioners hereby, in consideration of the premises, agree that the Brooklyn and Jamaica Railroad Company shall receive as compensation for compliance with this agreement and the provisions of said acts, and the surrender of the rights of said companies to use steam within the limits of the said city of Brooklyn, the sum of one hundred and twenty-five thousand dollars, to be paid in pursuance of the provisions of the said acts, and said Brooklyn and Jamaica Railroad Company hereby signify their assent to the provisions of the acts passed April 19th, 1859. And inasmuch as it has been thought advisable that the Long Island Railroad Company should assent to these presents, the said Long Island Railroad Company doth hereby fully assent to and confirm all and singular the matters aforesaid, so far as it has any right so to do, and so far as it has any interest therein.

In witness whereof, the said parties of the first part and second part have executed these presents, and the said Long Island Railroad Company hath assented thereto this twenty-eighth day of April, eighteen hundred and sixty.

E. B. LITCHFIELD, [L. S.]
President Brooklyn and Jamaica Railroad Company.

T. F. KING, [L. S.]
JOHN D. LAWRENCE, [L. S.]
JOHN WINSLOW, [L. S.]
Commissioners.

WM. E. MORRIS, [L. S.]
President Long Island Railroad.

Sealed and delivered in presence of (the sixth word on line six, subdivision five interlined before execution)

H. B. JOHNSON.

Subjoined is a copy of the assignment by the Long Island Railroad Company to the Brooklyn and Jamaica Railroad Company of its interest in the compensation to be paid to the Long Island Railroad Company for the removal of steam from Atlantic avenue, which was executed on the 26th day of April, 1860.

An assignment by the Long Island Railroad Company to the Brooklyn and Jamaica Railroad Company, and recorded in said Liber 525 of Conveyances, page 422, of which the following is a copy:

KNOW ALL MEN BY THESE PRESENTS: Whereas, An Act of the Legislature of the State of New York was passed April 19, 1859, entitled "An Act to provide for the closing of the entrances of the tunnel of the Long Island Railroad Company, in Atlantic street, in the city of Brooklyn, and restoring said street to its proper grade, and for the relinquishment by said company of its rights to use steam within said city," under which act Theodore F. King, John D. Lawrence, John Winslow have been appointed commissioners.

And whereas, A certain other act of said Legislature was passed on the 23d of March, 1860, entitled "An Act in relation to the collection, payment and application of certain assessments in the city of Brooklyn." And whereas, The Long Island Railroad Company has executed and delivered to the Brooklyn and Jamaica Railroad Company a grant and assignment of its right, title and interest in the tunnel in Atlantic street, in the city of Brooklyn, and also of its right to use steam forever within said city. And whereas, The contracts mentioned in the second section of the said act, passed 23d March, 1860, and referred to the fifth section of the said act of 19th April, 1859, has been executed and recorded as provided for in said acts respectively.

Now, therefore, these presents witness that, in consideration of the premises, and the sum of one dollar, duly in hand paid to the Long Island Railroad Company, parties of the first part, by the Brooklyn and Jamaica Railroad Company, parties of the second part; the parties of the first part hereby grant and assign unto the parties of the second part any right or claim it has or may have to receive the compensation payable under said acts, for the closing of said tunnel, and for the extinguishment of all right to use steam power within the limits of the city of Brooklyn, and also any rights it may have to an assignment of the assessment list, and the assessments made or to be made, under or by virtue of the said acts of the Legislature, or either of them, and also any rights it may have to receive from the commissioners appointed under said acts, the assignment of said assessment roll and assessment, as provided in said act, passed 23d March, 1860.

To have and to hold to the parties of the second part, its successors and assigns forever. It is expressly understood and agreed, however, between said parties, that the said Long Island Railroad Company is to be under no obligations or liability to the Brooklyn and Jamaica Railroad Company to collect such assessments, and that the latter company is to collect or enforce the same at its own risk and expense.

In witness whereof, the said Long Island Railroad Company hath executed these presents this twenty-sixth day of April, A.D. 1860.

WM. E. MORRIS, [L.S.]
Pres. Long Island R. R. Co.

Signed, sealed and delivered by the Long Island Railroad Company, in presence of

H. G. DE FOREST.

RESTORATION OF STEAM ON ATLANTIC AVENUE.

On April 5, 1855, the Brooklyn and Jamaica Railroad Company executed to Samuel Willetts, Robert Wray and Alexander Hamilton, Jr., as trustees, a mortgage to secure its bonds to the amount of $100,000. This mortgage covered all its property, including that which was leased to the Long Island Railroad Company, in accordance with the lease hereinbefore set forth.

The suit to foreclose this mortgage was brought in the Supreme Court, to which suit the Long Island Railroad Company was also made a party, and which latter company served an answer in such suit and set out the surrender of its lease to the Brooklyn and Jamaica Railroad, and its various contracts and agreements made under the act of 1859, hereinbefore set forth.

On the 21st day of March, 1872, a decree of foreclosure and sale in the action was made, such sale to be "subject to a certain "agreement or release made between the Brooklyn and Jamaica "Railroad and the Long Island Railroad Company, dated April, "1860; and subject also to the provisions of an act of the Legis- "lature of the State of New York, passed April 19, 1859 (this "being the act hereinbefore set forth for the closing of Atlantic "avenue and the removal of steam therefrom); and subject also "to the provisions of a certain other act of the Legislature pass- "ed April 16, 1860, entitled: 'An Act authorizing the Brooklyn "'Central and the Brooklyn and Jamaica Railroad Company to "'consolidate and to continue their roads so far as such provisions "'of said acts relate to the closing of the tunnel in Atlantic street

" 'in the city of Brooklyn and the relinquishment of steam power " 'within the limits of said city,' which acts are referred to in the " answer of said defendant, the Long Island Railroad Company."

Under this decree of foreclosure the property of the Brooklyn and Jamaica Railroad Company was sold on the 28th day of September, 1872, and at such sale one William Richardson became the purchaser thereof, the property being bought subject to the conditions named in the decree, and which are above recited.

On the 29th day of April, 1872, in accordance with the provisions of the act, entitled " An Act to authorize the formation of railroad corporations, and to regulate the same," passed April 2, 1850, this being the general railroad law, a railroad corporation was formed by the filing of a certificate, as required by law, under the name of " The Atlantic Avenue Railroad Company of Brooklyn."

To this corporation on the 28th day of February, 1874, William Richardson, the purchaser at the foreclosure sale, conveyed the property bought in by him, and which in the deed he gave is described as " All and singular the railroad of the Brook- " lyn and Jamaica Railroad Company, extending from its com- " mencement at the ferry at the foot of Atlantic street in the " city of Brooklyn, in Kings County, to its termination in the " village and town of Jamaica in the County of Queens, includ- " ing all its appendages, and the depot lots in the village of " Bedford, and the right to construct branches to Flushing or " Flatbush, as secured to the said the Brooklyn and Jamaica " Railroad Company by their act of incorporation."

On the 26th day of March, 1877, the Atlantic Avenue Railroad Company leased to the Long Island Railroad Company, " its successors and assigns, all the railroad of the party of the " first part (that is, the Atlantic Avenue Railroad Company), ex- " tending from its eastern terminus in the village of Jamaica, " westward to the city line of the city of Brooklyn in Atlantic " avenue, and thence along said avenue in the city of Brooklyn " 250 feet east of the easterly line of Flatbush avenue, said 250 " feet to be measured along a line in the center of Atlantic ave- " nue," and also sundry other property as in the lease specially provided.

In the month of April, 1876, an act having been introduced in the Legislature to authorize the use of steam power upon Atlantic avenue, the common council of the city of Brooklyn, on the 10th day of April, 1876, adopted the following ordinance :

WHEREAS, This Common Council did, on the 28th day of February last, adopt the following preamble and resolutions :

" WHEREAS, It is understood that the various steam railroads of Long Island are controlled in one interest, and that the opportunity is offered to the city of Brooklyn for direct steam railroad connection with all parts of Long Island ;

" *Resolved*, That the Railroad and Law Committees be and they are hereby instructed to confer on the subject with the persons controlling said railroads, and if such connection can be secured, to report thereon for the action of the common council at its next meeting," and

WHEREAS, On tne 6th of March, the said committees reported the following resolution, which was adopted at the regular meeting of the common council, held March 13th, by a vote of 23 ayes to 2 noes, and was approved by his Honor, the Mayor ;

" *Resolved*, That the permission and authority of the common council be and the same is hereby given, to the use and operation of steam and steam locomotives and cars on Atlantic avenue, between Flatbush avenue and the city line, by the Atlantic Avenue Railroad Company of Brooklyn, or any railroad company acquiring by lease or otherwise the right so to use and operate the railroad now on said avenue, and complying with any requirements of law arising in the premises, subject to such rules and regulations as to rate of speed and public safety, as from time to time the common council may prescribe," and

WHEREAS, A bill has been introduced in both the Senate and Assembly of this State, designed to promote and effectually carry out the object of the foregoing resolutions, entitled " An Act to authorize the use of steam power upon Atlantic avenue, east of Flatbush avenue, in the city of Brooklyn ;"

Resolved, That this common council does respectfully and earnestly urge the Senators and Members of Assembly from this county to use every honorable effort to secure the prompt and favorable action of the Legislature on said bill,

Resolved, That a committee of five, of which the President of this Board shall be chairman, be appointed to appear before the Senate Committee at Albany, on Tuesday, 11th inst., and advocate the aforesaid bill, and also to request of the Senators and Members of Assembly from this county therefor, said committee to report on the subject in full hereafter, at an expense not to exceed $100, which sum is hereby appropriated from the contingent fund,

Resolved, That the clerk be directed to forward, forthwith, a written copy of the foregoing preamble and resolution to Hon. John R. Kennedy, of the Senate, and Hon. Jonathan Ogden, of the Assembly, with a request to have the same read to their respective houses, and that a printed copy thereof, properly attested, be forwarded to His Excellency, the Governor, and to each of the Senators and members of Assembly of this State.

Alderman Shepard moved to strike out from the second resolution so much as related to an appropriation of $100 for expenses of the committee, which motion was agreed to by a vote of 17 to 5.

The resolutions, as amended, were then adopted.

Subsequently to the passage of the foregoing ordinance, on the 28th day of April, 1876, the Legislature passed the act therein named, to authorize the use of steam power upon Atlantic avenue, east of Flatbush avenue, as follows:

CHAPTER 187.

AN ACT to authorize the use of steam power upon Atlantic avenue, east of Flatbush avenue, in the city of Brooklyn.

Passed April 28, 1876.

The People of the State of New York, represented in Senate and Assembly, do enact as follows:

SECTION 1. It shall be lawful for the Atlantic Avenue Railroad Company of Brooklyn and for the Long Island Railroad Company as lessee from the Atlantic Avenue Railroad Company of Brooklyn of that part of the railroad of said Atlantic Avenue Railroad Company which extends from the junction of Atlantic and Flatbush avenues in the city of Brooklyn eastwardly along said Atlantic avenue to the city line, to run cars over said railroad, upon Atlantic avenue, from the city line of Brooklyn to Flatbush avenue, by steam power, subject to such rules and regulations as to rate of speed and public safety, as, from time to time, the common council of the city of Brooklyn may prescribe.

§ 2. All acts and parts of acts inconsistent with the provisions of this act are hereby repealed.

§ 3. The Legislature may, at any time, alter, modify or repeal this act; and all leases and contracts for the use of said avenue shall be subject to such modifications or alterations in said avenue and the improvement thereof as the Legislature may prescribe.

§ 4. This act shall take effect immediately.

Following this statute, on the 26th day of March, 1877, the Atlantic Avenue Railroad Company of Brooklyn entered into an indenture of lease with the Long Island Railroad Company, wherein the Atlantic Avenue Company demised and leased to the Long Island Company, its successors and assigns, all the rail-

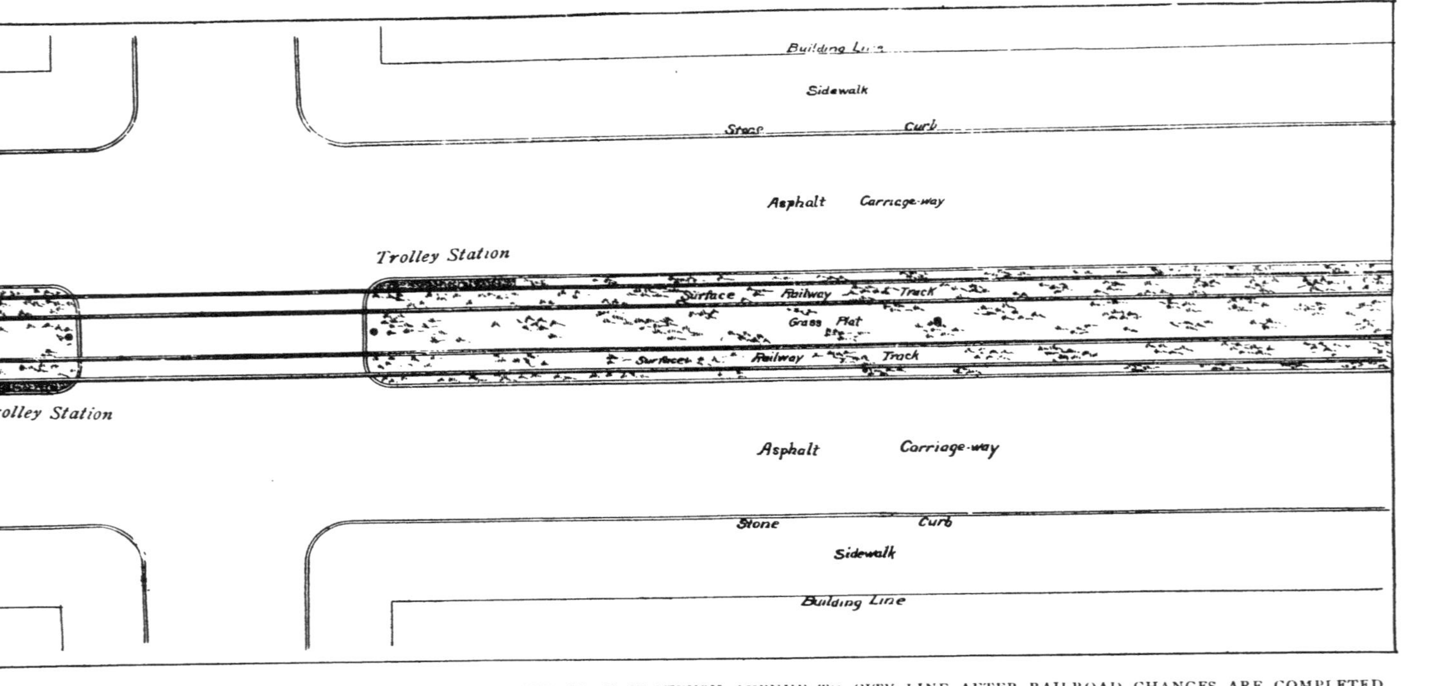

SUGGESTION OF MANNER OF IMPROVING ATLANTIC AVENUE FROM FLATBUSH AVENUE TO CITY LINE AFTER RAILROAD CHANGES ARE COMPLETED.

road which it held, extending from the eastern terminus in the village of Jamaica, westward to the city line of the city of Brooklyn, in Atlantic avenue, and thence along Atlantic avenue to Flatbush avenue, together with all the right of way, depot grounds, freight yards, gravel banks, and all lands owned by the Atlantic Avenue Company for the term of ninety-nine years, from the 1st day of June, 1877, which lease is appended:

This indenture, made the twenty-sixth day of March, one thousand eight hundred and seventy-seven, by and between the Atlantic Avenue Railroad Company, of Brooklyn, of the first part, and the Long Island Railroad Company, of the second part, witnesseth, that the said parties hereto, for and in consideration of the sum of one dollar, paid by each of said parties to the other, and for and in consideration of the mutual covenants and conditions and agreements herein contained, and by each of said parties to be observed and performed, have agreed and by these presents do mutually agree as follows:

First—The said party of the first part does hereby grant, demise and to farm-let unto the party of the second part, its successors and assigns, all the railroad of the party of the first part, extending from its eastern terminus in the village of Jamaica, westward to the city line of the city of Brooklyn, in Atlantic Avenue, and thence along said avenue to a point in Atlantic Avenue, in the city of Brooklyn, two hundred and fifty feet east of the easterly line of Flatbush Avenue, said two hundred and fifty feet to be measured along a line in the center of Atlantic Avenue; together with all right-of-way, depot grounds, freight yards, gravel banks, and all lands owned by the said party of the first part, and all the right, title and interest of the party of the first part, in any land used by it for railroad purposes, except as hereinafter provided; together with all its tracks, side-tracks, depots, car houses, water tanks, buildings and superstructure, owned by the party of the first part, easterly from the above named point, two hundred and fifty feet easterly from Flatbush Avenue, to the eastern terminus of its road in Jamaica, except the lands and right-of-way, not within the limits of Atlantic Avenue, in the city of Brooklyn, and also a plot of land in East New York, bounded on the south by Atlantic Avenue, and situated between Schenck Avenue and Barbey Street, are not included in this grant or lease. It is also understood and agreed between the parties hereto, that only a strip of land twenty-six feet in width along the northerly side of the right-of-way of the party of the first part in Atlantic Avenue, from the western terminus of the lands hereby demised, easterly to the easterly side of Washington Avenue, is included and intended to be herein granted. To have and to hold the above granted premises and property, together with its corporate rights and franchises therein, as lessee thereof, to be used and enjoyed for railroad purposes, as fully as the party of the first part might use and enjoy the same, for the full term of ninety-nine years, from the first day of June, one thousand eight hundred and seventy-seven.

Second—The party of the second part shall and will pay annually to the party of the first part, as and for the rental of the property and franchises above granted, out of all the gross receipts of the party of the second part, for passengers, baggage, express and all other business done on passenger trains from any station upon the lines now or hereafter operated by the party of the second part, to any station west of the village of Jamaica, upon the line of railroad hereby demised, and also from any station west of the village of Jamaica upon said line hereby demised to any station upon the line now or hereafter operated by the party of the second part, at and after the following rates upon such annual gross receipts: On the first one hundred thousand dollars of such annual gross receipts, at the rate of ten per cent. thereof; upon the second one hundred thousand dollars, at the rate of seven per cent. thereof; upon the third one hundred thousand dollars, or any part thereof, at the rate of six per cent.; upon the next two hundred thousand dollars, or any part thereof, at the rate of five per cent.; and at the rate of four per cent. upon all such annual gross receipts in excess of five hundred thousand dollars; and upon all freight receipts, to or from the same stations on the line of road hereby demised, to or from any station on the Long Island Railroad or its leased lines, the further sum at the rate of five per cent. upon the gross amount of all such freight receipts, exclusive of express freight receipts on passenger trains; provided, however, that the party of the second part hereby guarantees that the rents so to be received by the party of the first part shall not in any one year fall below the sum of twenty thousand dollars.

It is further agreed that a statement shall be rendered to the party of the first part, within fifteen days after the last day of August, November, February and May, of each year, of the said gross receipts for each preceding three months, terminating on the said last day of August, November, February and May of each year, and, with such statement, the money due the party of the first part for each preceding three months shall then be paid to the party of the first part. If with such statement, rendered fifteen days after the last day of August in each year, it shall be found that the total payment to the party of the first part for the preceding year, including the payment then to be made, shall not be equal to twenty thousand dollars, the deficiency shall be paid with the payment then accrued. At each quarter yearly settlement for the quarters ending the last days of November, February and May, payments shall be made allowing the rate per cent. above provided, upon one quarter of the above several sums of one hundred thousand dollars, two hundred thousand dollars, three hundred thousand dollars, five hundred thousand dollars, and all receipts above five hundred thousand dollars; and at the settlement made for the quarter ending the last day of August in each year, such sums shall be paid as shall make the total annual payments for the preceding year only, equal to the annual rent first above provided.

Third—It is further agreed by and between the parties to these presents, that in the event of the party of the first part neglecting or failing to pay the interest or interest coupons that will, from time to time, accrue on any of its bonds issued or hereafter issued, secured by a mortgage or mortgages on the demised premises, that the party of the second part may pay such interest or interest coupons out of the rents reserved as above, and such payments shall be a full discharge and acquittance of so much of said rent as shall be equal in amount to the interest so paid as aforesaid. And if such payment on account of interest or interest coupons shall be in excess of the rents due from the party of the second part, the party of the second part for such excess shall be subrogated to all the rights of the holders of such interest coupons; that in the event of the failure or neglect of the party of the first part to pay on maturity any bonds issued or hereafter to be issued, secured by a mortgage or mortgages on the demised premises, and in the event of the enforcement of said mortgage or mortgages by the mortgagees, by foreclosure thereof, or of either of said mortgages, the party of the second part may pay such matured bonds and be subrogated to all the rights of the holders of such bonds, and may enforce the payment of the same by foreclosure of the mortgage given for their security, or otherwise, as the party of the second part may then be advised.

Fourth—The party of the second part shall and will pay all taxes and assessments which may be lawfully levied and imposed upon the premises hereby demised, during the term of this lease.

Fifth—The party of the second part shall and will save harmless the party of the first part from any and all claims and demands which may be hereafter made against the party of the first part, by any person or persons, for any damage or injury arising out of the operation of the aforesaid railroad by the party of the second part during the continuance of this lease.

Sixth—The party of the second part shall, and will, run, during six months of the year, which shall include the summer months, not less than thirty trains daily, Sundays excepted, each way for local travel between the stations to be established at or near Flatbush Avenue, and the easterly limits of the city of Brooklyn; and for the balance of the year, within said limits, not less than twenty-six trains each way daily, Sundays excepted, for local travel, and will, also, run local trains on Sundays, as public convenience may require; and upon all such local trains the fare between any stations within the limits of the city of Brooklyn shall not exceed the amount of the lawful fare now allowed to be charged, or that may, from time to time, hereafter, be allowed upon other railroads within the limits of the city of Brooklyn.

Seventh—It is further agreed by the party of the second part, that the character of accommodation, the number of trains, and the facilities for travel from and to the station near Flatbush Avenue, in the city of Brooklyn, over and upon the line of the road hereby demised and leased, to and from all points beyond Jamaica, on the roads of the party of the second part, and its leased lines, shall be equal to the character of accommodation, the number of trains, and the facilities for travel furnished over and upon any route which is, or may be, operated by the party of the second part, between Long Island City or any other westerly terminus of said roads, and such stations on the roads of the party of the second part and its leased lines beyond said village of Jamaica. The rate of fare and tariff for freight transportation from or to any station on the lines of the party of the second part, beyond Jamaica and the city of Brooklyn, shall not exceed the rate of fare and tariff for freight transportation between such stations and Long Island City, or any other westerly terminus of the roads of the party of the second part on Long Island.

Eighth—It is further provided, that if the party of the second part, its successors or assigns, shall fail to perform the covenants and agreements herein required to be performed and fulfilled by the party of the second part, then, and in that case, the said party of the first part, its successors or assigns, may, at its or their option, enter upon the premises hereby granted, and thereafter hold, use, occupy, and enjoy the same in like manner as if this agreement had not been made; but no right of re-entry shall accrue to the party of the first part for the non-payment of any rent or rents, after the same shall accrue and become payable as above provided, until three months after written notice from the party of the first part, its successors and assigns, to the party of the second part, its successors and assigns, to pay the same, provided, however, that interest shall accrue upon all payments of rent after the same shall become payable as hereinbefore provided; and payment of such rent and interest may be enforced by the party of the first part by any suit or action that may from time to time be allowed by law.

Ninth—And the party of the first part, for itself, its successors, does hereby covenant and agree to and with the party of the second part, its successors and assigns, that the said party of the second part, its successors, paying the rents and performing the covenants hereinabove required, the said party of the second part, its successors and assigns, shall and may at all times, during the term hereby granted. peaceably and quietly have, hold and enjoy the said demised premises, without any manner of let, suit, trouble or hindrance, of or from the said party of the first part, or its successors, and will not transport passengers by any power or any manner, or aid, encourage, or abet their transportation by any person or persons or associations of persons, or body corporate, by any power or in any manner, eastwardly along Atlantic Avenue, to any point within the city of Brooklyn eastwardly to the eastwardly boundary line of Washington Avenue, so long as the party of the second part, its successors or assigns, shall occupy such aveuue; it being understood and agreed, however, that the said party of the first part reserves to itself, its successors and assigns, the right to run cars along the southerly side, but not on the strip hereby demised, as far eastwardly as to the eastward line of Washington Avenue.

Tenth—It is mutually agreed and understood between the parties to these presents, that if by an act of the Legislature hereafter passed, or by any lawful proceedings of the city of Brooklyn, or by virtue of a final judgment or decree hereafter entered by any court having jurisdiction of the matter, the party of the second part, its successors or assigns, shall be deprived of or adjudged not to be possessed of the right to run with its locomotives and cars along Atlantic Avenue, to its depot near Flatbush Avenue, or shall be adjudged not to be vested with such right, or if the said right to run by steam power within the limits of the city of Brooklyn as aforesaid, shall in any lawful manner be taken from the said party of the second part, its successors or assigns, then, and in that event, the party of the second part may, at its option, surrender to the party of the first part, for the unexpired portion of the term hereby granted, that part of the road within the city limits, but may continue to use and occupy that portion of the said demised premises, from the city limits eastwardly to the terminus in the village of Jamaica, paying therefor the same percentage of the gross receipts to and from that part of the said railroad, in the same manner as is above provided for the whole of the demised premises; except that, in such event, amount of annual rent guaranteed shall thereafter be the sum of ten thousand dollars; and all obligations and undertakings on the part of the party of the second part, its successors and assigns, to run trains within the limits of the city of Brooklyn, shall cease and determine.

Eleventh—The party of the second part shall not under-let the premises hereby demised for railroad purposes, or any part thereof, without the written consent of the party of the first part.

Twelfth—The party of the second part shall keep correct books of account of all moneys received by said party of the second part, and chargeable with the percentage above agreed to be paid, which books shall be open at any and all times, upon reasonable notice, to the inspection and examination of the party of the first part.

Thirteenth—The officers of the party of the first part, not exceeding three, shall have the privilege of riding free upon any and all regular passenger trains run upon any and all railroads operated by the party of the second part.

In Witness Whereof, the parties hereunto have caused these presents to be executed by their respective officers, and their respective seals to be hereunto affixed, the day and year first above written.

THE ATLANTIC AVENUE RAILROAD COMPANY OF BROOKLYN,
By Wm. Richardson,
President,
[SEAL.] N. H. Frost,
Treasurer.

THE LONG ISLAND RAILROAD COMPANY,
By D. N. Ropes,
President,
[SEAL.] E. B. Hinsdale,
Secretary.

A SUMMARY

OF THE STATUTES, ORDINANCES AND AGREEMENTS FOREGOING, SHOWING THE STATUS OF THE LONG ISLAND RAILROAD IN ITS RELATION TO TRANSIT ON ATLANTIC AVENUE.

---

1. Chapter 256 of the Laws of 1832, charters the Brooklyn and Jamaica Railroad Company, and authorizes it, among other things, to build a railroad from any convenient point, in the village of Brooklyn to the village of Jamaica (p. 160).

2. Chapter 178 of the Laws of 1834, incorporates the Long Island Railroad Company, and authorizes it to construct a railroad from any eligible point on Southold Bay, in or near the village of Greenport, through the middle of the Island to points on the water's edge in the village of Brooklyn, and the village of Williamsburgh, to be designated by the trustees of those villages (p. 164).

3. The Brooklyn and Jamaica Railroad Company afterwards built a road from the East River along Atlantic Avenue to Jamaica.

4. Chapter 94 of the Laws of 1836 authorizes the Brooklyn and Jamaica Railroad Company to sell or lease its railroad from Brooklyn to Jamaica to the Long Island Railroad Company (p. 171).

5. December 1st, 1836, the Brooklyn and Jamaica Railroad Company entered into an agreement with the Long Island Railroad Company, leasing to it the road from the South Ferry to Jamaica for the term of forty-four years and six months (p. 172).

6. March 29th, 1844, Ordinance of the Common Council, granting to the Long Island Railroad Company authority to construct the tunnel in Atlantic Avenue for the use of the railroad (p. 177).

7. Chapter 220 of the Laws of 1853 granted to the railroads on Long Island the right to use their roads in the same manner, and to propel their cars over the same through their entire length as that used by them at the time of the passage of the act.

§ 2. Provides that the act shall take effect only on condition that the strip of land owned by the Brooklyn and Jamaica Railroad Company on the south side of Atlantic avenue, between the Gowanus lane and Classon avenue, should be ceded to the city of Brooklyn as and for a public street (p. 179).

8. April 10th, 1855, an agreement was made, tripartite, between the Brooklyn and Jamaica Railroad Company, the Long Island Railroad Company, and the city of Brooklyn, wherein, in pursuance of the act last referred to, the Brooklyn and Jamaica Railroad Company ceded to the city of Brooklyn the strip of land on the south side of Atlantic avenue, between Gowanus lane and Classon avenue, for the purpose of a public street, forever, the city granting to the Brooklyn and Jamaica Railroad Company, its lessees, successors and assigns, the right to occupy a space of thirty feet in width in the center of Atlantic avenue after it shall have been widened to be used for railroad purposes, so long as the street shall be maintained as a public street, as fully as they had the right to use the strip ceded as aforesaid (p. 181).

9. Chapter 475 of the Laws of 1855 authorizes the Common Council to widen and extend Atlantic avenue, and to ratify and confirm the agreement tripartite last recited (p. 185).

10. Chapter 444 of the Laws of 1859 is supplementary to the Act chartering the Long Island Railroad Company (p. 188).

11. Chapter 484 of the Laws of 1859 provides for the closing of the entrances of the tunnel of the Long Island Railroad Company in Atlantic street, and restoring the street to its proper grade, and for the relinquishment of the right of the company to use steam power within the city limits (p. 189).

12. Proper proceedings were taken under the last named act for the removal of steam from the avenue, and the tunnel was closed and steam removed (p. 190).

13. Chapter 65 of the Laws of 1860 amends the charter of the Long Island Railroad Company, and authorizes it to change its terminus from the foot of Atlantic street to the East River at or near Hunter's Point (p. 195).

14. Chapter 460 of the Laws of 1860 authorizes the Brooklyn Central and the Brooklyn and Jamaica Railroad Companies to consolidate and extend their roads as one. It also provides that any agreement made with the Long Island Railroad Company or its assigns, or by the Brooklyn and Jamaica Railroad Company, or the consolidated company with the commissioners appointed under the act to provide for the closing of the tunnel, which shall release or prohibit the use of steam power within the city limits, shall be binding upon each of the companies, their successors and assigns, and repeals all laws authorizing the use of steam within the city (p. 196).

15. April 26, 1860, the Brooklyn and Jamaica Railroad Company and the Long Island Railroad Company entered into an agreement, whereby the Long Island Railroad Company surrenders the lease and all rights thereunder granted to it by the Brooklyn and Jamaica Railroad Company as previously recited (p. 197).

16. April 20, 1860, an agreement was made between the Brooklyn and Jamaica Railroad Company, the Long Island Railroad Company, and the commissioners appointed under the act providing for the removal of steam from Atlantic street, providing that the party of the first part should close the entrance to the tunnel, restore, pave and regulate the street, and should relinquish all right to use steam power within the city, and that it should do all things provided to be done by the Long Island Railroad Company, or its assigns, in the act of March 23, 1860, and that it should receive the compensation provided to be paid to the Long Island Railroad Company for the removal of steam from the avenue (p. 200).

17. April 26, 1860, the Long Island Railroad Company assigns to the Brooklyn and Jamaica Railroad Company its interest in the compensation to be paid to the Long Island Railroad Company for the removal of steam from the avenue (p. 203).

18. April 5, 1855, the Brooklyn and Jamaica Railroad Company mortgaged all its property, including that leased to the Long Island Railroad Company, to three trustees, to secure one hundred thousand dollars in bonds.

On the 21st day of March, 1872, this mortgage was foreclosed, and on the 20th day of September, 1872, the mortgaged property was sold in foreclosure, and William Richardson became the purchaser thereof.

On the 29th day of April, 1872, under the General Railroad Act, the Atlantic Avenue Railroad Company of Brooklyn was incorporated.

February 28, 1874, Richardson conveyed all the property purchased by him in foreclosure to the said Railroad Companv (p. 205).

19. April 10, 1876, the common council granted authority to the Railroad Company to use steam on Atlantic avenue (p. 206).

20. Chapter 187 of the Laws 1876 grants authority to the Atlantic Avenue Railroad Company to operate its railroad on Atlantic avenue by steam power (p. 207).

21. March 26, 1877, the Atlantic Avenue Railroad Company leased its road from Flatbush avenue to Jamaica to the Long Island Railroad Company for the term of ninety-nine years, from June 1, 1877 (p. 207), and under this lease the Long Island Railroad Company now occupies the avenue, operating its railroad by steam power.

DECISIONS BY THE COURTS

RESPECTING THE RIGHTS OF RAILROADS ON ATLANTIC AVENUE.

From an examination of the statutes, ordinances, contracts and agreements which have preceded, it is evident that all the right which the Long Island Railroad Company has to operate a railroad on the surface of Atlantic avenue with steam power is derived:

1. From the purchase by William Richardson, under the foreclosure of the mortgage made on April 5, 1855, by the Brooklyn and Jamaica Railroad Company to trustees to secure its bonds to the extent of $100,000, and which mortgage was foreclosed, and the property covered thereby sold on the 28th day of September, 1872; and

2. From the provisions of the act of the Legislature, passed April 28, 1876, known as Chapter 187 of the laws of that year, and entitled "An Act to authorize the use of steam power upon Atlantic avenue, east of Flatbush avenue, in the city of Brooklyn."

This act, as it will be seen, conferred upon the Atlantic Avenue Railroad Company, and its assigns, the right to operate a railroad by steam power from the junction of Atlantic and Flatbush avenues in the city of Brooklyn, eastwardly along the line of Atlantic avenue to the City Line, the Legislature reserving to itself the right at any time to alter, modify or repeal the act, and subject, also, to such rules and regulations as to rate of speed as from time to time the common council of the city of Brooklyn might prescribe; and making all leases and contracts for the use of the avenue by the railroad company subject to such modifications or alterations in the said avenue and the improvement thereof, as the Legislature may at any time prescribe.

The question as to the right of the Long Island Railroad Company to operate its railroad by steam power on Atlantic avenue has so frequently come before the courts in this state, that it remains now only to show what the course and tendency of the decisions of the courts have been with reference to that question; and it may be said that in most instances the courts have found some convenient way of avoiding a decision on the main question.

It appears that the earliest case which was brought to test this question is the case of Barnes and others vs. the Long Island Railroad Company, which was an action brought by the plaintiffs, consisting of property holders along Atlantic avenue, against the railroad company to restrain it from laying down its tracks and running its cars with steam power on Atlantic avenue, on the ground that the Act of April 28th, 1876, which purported to give the railroad company that right was in contravention of the Constitution of the State of New York and of the Constitution of the United States.

This case was tried before Judge Gilbert of the Supreme Court, and judgment was given for the railroad company. The opinion is not reported in any of the law reports, but the purport of it is that the company acquired the right under Chapter 187, of the Laws of 1876, to operate its road on Atlantic avenue with steam power, or rather that that Chapter of the Laws of 1876 was not inimical either to the Constitution of the State of New York or of the United States.

This case does not seem to have been appealed by the defeated party.

After this a case was brought by one Miller (a non-resident), a property holder on the line of the avenue, against the Long Island Railroad Company, in the Circuit Court of the United States for the Eastern District of New York, in which the attempt was made to enjoin the use of steam on the avenue and the fencing of the same, on the ground that the same was a nuisance and injurious to the interests of the property holders living along the line of the avenue.

The case was tried before the late Judge Blatchford July 13, 1880, and he held in brief as follows:

"1. Where a railroad is a lawful structure, and the use of steam is permitted by law, the use of the road and the use of steam on it independently of any abuse, is not a public nuisance to be enjoined. Where the abuse, if any, is general and common to all owners of adjacent property, the defendants can be called to account only by the sovereign authority.

"2. The fencing of a railroad in a city, with gates at the street crossings, is a regulation for public safety, and any incidental inconvenience is merged in the superior interests of the public."

It will be seen, therefore, that the Federal Court did not decide the question as to the constitutionality of the Act of 1876, authorizing the use of steam on the avenue, but held practically that private parties could not test the question in case the railroad was deemed to be a public nuisance, as was claimed, and that that question could only be raised by the sovereign authority, that is, in an action brought in behalf of the people of the State. This case is reported:

Miller vs. Long Island R. R. Co., 17 Fed. Cases, 333.

Judge Neilson, in the City Court of Brooklyn, in an unreported case, has made a similar holding, basing his decision on the cases of Barnes and Miller vs. the Railroad Company, already referred to.

The question came before the late Judge Westbrook in the Supreme Court of this State again in 1880, in an action brought by the People against the Long Island Railroad Company, in which it was sought to restrain the railroad company from operating its road by steam power on Atlantic avenue, on the ground that the proceedings which were taken under the Act of 1859, to provide for the removal of steam from the avenue, amounted to a contract between the property holders along the line of the avenue and the companies, not to use steam on the street. The Court decided in favor of the Railroad Company, holding:

1. That no contract whatever existed by force of the Act of 1859, which prevented the State in the future from conferring the right to use steam on Atlantic avenue upon the defendants; nor could one Legislature by a law prevent a succeeding one in a matter of public policy from changing or altering the enactment.

2. That no agreement has been made, either with the people, the city of Brooklyn, or the owners of the property in the district taxed under the Act of 1859, which will justify the maintenance of an action to prohibit the use of steam on the avenue.

3. That a railroad corporation cannot by contract, when no statute authorizes it so to do, bind itself to a particular mode of propelling power, regardless of the interests of the people, which may require it to adopt a different one.

4. The Statute (Chap. 187, Laws of 1876) under which the defendants claimed the right to use steam upon the avenue, is not obnoxious to Section 1 of Article 14 of the Constitution of the United States, declaring among other things that no State can deprive any person of life, liberty or property without due process of law; nor to Section 6 of Article 1 of the Constitution of this State, which likewise provides that no person shall be deprived of life, liberty or property without due process of law.

5. That when as against the owners of the land the right to operate a railroad has been acquired, the mode of such use, whether by steam or otherwise, is a matter within legislative control; and in regulating such use no right of property is infringed upon to which the above cited provisions from the Federal and State Constitutions are applicable.

6. The Act of 1876, Chapter 187, confers no right to lay down railroad tracks. The privilege so to do was one already enjoyed by both defendants as already existing railroad corporations. The Act gave legislative permission to use steam as a motive power on railroad tracks already constructed, the right to re-lay and repair which was an incident to the original grant. Such a legislative permission to an existing corporation is not covered by the above constitutional provision.

This case is reported as People vs. Long Island R. R. Co., 60 How. Rep., 395.

The people took the case to the General Term of the Supreme Court, and the judgment of the Trial Court was affirmed on the authority of the opinion of Judge Westbrook at the trial and is reported as People vs. The Long Island Railroad Co., 30 Hun, 510.

It was not appealed to the Court of Appeals.

The question arose again in a case brought by the People against the Brooklyn, Flatbush and Coney Island Railroad Co., which found its way to the Court of Appeals, and is reported as The People vs. the Brooklyn, F. & C. I. R. R. Co., 89 N. Y., 75.

This was an action brought by the State through its Attorney-General, against the Brooklyn, Flatbush and Coney Island Railroad Co., to restrain it from running its cars and locomotives along and upon Atlantic avenue in the City of Brooklyn. The Brooklyn, Flatbush and Coney Island Railroad Co. was running its cars from Flatbush avenue along Atlantic avenue, and then over the road known as the Brighton Beach Road, to Coney Island, by virtue of a lease or consent so to do from the Long Island Railroad Co.; and the action was brought against it instead of against the Long Island Railroad Co., the lessor.

The Court of Appeals held, among other things:

1. That the Act of 1876, permitting the use of steam on Atlantic avenue, was not violative of the provision of the State Constitution, Article 3, Section 18, which prohibits the passage of any private or local bill granting any exclusive privilege, immunity or franchise whatever.

2. That the question whether that Act was violative of the constitutional prohibition against legislation impairing the obligation of contracts, could not be presented in an action brought by the State against defendants, to which the assessed landowners, who alone had such contract rights, if any existed, were not parties.

3. That it was the duty of the Court to determine a constitutional question only when it is directly and necessarily involved in the issue to be determined; and this can only be done when some person attempts to resist the operation of an Act claimed by him to impair the obligation of a contract, and calls in the aid of the judicial power to pronounce it void as to him, his property or rights. The Attorney-General, in an action brought by him, represents the whole people and a public interest, and no question can be presented in such an action effecting only mere individuals and private rights.

This question came lastly before the Court, and was passed upon by the Court of Appeals in the matter of the proceedings of the Long Island Railroad Co., to acquire title to the real estate of Charles Horan (143 N. Y., 67).

The Railroad Company made an application under the General Statute to condemn the lands of Moran, on which the freight depots of the company are now situated, on the south side of Atlantic avenue, near Clermont avenue.

Moran defended against the proceeding and answered that the Act, Chapter 187, Laws of 1876, was unconstitutional, and that the railroad had no lawful right upon the avenue, for the reason that it had agreed by contract to withdraw steam from use thereon, and having no lawful right upon the avenue, it had not the right to condemn and take lands for its own use. The Court decided against Moran, and held substantially as follows:

"The charter of a railroad corporation may not be anulled or held forfeited "in part because of a violation by it of a private contract.

"So also the fact that such a corporation propelling its cars by steam, has, "by virtue of a private contract, surrendered the right to use steam on a small "portion of its road, and that it has violated this contract is no defense in pro-"ceedings instituted by it to condemn lands required and shown to be neces-"sary for its corporate purposes.

"The company's corporate rights of eminent domain are unaffected by the "breach of contract, and may still be exercised in a proper case.

"When, therefore, in such proceedings it appeared that the petitioner, that "is: the Railroad Company, prior to 1859, was lawfully running its trains along "an avenue in the city of Brooklyn; that pursuant to the provision of the Act 'of that year, Chapter 484, Laws of 1859, providing for the relinquishment of "the right to use steam power within the city, it entered into a contract with "the city by which it surrendered such right in consideration of a sum paid to "it, which was raised by assessment on property benefited; and thereafter the "common council of the city of Brooklyn adopted a resolution authorizing the "use of steam in running cars on said avenue, and the Legislature passed an "Act, Chapter 187 of the Laws of 1876, authorizing the petitioner, that is, the "Railroad Company, to run cars over its road on the avenue by steam power, "whereupon the petitioner resumed the use of steam power on the avenue.

"HELD that the question of the constitutionality of the Act last mentioned "was not presented; and that if unconstitutional, and the use of steam power "on the avenue illegal, this was no defense to the proceeding."

www.ingramcontent.com/pod-product-compliance
Lightning Source LLC
LaVergne TN
LVHW010559110826
845149LV00003B/709

* 9 7 8 1 4 1 8 1 8 7 5 4 5 *